On the Line

On the Line

Slaughterhouse Lives and
the Making of the New South

Vanesa Ribas

UNIVERSITY OF CALIFORNIA PRESS

University of California Press, one of the most
distinguished university presses in the United States,
enriches lives around the world by advancing scholarship
in the humanities, social sciences, and natural sciences. Its
activities are supported by the UC Press Foundation and
by philanthropic contributions from individuals and
institutions. For more information, visit www.ucpress.edu.

University of California Press
Oakland, California

© 2016 by The Regents of the University of California

Library of Congress Cataloging-in-Publication Data
Ribas, Vanesa, 1979- author.
    On the line : slaughterhouse lives and the making of
the new South / Vanesa Ribas.—First edition.
        pages cm
    Includes bibliographical references and index.
    ISBN 978-0-520-28295-7 (cloth : alk. paper)—
    ISBN 0-520-28295-7 (cloth : alk. paper)—
    ISBN 978-0-520-28296-4 (pbk. : alk. paper)—
    ISBN 0-520-28296-5 (pbk. : alk. paper)—
    ISBN 978-0-520-95882-1 (ebook)—
    ISBN 0-520-95882-9 (ebook)
    1. Foreign workers—North Carolina—Social
conditions.   2. Slaughtering and slaughter-houses—
North Carolina—Employees—Social conditions.
3. African Americans—North Carolina—Social
conditions.   4. Hispanic Americans—North Carolina—
Social conditions.   5. Minorities—Employment—North
Carolina.   6. Racism in the workplace—North
Carolina.   I. Title.
    HD8083.N8R53 2016
    331.6′209756—dc23

                                            2015019374

Manufactured in the United States of America

25 24 23 22 21 20 19 18 17 16
10 9 8 7 6 5 4 3 2 1

In keeping with a commitment to support
environmentally responsible and sustainable printing
practices, UC Press has printed this book on Natures
Natural, a fiber that contains 30 percent postconsumer
waste and meets the minimum requirements of ANSI/NISO
Z39.48–1992 (R 1997) (*Permanence of Paper*).

To the women and men whose vitality ebbs and flows with the workday at Swine's and who clamor to live and work with dignity and respect.

Contents

List of Illustrations

Preface

This is a story about people whose lives are on the line. They work in a meatpacking plant, on double-digit shifts, day after never-ending day. Bodies ache. Lives and limbs are in peril. Hours of repetitive, dangerous, grueling labor pounds their spirits. Their dignity is beaten down as a matter of business.

This is a story of how working-class immigrants from Latin America and native-born African American workers, who spend most of their waking lives working on the line, negotiate social boundaries and construct identities as they labor alongside one another. This is also a story of how I, as a sociologist, situated myself on the line to understand firsthand the nature of changing race and ethnic relations in the New South.

In the summer of 2009, when I was deciding on my dissertation topic, the American South was in the midst of a demographic and social transformation—one that brought several million Latino/a[1] migrants to work in a variety of industries and live in rural and urban communities with little or no collective memory of immigration. I wanted to know who these newcomers were and how they were becoming a part of the New South. I also wanted to better understand their incorporation experience in the context of a South that is historically defined by black-white relations, and more specifically by the structuring principles of white supremacy. I realized that Latinas/os' introduction to the South was playing a constitutive role in the spectacular transformation of the region's ethnoracial[2] panorama and systems of intergroup relations.

From earlier research on intergroup relations, I knew that these questions depended on the social relations and economic circumstances in which migrants were embedded. I realized that in order to really understand if and how Latinas/os were gaining a sense of belonging within the American racial and class stratification systems, I needed to go where working-class migrants and native-born Americans spend most of their waking hours: the workplace. Because the food processing industry, with its insatiable appetite for labor, has been such an important draw for Latino/a migrants and remains a significant employer for working-class African Americans, I decided to situate my research in this work environment. Finally, I wanted to understand at the ground level whether this New South was being shaped by rising tensions between Latino/a newcomers and African Americans, as some scholars have argued, and if so, how this related to Latinas/os' emergent sense of their place within the American stratified system of belonging.

To this end, I decided to get a job at a meatpacking plant in North Carolina. In July 2009, I packed up my belongings and moved to a rural community of around ten thousand people surrounded by hog and poultry farms and corn and tobacco fields. At the end of July 2009, after waiting in line overnight outside the factory gates with several dozen other people eager to apply for a job at Swine Inc., I was hired as a regular production worker.[3] I began my job as a meatpacker in the Marination Department in August 2009, where I worked for seven months before transferring to the Loin Boning and Packing Department, where I worked another nine months until December 2010. Marination was a small, majority–African American department with a white-dominated authority structure, while Loin Boning and Packing was a large, majority-Latina/o department with an African American–dominated authority structure. Although my initiation in the Marination Department was accidental—this was simply the department I was assigned to work in when I was first hired—my transfer to Loin Boning and Packing was intentional. I requested the transfer so that I could observe intergroup relations in a context that differed greatly in composition and working conditions. While I spent the preponderance of my time toiling in these two departments, I also had a chance to work in and become acquainted with other major plant departments, including the Kill Floor, Cut Floor, Hamboning, Bacon Slice, Pork Chop, Dry Salt, and Belly Conversion. Altogether, the data I gathered for this project comes from more than sixteen months of participant observation represented in five hundred single-spaced pages of field notes, as well as twenty-three in-depth interviews with Latina/o and African American workers collected from December 2010, when I quit the job, to April 2012.

Sitting on a beach in Wilmington with my girlfriend, just days before I was to start my job, we talked excitedly about this unexpected adventure—unexpected because I had not anticipated it would be so easy for me to get hired, and an adventure because it would be a foray into a world normally hidden from scientific observation. While I was deeply concerned that I would not make it beyond a few days, I was hoping I could last at the plant for a few months, enough time to observe intergroup relations and perhaps even develop casual friendships with coworkers. In the end, over my sixteen months, I developed intimate friendships with many people with whom I spent thousands of hours laboring on the line and eating, drinking, and dancing off the line. It was not easy. At times I was overwhelmed with loneliness, confusion, isolation, and frustration. At times my body experienced injury and pain to a degree I had never felt before and in ways I had not known were possible. The ruthless regimen of work and subjugation literally crushed my spirit, producing feelings of desperation, hopelessness, and anger, although these ultimately gave way to a kind of alienated self-discipline.

As a regular worker, first in Marination and later in Loin Boning and Packing, I directly observed and experienced the life of a meatpacking worker. As far as I know, management was unaware of my ulterior motives for working at the plant, so my status as a PhD student did not afford me preferential treatment. The Human Resources recruiter who interviewed me barely glanced at the education and work experience I listed on my application, and didn't inquire about the sociology professor listed as my reference, Jacqueline Hagan. I was seemingly just another warm body. But because I was identified by others as white, "from here," and possessing bilingual skills, I received preferential treatment relative to other Latina/o newcomers. Supervisors shielded me from the toughest jobs, personally warning me that work on the straight knife or whizard knife would "ruin" me. Apparently, they were less concerned about the hundreds of other women and men, mostly Central American and Mexican, who worked knife jobs. Those were perhaps not fully persons, and their bodies perfectly suitable for ruining.

Because I am a native Spanish speaker from Puerto Rico, I was frequently called on to translate supervisor speeches and reprimands, and sometimes to gather signatures from Spanish speakers for weekly "safety training" forms. Usually I did these tasks with displeasure because I didn't want to be seen by workers as management's favorite, and supervisors wondered out loud why I would not be ecstatic to get a moment's break from real work. And when I sought medical treatment for my hands—I acquired occupationally induced carpal tunnel syndrome in a matter of weeks following my transfer to the brutal Loin Boning and Packing Department, and six of my fingers were numb for several months from bagging those loins—I insisted (without much resistance) that I be moved to a different job. Nobody in Human Resources challenged the medical leave I got from an outside doctor. In stark contrast, many foreign-born workers were afraid to seek care even from the company nurses, who generally provided no medically significant assistance anyway (hot-wax hand baths being their universal therapy) and probably unlawfully impeded actual treatment. They were convinced that seeking medical attention would get them fired, especially if they were unauthorized workers. Indeed, Human Resources staff told them as much.

At around twenty-one hours and $250 per person per year, the company pockets nearly $300,000 a year in but one routine practice of wage theft. To that sum must be added the hundreds of thousands of dollars in *value* that 1,200 workers produce for the company in those five minutes of lunch break that they are usually robbed of, being expected back on the lines in thirty minutes, not the thirty-five they are supposedly due. And just like that, in one fell swoop the vulture seizes scraps of profit from the workers' tenuous grip; what at first glance seems a petty complaint turns out to be a million-dollar pilfering. But the real injury is not felt in lost wages. Those precious few minutes of rest and respite that daily are taken through threats and intimidation exact a psychological, emotional, and physical toll that has no dollar value.

How does one put into words the rage that workers feel when supervisors threaten to replace them with workers who will not go to the bathroom in the course of a fourteen-hour day of hard labor, even if it means wetting themselves on the line? Or the despair a worker feels as she realizes at the twelfth hour of unremitting labor that there is a lot of work still to do, and then she has to pick up her children from the babysitter, prepare a meal for her family, and be ready in a handful of hours to do it all over again? Or the pain a worker goes through in submitting her hands to the brutal repetitive trauma of cutting or packing meat, helpless as her nails turn purple and fall out from sheer effort, or the muscles in her hands contract and spasm uncontrollably, or protu-

berant knots develop along the joints in her fingers and wrists that are
visible to the naked eye? Then there is the throbbing discomfort of damp,
freezing hands and feet that workers endure while laboring in wet,
below-40-degree temperatures. The recurring sinus infections. The stab-
bing back pain. The scorching fury that swells inside from the incessant
assaults to workers' dignity as supervisors subordinate their humanity to
the value of hogs so that consumers can have fresh pork on their tables.

These are the jobs that don't go away. This is the kind of work that
hasn't changed all that much despite a century of astonishing techno-
logical innovation. Many of these jobs would be immediately recognizable to Upton Sinclair, for their reliance on sheer effort and physical
resilience makes this modern packing plant a hostile jungle to cut
through. The workers say these are the good jobs, the ones that pay
mucho dinero, but they sacrifice a lot to make that money. This is the
most onerous work a long-slogging migrant has ever had. This work is
for people who just got here and still owe their coyote, I am told. These
are the good jobs, but not for anyone's kids, my coworkers clarify. This
work is for people who don't have papers, the people without papers say
with resignation. This money is costly to earn. On a particularly bad
day, the workers say, the devil might as well whisk you away like that
old Ramón Ayala *corrido* laments. Good luck to the departed, and *bien-
venido* to the ones who just arrived! Tomorrow no one will remember
you were here, but for a few moments you felt indispensable to the mission of production. These jobs can be more like a strange supermarket
gig or more like slavery, but you probably won't get to choose. These
jobs are depressing. After this, there's nothing left to do but go back to
the country you came from because not even the animal farms will hire
you these days. After this job, that door will be closed forever, so you
better save it for when you are sure it's the best shot you've got in life. I
know these are the jobs that people with PhDs designate as "unskilled,"
but most of those skillful geniuses wouldn't even be capable of *learning*
how to do the work properly if they were given a month to train and a
manual filled with diagrams to study (and they would never be afforded
such luxuries). These are the jobs one cannot believe haven't been mech-
anized. These are the good jobs, the ones that command workers respect
in their communities, but never respect on the job.

I could not truly have understood before how the experience of
oppressive exploitation profoundly shapes how Latina/o migrants view
their position within a stratified system of belonging, and how it all is
inextricably tied to their perceptions about the positions occupied by

other groups with whom they are meaningfully engaged, such as African Americans. The abusive treatment, the routine indignities, the incessant surveillance by supervisors steeled my determination to be a witness. The constant jibes from fellow workers about those who couldn't hack it and quit made it difficult to give up, if only out of a sense of shame and personal failure. Whenever a new worker started, my coworkers sized him or her up—in terms of work ability, effort, and ethic—and most often they decided the worker was going to quit very soon, maybe even that same day. Sympathy was necessarily in short supply, rationed out in small doses and reserved for the gloomiest of situations, such as death or deportation or natural disasters. As much as my coworkers understood how tough the work was, slackers and quitters drew their ridicule and scorn. Being able to withstand the hiding of a workday at Swine's was a badge of honor, its perverse reward the distressing certainty of another hiding to come. Every so often, a worker would tell me how surprised she or he was that I was still working there. When I came back to work after my one-week medical leave, many said they were sure I had quit, and when I was still there months later, they would say "*Ya te acostumbraste a este abuso ah!*" (You've gotten used to this abuse, huh!).

I felt an unceasing commitment to my project, a sense that I was experiencing something that few social scientists ever had or would. At times I felt sudden surges of sheer euphoria, emerging from a work-induced automaton mode to regain my sociological senses and see all around me the nearly synchronized movements of hundreds of bodies, hear the rhythmic clanking of machinery, feel the shock of cold air on my face and the nearly frozen wet meat turning my fingers into popsicles under damp gloves. There was a mesmerizing quality to the everyday shop-floor performance: the loin boners leaning in sequentially to make their cuts as sixteen thousand loins made their way down the lines like a choppy succession of waves; saw operators towering over the boning lines where the leftover ribs were separated from backbones, like conductors at a meat symphony; packers with unseen strength stuffing and shaking huge anaconda-like loins into torturously small bags. At other times, anticipation of the verbal lashings that punctuated the entrancing choreography of ceaseless production was all that kept the mind from surrendering to a deep slumber.

Swine's was more than just a factory where 1,200 people disassembled hogs and assembled meat products on the line. Because the workday could be so eternal, social functions that might ordinarily take place outside the workplace—everything from dating to purchasing goods—took place inside the factory gates. On short breaks, a young couple might share a coffee or some fruit, squatting together under a line of lunch boxes that hung across the walls like the industrial version of mistletoe. On a daily basis, in the locker room shared by Loin Boning, Cut Floor, and Kill Floor workers, the last few minutes of lunch break took on the haggling air of a flea market. Women gathered around workers who sold bras and thongs, perfume, shoes, Mary Kay products and other assorted cosmetics, and even magical potions advertised as far superior to the HerbaLife that others offered, promising rejuvenation and vitality. Several women sold numbers for an informal lottery the Hondurans had set up (*chica*), tempting would-be buyers with inside information about numbers thought to be especially lucky. Other women collected money from contributors to the *tanda,* a cooperative lending scheme many Honduran workers participated in. Doña Isadora had no trouble selling any *baleadas,* a typical Honduran breakfast dish, left over from her morning sale; these would be surreptitiously slipped into a locker to be eaten at third break.

Just before lunch break would end, as the uproar from supervisors pacing the halls outside the locker room intensified and full-throated shouts of "Let's go, Boning! Let's go, ladies!" got louder and closer, the locker room took on the frenzied air of a theater backstage as women hurried to reapply their makeup, blow their runny noses, rinse tidbits of food from their teeth, refasten the colorful bandanas worn beneath their hair nets and hard hats, and perhaps grab a clean white butcher coat, dousing it with perfume. There was most definitely a meatpacker style, carried off with a proud swagger, and Latinas set the fashion trends, scrutinizing deviants with a contemptuous glare and pitying the sorry, disheveled appearances of the new hires with their lopsided hard hats, butcher coats drenched in blood, snot-encrusted nostrils, and wax-coated earplugs dangling freely.

Even in the harsh work environment of the meatpacking plant, workers found ways to make the day more bearable, chatting with whoever worked alongside them even if it meant inventing hybrid tongues ("You like *mucho chaca chaca*?"), posing exhibits of various cuts of meat arranged in obscene ways to get a laugh (pork tenderloin penis with meat scrap testicles was a crowd favorite), dropping double entendres like only a job packing meat allows ("*No me lo estás metiendo bien!*" [You're not putting it in right!]). Crude humor, especially of a sexual nature, was commonplace, and an important avenue for communication between Latinas/os and African Americans, perhaps because laughter and sex have universal appeal. Every so often, workers spontaneously disrupted the numbing monotony, howling plaintively into the frosty air like jungle beasts to elicit the echoing howls of other worker-wolves far out of sight, the melancholic lament of the forsaken fading into the humming background of moving parts ("AAAUUUUU!"). These were necessary diversions, the delirium of outrageous performances far more desirable than dreary hours of deafening silence. Comedic absurdity offered fleeting moments of cheer, and we celebrated the irreverent cries of the floor man, who serenaded us with his broom-cum-guitar and greeted his audience of workers with the surreal proclamation "¡¿Cómo están mis ovejitas?! Yo soy el buen pastor" (How are my little lambs?! I am the good shepherd). Candy, forbidden currency on the shop floor, was highly coveted by workers, a valued commodity that enhanced the popularity of frequent givers. Candy staved off hunger and kept drowsy workers alert. More importantly, I came to believe, candy disguised the wretched breath that could disgust workers laboring in close proximity to one another, and which no one wanted to be associated with lest they get a reputation for being a *chancho* (pig).

On Thursday mornings, a stream of new hires coursed through the plant, their wide-eyed ranks dwindling as the purple-hatted trainer assigned them to their respective stations. As they were paraded around the production floor like fresh jailbait, the lines erupted into raucous hooting and hollering, knives and meat hooks banging loudly on steel. If they made it, in the next month of their lives the work schedule would reset their bowel movements and make them uniquely aware of the precious value of time. The full-body throttling of packing enormous whole loins would literally shake the farts out of them. The unremarkable but recurring act of clenching their hands as they grabbed hold of a knife or loin or bag would reveal its true viciousness overnight, when the pulpy muscles of the palms became so tender that turning a doorknob was an excruciating feat. If they made it through that first month, they would have come to know what it feels like to wear away with work the very fibers of one's being.

Over time, I developed close friendships with people I cared about, six of whom (Cristina, Thomas, Linda, Rosa, Vincent, and Claudia) will be featured prominently throughout this book. Workers gave me nicknames such as "Scrappy" (because of my squirrelly fighting moves), "La Doctora" (because I was getting a doctorate degree), "Flaca" and "Skinny

Winny" (because people thought I was thin), "La Boricua" (because I am from Puerto Rico), and "Cuca" (because a Salvadoran woman called everyone "*cara de cuca*" [pussyface] and soon "Pussy" evolved into a term of endearment). As I developed relationships with workers who I felt could be key informants for my research, I explained my status as a sociology student and my purpose in working at Swine's. This "coming out" process was repeated several dozen times throughout my fieldwork , and continued after I quit the job and proceeded to collect interviews with selected workers. Especially while working at Swine's, I wrestled constantly with my multiple simultaneous roles as a researcher, worker, and friend, and the difficulties and dilemmas I faced come through in some of the data I present in the chapters to come.

Over the course of my time in the field, as I got to know these worker-friends while working at Swine's and even after leaving the job, I went to lakes, beaches, amusement parks, soccer fields, and county fairs with them. I went to malls, airports, laundromats, drug houses, strip clubs, and movie theaters with them. I went to obstetricians, pediatricians, orthopedists, and ophthalmologists with them. I went to hospitals, social service agencies, courts, and lawyers' offices with them, and I went to jail to bail them out. I went to birthday parties, baby showers, Halloween trick-or-treats, and New Year's festivities with them. I went to "Mexican" *discotecas* where I learned to dance *rancheras* and *corridos* and got used to the usual drunken brawling. I went to Latino/a nightclubs where I was continually shamed for not knowing how to dance *bachata*. I went to an after-hours dive run by a transgender runaway from Honduras where Latino men paid $20 a drink for the company of a woman. I went to "Black" clubs where handfuls of cash were traded for bottles of Grey Goose and the smell of weed saturated the air. I went to pool halls in Mexican restaurants and "Black" restaurants. I was teased and hazed for being a *culera/tortillera* (dyke), "masculine," hairy, flat-assed, a slacker, a slut, talking "white," talking "Black," talking unintelligible "Boricua" Spanish, possibly being unauthorized, and being naive. I cried, laughed, and got angry with my worker-friends, and they with me. I slept in my worker-friends' beds and they in mine. And while much about these experiences didn't make it into this book, the ass-slapping, dirty jokes, flirtations, banter, and small subversions on and off the line, in the locker rooms, in break rooms, and outside the factory infused each day with levity and added a whole other layer to the social side of laboring.

With time, I came to realize how extensively I had embedded myself in the social world of the factory, and I shuddered at the thought of leaving it all behind. My graduate adviser, Jacqueline Hagan, and my family grew anxious about my reluctance to leave the field. I dreaded the end to what I knew would be a life-defining experience. Even now, it astounds me that over the course of nearly a year and a half working as a meatpacker I managed to avoid "pointing out," as a majority of new hires do (this happens when you accumulate six points at any given time due to absences or leaving before your shift ends). And yet, what I went through physically, mentally, and emotionally pales in comparison to most workers' experiences. Workers in some departments left a twelve- to fifteen-hour day of punishing physical labor and emotional duress, knowing that their best hopes for earning a living wage that could provide for their family depended on their ability to relive that day indefinitely. With only a handful of hours to sleep, who had the wherewithal to contemplate alternatives, anyway? Many women left work only to get home to children and a husband who had to be cooked for and taken care of, and a home that had to be tidied. The unluckiest, who were many, found themselves either currently or in the recent past locked into extremely unequal domestic arrangements with men who all too often were physically abusive. Some workers added to their already-endless workday an hour-long commute. Like many migrant workers in the New South, some dealt with the precarious condition of being an unauthorized worker.

Current research on the incorporation experiences of Latino/a migrants in the New South paints a mixed picture of the phenomenon. While most scholars would probably agree that Latinas/os have contributed immensely to economic growth in the region and constitute an important segment of the new Southern working class, some research suggests a far less optimistic outlook regarding relations between Latino/a migrants and native-born groups, especially African Americans. If this contentious, but rather superficial, portrayal accurately reflects the character of social relations between Latino/a migrants and native-born groups with whom they are meaningfully engaged, this would undoubtedly influence the ways in which Latinas/os in the New South develop an understanding of their position as a group within the American stratified system of belonging. In taking my place on the meatpacking lines, laboring alongside Latina/o and African American women and men, I hoped to gain a firsthand understanding of this phenomenon, situating it in the most crucial social domain of working-class lives: work. The stories that unfold throughout the book cast a harsh light on the very

palpable struggles to make it in which Latinas/os find themselves playing a starring role, far beyond an objectified view of them as mere cogs
in a wheel. The reader will find neither saints nor villains in these narratives, but simply people who struggle, with whatever resources are
available and under conditions not set by them, to survive inside the
belly of the beast.

Acknowledgments

Many people have inspired, supported, and assisted me in carrying out the research and writing for this book. UC Press editor Naomi Schneider has been a wonderful guide throughout the manuscript preparation process, and I'm thankful for her enthusiasm in promoting my project and for the diligent assistance of Ally Power and my copy editor Lindsey Westbrook. I have also benefited enormously from comments on earlier drafts of this book from Cecilia Menjívar, Seth Holmes, and an anonymous UC Press reviewer. In addition, I thank Roger Waldinger for his careful reading, critical reactions, and enthusiastic support of this research. The final manuscript also was improved thanks to feedback from Mara Loveman and Helen Marrow. Generous grants and fellowships from the Graduate School at the University of North Carolina, the Center for the Study of the American South at UNC, the National Science Foundation, the UCLA Institute for Research on Labor and Employment, and the Faculty Career Development Program at UCSD have provided much-needed assistance along the way.

I have been extremely fortunate in life to have the mentorship of two extraordinary scholars. Shahnaz Rouse, my mentor at Sarah Lawrence College, sharpened my analytical senses and nurtured in me an outrage toward injustice. Shahnaz taught me that the best questions are difficult to answer and that there are only better answers to difficult questions. Her intellectual integrity and passion for teaching are legacies worth emulating. My doctoral advisor, Jacqueline M. Hagan, was a stalwart advocate on my behalf from the time I began my graduate studies at Carolina. Dr. Hagan traveled a long road with me over the seven years it took me to complete the PhD and remains a caring mentor and friend. I owe Jackie an enormous debt of gratitude for the many, many hours that she devoted to advising me, deciphering my ideas and helping me develop them, and pushing me to write the stories contained in this book as they deserve to be told.

I am also thankful to have had the support and critical feedback of Arne Kallenberg, Ted Mouw, Charlie Kurzman, Kenneth (Andy) Andrews, and Jacquelyn Hall on my dissertation committee at UNC. I also appreciate the comments and suggestions of Karolyn Tyson and members of the UNC Race Workshop. My colleagues in the sociology department at UCSD have also provided much encouragement and guidance in the book writing process, especially Amy Binder and Jeff Haydu, and also David Fitzgerald and Tom Medvetz.

My mom, Gayle Ribas, and sister, Mel Ribas, provided stable anchors outside the world of hog country during the course of fieldwork for this book, and have been constant sources of support and confidence throughout this long process. Beyond that, I am thankful to my mother for always allowing me to pursue my intellectual curiosities wherever these took me, and for the many sacrifices she made without a second thought in order to make that possible.

I reserve the deepest admiration for the women and men with whom I worked at Swine's and who assisted me in one way or another in my research. It is my hope that at least some small benefit can come their way from the publication and dissemination of this book, although my personal debt to them can never be repaid. I feel the sincerest gratitude and affection for those close friends I made while living and working in rural North Carolina. I learned more about strength and perseverance through pain and difficulties, and about the life-affirming properties of humor and humility, from these worker-friends in a couple of years than I had in my entire life. The irony of not being able to properly name these women and men in my acknowledgments does not escape me. The unmatched kindness and generosity that Mayra, Ivonne, and Gladys showed me is not to be forgotten. It was also my good fortune to get to know Pete, La Siquitraqui, Berta, and Kiki, all of whom immensely enriched my experiences on and off the line.

CHAPTER I

Introduction

*Lives on The Line: Carving
Out A New South*

It is Friday morning and there are seven of us working a rib trimming line: Cristina, Thomas, Rosa, Linda, Vincent, Claudia, and me. These workers—some Latina migrants, others native-born African Americans—would be some of my closest coworkers, my good friends, and my key confidants, and their experiences in the plant and in North Carolina and beyond more generally guide the narratives of this book.

On this particular Friday morning, with knife in hand, Cristina draws the rationale behind her decision to migrate on the table in hog blood. In Honduras, she can hope to make around 700 lempiras per week sewing garments at a maquiladora. As Thomas, Linda, Rosa, and I look on, she scrawls the exchange rate in diluted red numbers: 18 lempiras to 1 dollar. Cristina never imagined she'd end up here in this countryside breaking her back working a knife job. If anything, she tells me with a chuckle, having worked at a Korean-owned garment factory outside San Pedro Sula for seven years from the age of fifteen, she had entertained fantasies of running off to Korea. Her husband, Ernesto, arrived in North Carolina in 1998, right before Hurricane Mitch devastated Honduras, leaving the mines, cattle ranches, and dense forests of Olancho to follow his brothers to work in the pork, turkey, and chicken processing plants, livestock farms, and agricultural fields that dot the landscape and are the backbone of this Southern economy. Cristina joined him seven years later, in 2005.

At thirty-three, she has worked at Swine's deboning small hams and trimming ribs for two years without missing a day of work, and before this she worked on the knife for two years at Fresh Birds, a large poultry processing plant in Linden. She works without authorization, and has borne and shed three identities other than her own while eking out a living in North Carolina. Today, Cristina and Ernesto are part of a large Honduran community that lives in the multicounty catchment area of the plant, proportionally among the greatest in the country. Cristina prides herself on the quality of her work, relishing the praise of Quality Assurance staff and deriding other workers' knife skills—like those of Thomas and Rosa—from sharpening the knife to actually using it. Cristina left behind a four-year-old son and a five-year-old daughter with her in-laws in Olancho, whom she had lived with after Ernesto left, in what she depicts as conditions of servitude. Her daughter made the dangerous journey with another of her husband's brothers several years later, and now, at twelve years old, she says without a hint of irony, but much to her parents' amusement, that she wants to be an FBI agent when she grows up. Cristina's youngest daughter was born in North Carolina, so her children span the spectrum of migration statuses. Outside the plant, she lives in fear of police checkpoints and deportation, which would mean permanent separation from her husband and children, topics we regularly discuss at the table where I bag or box the ribs she trims.

Working alongside Cristina at the ribs station this Friday morning is Thomas, who like many coworkers respects Cristina's knife skills, often depending on her to sharpen his knives. Thomas is a fifty-three-year-old African American man who grew up in a nearby rural North Carolina town. In the 1990s, he worked for Hansen Farms with a night crew loading turkeys from farms across North and South Carolina. At that time, the loading crews were composed mostly of local Black men and the poultry farm labor was heavily Latino/a. The pay was by the load, and Thomas says it averaged out to a good wage. In a very matter-of-fact tone, Thomas attributes shifts in the composition of labor across animal farming and processing industries to increased competition for jobs due to the influx of Hispanics and their growing share of the applicant pool in the context of regular turnover in these jobs, in almost exactly those words. After a brief move to Virginia, where he followed his substance-abusing partner and worked at a large distribution center as a forklift operator, Thomas returned to North Carolina and started to work at Swine's in 2001.

Sometimes Thomas works with the knife, trimming ribs. Other times, he is able to escape knife work and instead bags ribs, which is considered a lighter task. But there are also times when he has to lead in producing huge orders of "curlies"—a rib that is skinned on the backside using a small handheld hook, and that Cristina says is for rich people. The work is grueling, *un trabajo perro* (dog's work, hard work), as Salvadoran fellow rib trimmer and skinner Hernán calls it, but Thomas is the fastest at this work. His form, efficiency, and speed are impressive to watch, as he skins ribs and fills giant combos at twice the rate of the next-fastest worker. No matter what type of work he is doing—whether trimming, bagging, or skinning—Thomas's laboring has a distinctive rhythm to it, a certain swaying or rocking of his tall, lanky body to the cacophonous melody of machinery. On lunch break, he hurries out to the parking lot across from the factory, immersing himself in the quiet solitude of his pickup truck. Aisha, a young Black packing worker, insists she has smelled liquor on his breath, but it never does waft my way. On short breaks, Thomas leans into the chain-link fence outside the factory while smoking his cigarette, staring through the links at the outside world, rebuilding his momentum, lost in thought, forlorn.

Just as she is this Friday morning, Rosa usually works alongside Cristina either at the ribs station or on the ham-end boning line. Rail-thin and slightly hunchbacked, Rosa has receding gums that give her mouth a concave appearance, like she is missing all her teeth, not just the bottom set. She is a forty-five-year-old Salvadoran who migrated first to Los Angeles from Santa Ana, living there for ten years before returning to El Salvador in order to regularize her status through her then-husband. She returned in 2006, later bringing her three American-born but Salvadoran-raised daughters to live in North Carolina, and they remind Rosa how much they resent her for having left them in El Salvador every chance they get. Despite her efforts to steer them toward righteousness through her Evangelical church, each of her daughters compounds her troubled life, one with a violent and substance-abusing spouse, another with marital dissolutions and consecutive childbearing, and the youngest with school desertion, drug arrests, and general teenage defiance. Rosa also has a three-year-old son with her most recent husband, a twenty-five-year-old Honduran man who works on the boning line and who abandoned her for another woman, though she still meets him clandestinely against her better judgment and maintains a bitter feud with his new *vieja*. She is a rebellious yet individualistic worker, unexpectedly hilarious and foulmouthed, though she is quick to clarify that her ex-husband never knew her that way. Calling people *cara de cuca* (pussyface) is a habit of hers, one that Latina coworkers have picked up as an affectionate nickname (now it's *my* nickname), and it's a Spanish phrase that, like *chaca chaca* (slang for "sex," like "hanky panky"), African American coworkers have become acquainted with. A reporter of all Swine-related gossip and news, Rosa's loose lips are immortalized in her nickname, Radio Bemba. She has been working at Swine's since 2006, deboning small hams and trimming ribs, or bagging ribs when she can avoid knife work, which she frequently attempts to do, leading to confrontations with supervisors. Rosa is a coffee fiend, and on the unsanctioned and ever-contentious midmorning bathroom break she will take her contraband thermos out of her locker and into a stall, where I imagine her sitting on the toilet seat, sipping subversively.

Linda, an African American woman born in North Carolina but raised in New Jersey, often pairs with Cristina or Thomas at the ribs station, as she does on this Friday morning. Linda recently turned sixty but seems to be going on thirty. She is such a motivated worker that not only is she exempted by Latinas/os in their usually-critical characterizations of African Americans' work performance, but some even resent her for being such a *cagapalo* (stick shitter), making sure every last bit of meat gets processed, and concerning herself more than others with product specifications and quality. Despite getting annoyed with her for this, some Latina coworkers, especially Rosa, tell her in choppy English and crude sign language about the troubles they are having with their kids or husbands. Linda is a proud worker, and her high self-regard is evident when she describes Cristina and Rosa as "the women who cut meat for me" instead of herself as packing meat for them. Although she has roots in rural North Carolina, Linda spent much of her adult life in New Jersey, which is reflected in her accent, made even more distinctive by her deep, raspy smoker's voice and gravelly laugh. These days she makes it up to Atlantic City from time to time to hit the casinos with her sister, riding one of those chartered tour buses all the way up north for a quick weekend getaway, and she is a regular at the slot machines at the local no-name "Internet Sweepstakes" joint. Her lips shimmer with a berry-infused gloss, the smell of which can become dizzying after hours of direct inhalation while paired with her to bag ribs or loins. Before starting at Swine's in 2008, she managed a liquor store in Parsons but lost that job, I am told, after she punched out a rude customer. She is a chatty worker unless she is in a bad mood, and her tendency to want to coordinate and lightly control the work process ("Come on, baby! What's wrong?") has earned her the uncomplimentary nickname "Grandma" from some of the younger Black workers.

Vincent is a twenty-nine-year-old African American from Wadeville, North Carolina, who trims ribs at a table near Cristina and Linda. I am sometimes paired to work with him, but he is paired with someone else on this Friday morning. He has a thick country accent and a peculiar laugh as though his jaw was wired shut. His mouth barely opens to let out his characteristic cackle, which turns out is because of oral surgery he had a few years back. He once did a two-year stretch in jail on a drug charge and has worked at Swine's since 2009. Although Vincent normally works on the knife, trimming ribs, he is called on to cover for others from time to time as a pallet jack driver or as a trimmer on the loin boning line, jobs he previously held. His cousin Kim worked with me in the Marination Department before my transfer to Loin Boning, and he is shocked that she lasted as long as she did because, in his words, she can't keep a job. Another of his cousins, a lesbian nicknamed Little G, who he and others think is "lazy as hell," is a packer in Loin Boning as well.

Vincent seems self-conscious about the fact that he has four kids with four different women, but is also proud to be a responsible provider for his girls (and the young boy he recently found out about). He is a very funny guy, and part of his routine is an incessant sexual bravado and banter that is more comical than threatening, but sometimes irritating and tiresome ("Oh, come on. You trying to tell me you never sucked dick?"). Vincent is a lay social scientist, constantly raising social and political topics of conversation, drawing on his perceptive observations. His conversational, jokester personality makes it so he is not taken so seriously by coworkers. Vincent, some Latina coworkers have remarked more approvingly than not, gets the work out even though he doesn't pay attention to the quality; still, others call him a *pendejo huevón* (lazy ass). In the summer of 2011, Vincent lost his home to the devastating tornadoes that swept through North Carolina, days after calling to tell me he won the job bid for a coveted position as a mechanic in the Maintenance Department.

Claudia is at the end of the line this Friday morning, as always, operating the *tortuga* (literally "turtle"), the machine that seals the bags containing ribs and other meat products before these go into boxes for shipping. She has worked at Swine's for nine years, and started out bagging loins on the line. Previously she worked at an appliance factory in Roseville, though she is always quick to remind me that she had been a secretary, along with her mother, in the town hall in Aguilares, El Salvador. She made the arduous journey to North Carolina in 1999 from her small town near San Salvador to reunite with her then-husband, Marcos, a man who has mostly dedicated himself to activities in the underground economy of migration, spent time in a U.S. prison, and was once deported. She finally left him because he was cheating on her. Four years after her arrival, Marcos's sister brought the couple's six-year-old son along with her on an undocumented journey to the United States.

After an earthquake struck El Salvador in 2001, Claudia and her son received Temporary Protected Status, which they must renew every eighteen months at a cost of around $900. She and her husband later had a daughter, who at nine years old expresses the multiple and conflicting ideas she learns at home, at school, in the community, and in the media with such direct, deceptively simple questions as, "Hey, Janet [my first name, and the one printed on my hard hat], is racism bad?" Claudia is deeply enamored of all things Mexican, from the music to the men (but not the women, who she jokes all have moustaches they can twirl around their fingers). On the weekends it is typical for her to go to a *disco mexicana* with friends or a boyfriend and dance to *música norteña* all night while slinging Modelos. She is an attractive, alluring thirty-six-year-old who prefers to date much younger men, preferably around half her age. Claudia is besieged at her workstation on a daily basis by a stream of admirers, regular workers and supervisors alike, be they Latino, African American, or white, married or not, young and old, who shower her with offerings of chocolate, romantic CD mixes, religious charm bracelets, and pledges of much more.

This is the new Southern working class. Cristina, Thomas, Rosa, Linda, Vincent, and Claudia illustrate the immense diversity of social positions and experiences that exist in this context both across and within racial/ethnic groups. The U.S. South has changed dramatically over the last twenty-five years. The historical racial binary made up of African Americans and whites has given way to a new configuration that now includes Latino/a migrants from Mexico, Central America, and traditional gateway states such as California and Texas. In North Carolina, the Latino/a population grew from 76,726 to 506,206 between 1990 and 2004 (Kasarda and Johnson 2006). By 2010, Latinas/os made up 8 percent of the state's population, and between 15 and 20 percent of the population in some counties, such as "Clark" County, where I conducted my research (United States Census Bureau 2001). (I will henceforth use this name, and the town name of Perry, to refer to the location of Swine's.)

Impressive as they are, these figures do not adequately convey the fine-grained and multidimensional diversity of this area, which is probably imagined by outsiders to be quite homogenous, dull, and old-fashioned. At Swine's I met people with origins in ten different Latin American countries; multiple generations of international migrants and their descendants (of all varieties of legal status); African Americans who had never left North Carolina, and others who had returned to their Southern roots after living in New York, New Jersey, or Washington, DC; Coharies and other Native Americans; and even, most exotically among the workers, a few whites. Among my fellow workers there were said to be ministers, heathens, mystics, reformed prostitutes, ex-cons, and fugitive gun dealers. Some had been Central American rebel fighters, while others were right-wing sympathizers. And, to my surprise, there were many (mostly African American) gays, lesbians, and bisexuals.

Unlike the majority of studies of new migrant destinations, in which Mexican migrants are the sole group of interest, Hondurans, Salvadorans, and Mexicans are all important for understanding emerging social realities from Knobbs to Knoxville, Boyd to Bennettsburg, Hensley to Kerr Hill, Leesville to Linden, Gardenia to Roberts Grove, Faircloth to Fall River. In fact, the multicounty region in North Carolina that forms a single labor catchment area for the poultry and hog production and processing industries includes communities with some of the country's highest proportions of Central Americans, contributing to the 25 percent of non-Mexican, Puerto Rican, or Cuban-origin Latinas/os living in the state in 2000 (United States Census Bureau 2001). Some are newcomers; others are long-term settlers, many with growing families, making the South both an area of new and *maturing* destinations. The African American population in the South is increasingly heterogeneous as well, as Black Americans have been leaving northeastern cities to (re)settle in the South since the latter part of the twentieth century, and at an accelerated pace in the last decade, resulting in the highest percentage of Black Americans residing in the South since 1960. Indeed, for some Black Americans who have moved to cities such as Atlanta and their suburban enclaves in search of better job opportunities, the economic, political, and cultural changes that have transformed this region represent the hopeful promise of a New South (Tavernise and Gebeloff 2011; Hunt, Hunt, and Falk 2008).

Through the present ethnography of a large hog processing plant in North Carolina that has been undergoing demographic and economic restructuring for at least twenty years, where I worked approximately 3,500 hours over sixteen months at several entry-level jobs, as well as twenty-three in-depth interviews with workers and innumerable hours of ethnographic observation in informal settings over three years, I examine how the social organization of labor shapes the social and economic incorporation experiences of Latinos/migrants in the contemporary American South. In most literature on immigration, incorporation is a general concept that refers to the ways in which "outsiders" are brought into the national fold of immigrant-receiving countries, with an emphasis on outcomes as incorporation occurs in various domains of life (e.g., socioeconomics, health, education) or through particular paradigms or modes of incorporation (e.g., assimilation, segmented assimilation).

These are no doubt important angles from which to study incorporation, but my contribution is a renewed attention to the real-life contexts in which migrants' lives are embedded, and to the real-life encounters with other people that imbue Latina/o migrants' experiences in the United States with collective definition. I seek to refocus the study of incorporation, viewing it as an ongoing and active social process of mutual adjustment by which groups both achieve and are assigned particular social locations in a stratified system of belonging. Further, I refer to the more narrow specification of the dynamics of incorporation that pertains to intergroup relations as *prismatic engagement*. The concept of prismatic engagement recognizes that intergroup relations—especially among subordinated groups—are mediated by the statuses and signifiers that dominant groups, here white Americans, overdetermine. Yet encounters between such groups are ongoing, and the positions they occupy within a shifting and stratified system of belonging are necessarily emergent rather than resolved. The position of whiteness at the core of this system means that subordinated groups' relations with one another are refracted through their relations with whites and whiteness. Expanding on what the critical race scholars Barbara Flagg (1993) and Ian Haney López (2006 [1996]) have termed the "transparency phenomenon," intergroup relations among subordinated groups in a system structured around white dominance take on what I call prismatic qualities.

Refocusing the study of intergroup relations in the incorporation process as prismatic engagement reveals the dynamic qualities of incorporation as an active process rather than a series of outcomes, calls attention to the fact that incorporation is a group-based process involving both the particular group of interest and those groups that meaningfully engage with it, and recognizes that the social system into which a group becomes incorporated is characterized by positions of unequal status. Viewed through the lens of prismatic engagement, the process of incorporation is bound to be rife with struggles over the positions that groups occupy within such a system. Work is a key interactional arena for the *mutual* construction of group identities through boundary processes, which in turn contributes to the broader incorporation process, that is, to the emergent "structures of feeling"[1] composed in part by multivalent intermediating relationships between groups. This study treats work as a field of human life rich in meaning-making through interaction across vertical and horizontal relations defined by the particular social roles, statuses, and relationships being examined, which include but are not limited to class, relation to authority, nativity, citizenship and authorization status, racial ascription, and gender.

Situating this study of active and ongoing incorporation processes through attention to intergroup relations, or what I refer to as prismatic engagement, in the context of work is crucial for several reasons. At the most basic level, work is where working-class people spend the majority of their waking hours, and it is the context through which different groups are most likely to encounter one another in structured and structuring ways. In the case of certain departments at this plant, such as Loin Boning, where I worked for nine months, workers spend a majority of the hours in their day at this single location: between twelve and fifteen hours each day, five to six days a week. Work is also a context in which a set of observable conditions are structured that likely shape how people understand and give expression to group boundaries. In particular, the racial/ethnic composition of labor and the authority structure, social perceptions about the nature of particular kinds of work and the ascribed qualities of particular types of workers, and variation in labor discipline regimes are important dimensions that shape how Latinos/migrants carve out their place in the New American South.

Contrary to the suggestion by some scholars that neighborhoods and public spaces such as Walmart are now the key sites for studying social relations involving Latinas/os, I argue emphatically that *work*—as setting, structure, and process—remains singularly important for understanding the incorporation experience of working-class Latino/a migrants, who are, after all, labor migrants. Although preconditioning factors such as racialized stratification systems in origin countries predispose Latino/a migrants to view groups linked to value-laden categories such as blackness and whiteness in particular ways, it is their education and their experiences in American workplaces that fundamentally mold their emergent sense of group position within the American stratified system of belonging. Untangling the variety of factors that condition this complex portrait of intergroup relations and incorporation processes is a primary objective of this project. This volume, then, is not just an ethnography of a meat-packing plant, but an ethnography of the social relations—fundamentally conditioned by the social organization of labor—that shape the incorporation of Latino/a migrants.

The section that follows offers a brief description of the context that frames the demographic and economic restructuring of the American South around the turn of the twenty-first century. In particular, it discusses the burgeoning agro-industrial development that depended on drawing an abundant supply of labor to areas that had previously known little of international migration. It explains the significance of the site I selected for studying the social and economic incorporation of Latina/o migrants, in particular through attention to their relationships with native-born non-Latina/o groups in the important social domain of work. The third section returns to the encounter that opens this chapter, elaborating on its significance for understanding social relations between Latinas/os and African Americans, the native-born group with whom they most overlap in the workplace. The fourth section gives readers a sense of the analytical framework that informs this study, and introduces the concept of prismatic engagement with which I propose to capture features of relations among subordinate groups encountering one another through the refractory lens of white dominance. The fifth section lays out the state of current research on Latino/a migrant incorporation in the U.S. South and relations between Latinas/os and native-born groups, pointing to strengths and limitations in this research that will be addressed throughout the chapters that follow.

DEMOGRAPHIC AND ECONOMIC RESTRUCTURING IN THE U.S. SOUTH

Researchers have documented the transformation of the U.S. South as a "new destination" for migrants, showing how a combination of factors, including the 1986 Immigration Reform and Control Act, the subsequent militarization of the U.S.-Mexico border, the increasingly adverse context of reception in traditional destinations, and the growing demand for less-skilled, low-wage labor partly resulting from the relocation to and concentration of certain industries in the region, have drawn millions of Latino/a migrants to the South (Massey, Durand, and Malone

2002; Zúñiga and Hernández-León 2005; Massey 2008; Hagan, Eschbach, and Rodríguez 2008). Although economic restructuring has devastated older industries in the South, notably textiles, new sources of economic investment have flocked to Southern states seeking cheap labor, new markets, and business-friendly policies. While manufacturing has declined steadily nationwide, the South has seen significant growth of the food processing, construction, and hospitality industries (Mohl 2005; Parrado and Kandel 2008; Hagan, Lowe, and Quingla 2011). Given these dramatic and ongoing transformations, researchers have had the opportunity to document the erosion of the historical racial binary between African Americans and whites and the development of an even more complex system of race relations, especially at the strategic site of the workplace, as newcomers become incorporated in Southern destinations.

At a time when large agro-industrial concerns were looking to consolidate their market control and expand production in new peripheries that had traditionally been beyond the reach of organized labor (Gray 2014; Stuesse 2009; Mohl 2009; Brueggemann and Brown 2003; Fink 1998; Stull, Broadway, and Griffith 1995; Andreas 1994; Broadway and Ward 1990), North Carolina proved to be fertile ground for growth (Griffith 2005). By most accounts, the 1990s were a nearly uninterrupted boom period for business. With the lowest unionization rate in the country, and union-busting "right-to-work" laws that were the icing on the big-business-friendly cake, that decade saw the world's largest pork processing plant open its doors in a state that already hosted the world's largest turkey processing plant. The "total vertical integration" system pursued by the big packers means that companies increasingly control animal production and processing, from pre-conception through slaughter. Between 1990 and 2004, one leading company expanded by 1,000 percent (Tietz 2006). This expansion is reflected in the growing centrality of animal production and food manufacturing to the North Carolina rural economy while other industries, such as textiles and furniture manufacturing, were on a steep decline. Yet if agro-industrial development on such a large scale was going to succeed, capital would need to draw, secure, and promote a steady and growing supply of labor of the sort it had a preference for: namely, the labor that was most exploitable.

Thus commenced in the hog processing industry what had already begun in the chicken, turkey, and hog farms and poultry processing industry up and down the Eastern seaboard and Sunbelt in the late

1980s and early 1990s: a process of "ethnic succession" through which Latino/a migrants increasingly came to occupy positions previously filled by native-born African Americans and whites.[2] In the case of Swine's, the chief protagonists of this demographic restructuring were Hondurans (along with Mexicans and Salvadorans) and African Americans, though without a doubt the main architects of the changes were the company's Human Resources personnel. Little is known for certain about the conditions that framed the initial recruitment efforts that drew Hondurans to Swine's specifically, but the expanding agro-industrial sector lured an early wave of Honduran men to the area in the early 1990s. As the twenty-first century began, Latino/a migrants had established themselves as the stable majority of the Swine's workforce. After 2000, women made up an increasing share of Honduran migrants, pushed by deteriorating economic opportunities following the devastation of Hurricane Mitch, but also wishing to reunite with spouses and family members whose planned temporary migrations had become increasingly permanent (Pastoral Social/Caritas 2003). Employment in the agro-industrial complex was abundant and easily attainable regardless of authorization status. But less than a decade later, dramatic shifts in the legal and political environment dealing with unauthorized migration lay bare the fragile position of this group in American workplaces and in the broader society. These economic, demographic, and political dynamics of change are the broader context within which incorporation processes take place, just as the prismatic engagement of groups configured at the level of the workplace and conditioned by the social organization of labor are critical to understanding how Latino/a migrants articulate their place in American workplaces and beyond.

These unprecedented transformations have spurred a large volume of scholarship on Latino/a migration and the New South, much of which addresses one of two issues. On the one hand, researchers have been busy documenting the growth of the Latino/a population in nontraditional destinations, assessing the kinds of "challenges" that large-scale change of this sort poses for communities unaccustomed to dealing with immigration, and for the well-being of new Latino/a communities. On the other hand, researchers who study race relations, migrant incorporation, and work have viewed the phenomenal transformation of the region's demographic composition with some weariness, concerned about the prospects for Latino/a migrants' successful incorporation into the social and economic landscape of the U.S. South, and about the competitive pressures they pose and potentially conflictive relations they portend vis-à-vis the region's African American working class. These twin concerns, and others, have been compiled in numerous edited volumes on Latino/a migration to nontraditional destinations, especially the U.S. South (Anrig, Wang, and McClain 2006; Zúñiga and Hernández-León 2005; Arreola 2004; Sills 2010; Hill and Beaver 1998; Stull, Broadway, and Griffith 1995; Gozdziak and Martin 2005; Hamamoto and Torres 1997; Jones 2008; Johnson-Webb 2003; Odem and Lacy 2009; Mantero 2008; Massey 2008; Murphy, Blanchard, and Hill 2001; Peacock, Watson, and Matthews 2005; Smith and Furuseth 2006; Gill 2010).

Recent research suggests that, while Latino/a migrants are "successfully" becoming a part of the Southern working class, African Americans facing a threat to their sense of group position resulting from socioeconomic competition react with an exclusionary posture toward them. Latinas/os, surprised to experience substantial discrimination as "outsiders" from African Americans, report comparatively more positive interpersonal relations with whites. Compounded by racial hierarchies from origin countries, which despite their differences from the American racial order concur in devaluing blackness, and by a class structure in the U.S. South that places them in competitive conditions vis-à-vis African Americans rather than whites, some scholars see mounting evidence in new destinations for an emerging Black/non-Black racial divide in the United States (Marrow 2011; Marrow 2007). Researchers have taken notice of important factors to explain the nature of intergroup relations in a drastically transformed South. From these accounts, in turn, scholars have drawn implications regarding the eventual form that the incorporation of Latinas/os into American racial and class stratification systems will take. Missing from this growing body of research is attention to how Latino/a migrants *themselves* articulate boundaries vis-à-vis native-born groups with which they are meaningfully engaged in fundamental domains of life, a dynamic that critically shapes how they come to view their position as a group within the American stratified system of belonging.

Studies have looked at the opportunities for social mobility offered by different types of work in the South (Hagan, Lowe, and Quingla 2011; Chavez, Mouw, and Hagan; Marrow 2011; Striffler 2005; Kandel and Parrado 2004), but we do not understand how specific critical dimensions of work affect the boundary-making processes that shape intergroup relations and produce or reinforce groups' sense of their position. While several studies have looked at whether the particular industries being examined are declining, stagnant, or growing for purposes of hypothesizing about whether ethnic succession via replacement as opposed to displacement is occurring and, hence, whether social relations are expected to be rife with conflict or not (Skaggs, Tomaskovic-Devey, and Leiter 2000), or for purposes of ascertaining the potential for social mobility migrants may experience (Marrow 2011), I am not aware of studies that have taken account of actual structural and organizational features of work that shape the context for relations among workers. The dimensions I take account of are (1) the composition of labor and the authority structure in a workplace, (2) social perceptions about the nature of particular kinds of work and the ascribed qualities of particular types of workers, and (3) labor discipline regimes. Bringing to the fore features prominent to the social organization of labor responds to the call of labor scholars to renew a focus on the work process (Juravich and Bronfenbrenner 2005; Reskin, McBrier, and Kmec 1999) and fills an urgent need in the contemporary literature on Latino/a migrant incorporation and intergroup relations for in-depth studies of the crucial domain of work.

By selecting sites that vary across theoretically meaningful dimensions pertaining to the social organization of labor—in this case departments within the same hog processing plant with different racial/ethnic compositions—my research considers the possibility that the features and salience of ethnoracial boundaries, and of the symbolic resources by which they are expressed, created, maintained, and transformed in the context of dramatic demographic change in workplaces, are in part conditioned by the actual context within which social relations take place (Lamont and Molnar 2002). Further, by drawing a focus on the compositional structure of sites at the micro level (i.e., departments in a single plant), I am able to build on pioneering work that shows that the relative size of groups is an important factor that explains patterns of intergroup relations in the contemporary U.S. South (Marrow 2011). A critical contribution of this study is that prolonged and deep immersion through participant observation makes it possible to simultaneously evaluate what Latinas/os (and other groups) say about one another as well as how they behave. I follow the lead of both pioneering and recent scholarship that understands participant observation to be the most appropriate method for taking account of the many dimensions of work as a structure, process, and setting (Burawoy 1979; Fantasia 1988; Leidner 1993; Fink 1998; Striffler 2005; De Genova 2005; McDermott 2006; López-Sanders 2009; Pachirat 2011).

FIGURE 1. Partial exterior view of Swine's from a parking lot.

FIGURE 2. Tobacco fields alongside the roads of Clark County.

FIGURE 3. Exterior view of turkey farm enclosures alongside the roads of Clark County.

SITUATING INCORPORATION: ENCOUNTERS ON THE LINE

The scene that opens this chapter introduced six individuals, some Latinas and some African Americans, with whom I worked regularly on a meatpacking line at Swine's. Now let me turn to an analysis of the encounter that Friday morning, since these interactions hint at the themes that run throughout this book. That Friday morning on the rib trimming line, when Cristina scribbled the Honduran exchange rate onto the table in blood with the handle of her knife, her African American coworker Linda exclaimed with astonishment, "Oh, I gotta go there!" Realizing Linda's confusion—that she had misinterpreted the exchange rate to mean she earned a lot more in Honduras—Cristina shook her head and explained what a typical take-home pay was in dollars, around $40 a week. Rosa chimed in that it was the same where she was from in El Salvador. "Oh no! That's why they come here. I would too!" Linda responded with outrage.

An older African American worker, Thomas, seemed curious, a shy smile on his face as he periodically looked up from the ribs he was cutting, glancing at Cristina with soft eyes: "Can they use dollars over there? Can they keep dollars in banks over there?" he asked. Linda was determined. "Elvia here [pointing to Cristina and using her real name] needs to start being real. Elvia needs to start being Elvia. So how much would it cost for her to get her papers?" she asked ingenuously. At a table nearby, a young African American worker named Vincent was trimming a different rib and looking over at us, provocatively pouting his lips behind his meat-smeared beard net. Claudia, a Salvadoran operator, was peeking under the wall where she worked at the machine sealing bagged meat, gauging the amount of bellies, shoulders, and ribs barreling down the line toward her. The day, cold and eternal, was like any other in the Loin Boning and Packing Department at Swine's. Michael, a freckle-faced African American floor supervisor, paced frenetically from the boning lines to the packing lines, throwing his hands up, bellowing in frustration, "Let's go, Boning, let's go!"

The scene conveys the kind of spontaneous interactions between Latina/o and African American workers laboring on the line and at tables that I observed over my sixteen months working at entry-level jobs at this meatpacking plant. That Friday morning, an unauthorized Honduran worker explained to African American coworkers through a combination of minimal English, pantomime, and basic math why people like her come to work in the United States. The frankness with which Cristina approached this shop floor discussion was evident in other encounters with Black workers, where she found ways to make light of her unauthorized condition, pointing at the assumed name on her hard hat and announcing comically that she was not really Cristina, much to their amusement. The relative lack of knowledge, but also curiosity and even sympathy, of these Black workers was evidenced in Linda's belief that Cristina's legal status problem was solvable with money, and her conviction that Cristina should be able to live normally as her real self, Elvia.

The subtle significance captured in this encounter contrasts with the blunt, partial, and unsituated understandings conveyed in much of the interview data other researchers have relied on, and elucidates the enigmatic contradictions found in survey research. Such scholarship has attempted to describe and explain relations between immigrants and native-born groups, and to examine their implications for the long-term incorporation of Latinas/os into American systems of racialized stratification. But this scene is also a single snapshot. If I had observed just this one encounter, I might have been left with the impression that attempts at mutual understanding despite communication barriers fully characterize relations between Latinas/os and African Americans in Southern workplaces. This conclusion would accurately depict one interactional mode that prevails between Latina/o and African American workers, but it would misapprehend a major thrust of intergroup dynamics gleaned from the hundreds of encounters, conversations, and comments to which I was privy.

Extrapolating a general conclusion about relations between Latinas/os and African Americans from this opening encounter would miss the fact that Cristina regularly referred to Thomas pejoratively as *el moyo*, a popular designation for African Americans, instead of by his name, and that she told Black workers they were lazy to their faces. It would miss the fact that nine years into working at this factory, Thomas didn't know what *moyo* meant until Vincent carefully explained it to him. It would miss Vincent's concern over whether Cristina was going to be "exported" following her arrest at the factory, and his muffled laughter at the idea that a raid would finally reveal everyone's real names. It would fail to recognize the verbal jostling between Rosa and Vincent, flinging accusations of laziness at each other that played on very different discursive materials, but often with similar comical tenor. It would neglect the explosive conflicts between Claudia and Lauren, her Black female coworker, and their unequal bargaining power with white male authority figures. Most importantly, it would ignore altogether the great sense of oppression felt by Latinas/os who perceive that they are the most exploited and powerless workers, and that African Americans are privileged at their expense. In short, it would oversimplify, and perhaps misrepresent, the major contours emerging from the prismatic engagement between Latinos/migrants and African Americans in the American South at the beginning of the twenty-first century.

A FRAMEWORK FOR STUDYING INCORPORATION IN A TIME OF CHANGE

My research attempts to synthesize and extend several important but disconnected theoretical traditions in the field of ethnic and racial studies, applying these to the study of intergroup relations and Latino/a migrant incorporation in the contemporary South. The sociologist Roger Waldinger's (1996) "ethnic succession model," which builds on Lester Thurow's (1975) queue model of labor markets and Stanley Lieberson's (1980) landmark study of the "new immigration" to New York City, attempts to account for the motivation and persistence of discrimination by employers as well as the salience or relative absence of competition and conflict between workers in the context of workplace compositional change. Several studies have applied the general logic of the ethnic succession model to analyzing the impact of migrants on the composition of labor markets in the U.S. South and the quality of relations between African Americans and Latinas/os. Although conclusions about the extent to which Latino/a migrants displace or replace native-born whites and African Americans are not in any way definitive, studies have tended to interpret the evidence as supporting replacement (Griffith 1995; Skaggs, Tomaskovic-Devey, and Leiter 2000; Rosenfield and Tienda 1999; Kandel and Parrado 2004; but see López-Sanders 2009 for a clear case of employer-initiated displacement).

While the ethnic succession model would *expect* little conflict in situations of replacement as opposed to displacement, few studies shed light on the *actual* character of social relations among groups encountering one another at work in the contemporary U.S. South at a time of massive demographic change. This volume builds on research that shows how ethnic succession processes are shaped, not just by the preferences of employers and the social closure that migrant networks permit, but also by the managerial policies and broader sociopolitical environment that enable or constrain these mechanisms. While the ethnic succession model is useful in explaining compositional change, especially of the large-scale aggregate sort, I argue that it has limited utility for understanding the dynamic features of intergroup relations given its built-in assumptions. I view incorporation as a process conditioned by context through which groups struggle to define their place in a stratified system of belonging. In doing so, I retreat from the focus on outcomes in general, and the emphasis on competition-based conflict narrowly construed in particular, that inheres in the ethnic succession model. Instead, I propose viewing relations among subordinate groups as prismatic engagement, in which ongoing iterations and encounters in crucial life domains are patterned into an emergent sense of group position, whose social boundaries are expressed symbolically, and which is mediated by dominant groups who form the core of stratification systems.

Some scholars have approached the question of social relations between Latino/a migrants and nonmigrant whites and African Americans by evaluating competing hypotheses relating to factors thought to give rise to intergroup conflict, with several important works advancing Herbert Blumer's (1958) "sense of group position" approach. Although Blumer's concept refers to the positional relationship between dominant and subordinate groups, and the mechanism that produces dominant-group prejudice toward subordinate groups (i.e., perceived threats to their position), scholars since have extended his group position approach to the study of intergroup relations and prejudice among subordinate groups (Bobo and Hutchings 1996) and within class-stratified contexts (Waldinger and Lichter 2003). While this approach has become popular, I argue that integrating the "group position" perspective with a "boundaries" approach, which can account for the social relational processes tied to patterns of structural transformation, yields a more robust explanation of the inter-group relations that shape incorporation in the context of dramatic demographic, economic, and legal-political change in the South. Indeed, curiously, the way in which Blumer's conceptualization dovetails with one strand of literature that draws on the anthropologist Fredrik Barth's (1969) view of ethnic groups as boundaries has not been acknowledged, as far as I know.

Barth's work has inspired cultural sociologists interested in the study of social and symbolic boundaries. In his (1969, 10) critique of viewing ethnic groups as "culture-bearing units," he underlined a shift in focus from cultural *forms* to generative *processes* of ethnic boundary creation, maintenance, and change. Drawing on Barth's original analysis of boundary formation and maintenance, and Pierre Bourdieu's (1984) advances in these areas, Michelle Lamont (2000; 1999; [with Fournier] 1992) has established a strong research program in boundary processes or boundary-work. This literature is concerned with how symbolic resources contribute to the creation, maintenance, contestation, and dissolution of institutionalized social differences (Lamont and Molnar 2002). According to Lamont and Virág Molnar (2002), boundary-work in general consists of categorical schemes around perceptions of similarities and differences that groups use to identify who they are. In their analytical focus on groups, scholars who study boundary-work are more interested in "the *content* and *interpretive dimensions* of boundary-work than with intra-individual processes" (171).

A number of scholars have examined the kinds of boundary-work through racialization that tie certain groups to certain jobs and to particular tasks within an occupation (excluding others), and have analyzed what these associations suggest about relations among different groups of workers and between workers and bosses (De Genova 2005; Striffler 2005; Waldinger and Lichter 2003; Hondagneu-Sotelo 2001; Wrigley 1999; Waters 1999). According to Nicholas De Genova (2005, 2), *racialization* refers to "the dynamic processes by which the meanings and distinctions attributed to 'race' come to be *produced* and continually reproduced, and more important, are always entangled in social relations and conflicts, and thus retain an enduring significance because their specific forms and substantive meanings are eminently historical and mutable." Such distinctions take on both structural and symbolic manifestations, as the physical attributes, social meanings, and material inequalities that are inscribed in "race" situate groups in relation to one another in a constellation of positions (Omi and Winant 1994; Kim 1999; Haney López 2006 [1996]) within which whiteness retains a central, and (I emphasize) prismatic role.

Though recently a number of scholars have turned to Blumer's (1958) "sense of group position" approach to explain how ethnic/racial groups view their own and other groups' location in such a complex hierarchical map of intergroup relations (Bobo and Hutchings 1996; Waldinger and Lichter 2003; Marrow 2007), attention to boundary processes sheds light on how and why such a map is produced and reproduced in different contexts, and on what the specific social and symbolic markers in distinct regions of the map convey (Wimmer 2008; Loveman and Muñiz 2007; Brubaker and Cooper 2000; Lamont and Molnar 2002; Loveman 1999). Lamont and Molnar (2002) call for studies of the content of, and mechanisms linked to, boundary-work that generates and mirrors social boundaries. In attending to the boundary formation processes tied to prismatic engagement between Latinas/os and African American workers in a Southern meatpacking plant, this research contributes to our understanding of the production of contemporary group-based inequalities.

INTERGROUP RELATIONS AND LATINO/A MIGRANT INCORPORATION IN THE U.S. SOUTH

Latino/a migration to nontraditional destinations has produced a wealth of volumes documenting the unprecedented transformation of the American heartland and Bible Belt regions (Anrig, Wang, and McClain 2006; Zúñiga and Hernández-León 2005; Arreola 2004; Sills 2010; Hill and Beaver 1998; Stull, Broadway, and Griffith 1995; Gozdziak and Martin 2005; Hamamoto and Torres 1997; Jones 2008; Johnson-Webb 2003; Odem and Lacy 2009; Murphy, Blanchard, and Hill 2001; Mantero 2008; Massey 2008; Peacock, Watson, and Matthews 2005; Smith and Furuseth 2006; Gill 2010). The vast majority of research on Latino/a migration to the U.S. South consists of case studies of particular localities, often painting a portrait in broad strokes of small-town demographic and economic restructuring that highlights the significant contributions Latino/a migrants have made to the agro-industrial labor force. This growing literature has addressed the "challenges" that such changes pose for places with little recent historical experience with immigration, and reveals an undercurrent of concern over the destabilization of long-standing binary intergroup relations and the ongoing configuration of a new, more complex system of intergroup relations now featuring whites, African Americans, and Latinas/os. The concern over potentially conflictive relations between Latinas/os and African Americans, in particular, is based on the idea that while studies generally show the net economic benefits of immigration to the U.S. economy, labor migrants might compete with less educated, more disadvantaged native-born groups (Holzer 2011; United States Commission on Civil Rights 2010; Smith and Edmonston 1997).

With respect to the latter concern, a number of scholars have undertaken analyses of intergroup relations across a plethora of rural and urban Southern locales. To this point, most studies report cause for concern over the quality of relations between Latinas/os and African Americans (McDermott 2011; Marrow 2011; López-Sanders 2009; Gordon and Lenhardt 2007; but see Jones 2012). For example, Marrow (2011; 2007) interviewed more than a hundred Latino/a migrants and native-born whites and African Americans in two North Carolina counties, across a variety of industries and institutional arenas. She found that Latino/a migrants sense greater discrimination from African Americans than from whites, and she explains this using a group position model, since African Americans are mostly at the bottom of the social class structure, while whites are generally split between working and middle class. She contends that African Americans, feeling a threat to their sense of group position, react in an exclusionary fashion toward Latinas/os, a socioeconomic competition–based threat exacerbated in areas with higher African American population levels. According to Marrow, "Hispanic newcomers experience discrimination and exclusion not just along one vertical skin color axis along which white natives can mark them as racially inferior, but also along a separate horizontal (non)citizenship axis along which both white and black natives can mark and ostracize them as undeserving civic and cultural 'outsiders.'" She says this axis is experienced most strongly by Latino/a migrants, and that Blacks are seen as its "worst perpetrators" (30). The anthropologists David Griffith (2005) and Steve Striffler (2005) report similar findings from their interviews with Latinas/os involved in poultry processing in Arkansas and North Carolina. To Marrow and others, these findings point to the role of African Americans in excluding Latinas/os, and "helping to speed up Hispanic newcomers' incorporation into 'mainstream' rural Southern society as 'nonblacks'" (2007, 30).

The problem with these studies is that they draw conclusions based on an incomplete picture of the dynamics that are at play. With respect to relations between African Americans and Latino/a migrants, scholars have tended to focus on one dimension of the relationship: African Americans' supposed attitudes and behavior toward Latino/a migrants. From this perspective, "conflict" is expected to stem from the former's feelings about the competitive threat posed by the latter. But from an *incorporation* perspective, Latino/a migrants' understandings about African Americans take on equal significance, and these understandings are likely tied to how Latinas/os view their own group. From this perspective, socioeconomic competition per se may not be the operative factor driving the character of intergroup relations.

Critically, previous research relies almost exclusively on interview data, mostly with Latino/a migrants embedded in a variety of arenas. Although interview-based research conducted with Latinas/os may elicit information about the stereotypes or other sources for attitudes they have toward Blacks, such data is no substitute for observational data that captures unprompted and spontaneous encounters between Latinas/os and African Americans in crucial and delimited contexts such as work. Indeed, studies that have gone beyond largely assumptive claims about socioeconomic competition, and which have considered actual workplace relations, suggest the significance of perceived disparities within the social organization of labor for conditioning relations between Latinas/os and African Americans in ways that foreshadow my argument (Stuesse and Helton 2013; Stuesse 2009).

Further, while such interview-based research yields rich data on the perceptions of Latinas/os across a broad range of social situations about whether they experience discrimination and to whom they attribute it, it is important to distinguish between a statement about Latinas/os' perceptions, whatever their actual experiences, and a statement about the fact of African Americans' role in essentially pushing Latinas/os to embrace a position closer to whites. After all, the built-in incentives Latinas/os have—and were likely well aware of before arriving—to distance themselves from Blacks and other highly stigmatized groups and identify with whites cannot be underestimated, and immigrant groups may "overlook" the slights and injustices perpetrated by dominant groups while exaggerating those of others (see Hondagneu-Sotelo 2001). Although some efforts have been made to give analytical attention to whites and whiteness in the study of Latino/a migrant incorporation in the South and the reconfiguration of racialized systems of stratification (see Marrow 2011, chapters 4 and 5), there is still a tendency to study intergroup relations dyadically. This is so because it is difficult to both conceptualize and operationalize the multiple configurations in which intergroup relations are actually organized. Unfortunately, this has obscured the powerful, if often intangible, intervention of whiteness, the opaque shadow of which looms over the whole system of racialized stratification (Haney López 2014; Lipsitz 2006 [1998]; De Genova 2005; Kim 1999).

Indeed, my argument here is prefigured by the "revisionist" history of scholars who rebuild the incorporation experiences of earlier migrants from Europe, who moved from "racial in-betweenness" to unambiguous whiteness, not just because employers placed them at the front of the queue ahead of African Americans, but through the very real struggles among workers themselves over jobs—"brutal, group-based competition" where it was widely known that Black workers fared much worse than any other native-born group (Barrett and Roediger 1997, 18; also Roediger 2005; Jacobson 1998; Brodkin 1998). Although the basis of these struggles today may be different, and their eventual outcomes remain uncertain, the dynamics themselves are remarkably similar. I draw attention to the study of incorporation as an ongoing social process of prismatic engagement that involves both action and reaction on the part of Latino/a migrants *and* native-born groups, such as African Americans, with whom they are meaningfully engaged in the crucial setting, structure, and process of work. By also situating this analysis within the backdrop of a broader system of racialized stratification characterized by white dominance, I hope to contribute one piece to the still-unresolved puzzle of who Latinas/os are becoming.

Laboring alongside Latina/o and African American meatpacking workers and getting to know them outside the factory left me certain that understanding how these groups encounter one another, and assessing what the character of these encounters suggests about how Latinas/os in the contemporary South are becoming incorporated into American racial/ethnic and class stratification systems, is a messy endeavor with surprising findings that are at once encouraging and deeply troubling. In marked contrast to the fears of some scholars and pundits, and against the conclusions put forth in recent research on the topic of intergroup relations in the U.S. South, African Americans working at Swine's do not talk or behave as if they are especially threatened by economic, political, or cultural competition from Latinos/migrants despite the fact that at least some of the necessary conditions are met, and this finding holds regardless of whether African Americans are the majority or minority in the department they work in.

On the other hand, Latinos/migrants deploy an elaborate array of racialized actions that are substantially inflected negatively toward African Americans. This reflects and reinforces ethnoracial boundaries between Latinas/os and African Americans, appears to represent Latinas/os' determination to achieve incorporation as non-Blacks, and may bolster the hegemony of whiteness in the emerging order. Yet the qualitative range within and across distinct modes of action—how Latinas/os and African Americans talk about and behave toward one another—reveals contradictions and disjunctures that complicate any sweeping generalization based on even the major tendencies I observed. It also serves as a reminder that in a context that demands prolonged physical proximity and collaboration, antagonism is likely to coexist with various forms of cooperation and even affection. As Yanira, a young Dominican packer, put it, "If you work with one person so closely, constantly, daily, hour after hour, thirteen-hour after thirteen-hour, you're going to get to be friends with that person one way or another, you're going to start fighting with that person, and then you're going to make friends again."

OUTLINE OF THE BOOK

Chapter 2 addresses the broad social and economic contexts in which Latino/a migration to the American South has unfolded. It discusses the arrival stories of Latino/a migrants, focusing especially on the experiences of women and Central Americans, as both of those groups have received less attention than their male and Mexican counterparts. This chapter first delves into the social and economic contexts of origin communities that framed the migrants' decisions to leave. It then discusses the Latina/o migrants' labor market experiences in the United States that shaped their eventual insertion into the South's agro-industrial labor force. Following this, it examines the history of compositional change at Swine's, of which these Latina/o migrants are the chief protagonists, linking such changes to the broader sociopolitical and economic environment and to the labor-relations context of Swine's from the 1970s to the present. It argues that compositional change or "ethnic succession" at Swine's can be attributed to a combination of replacement and displacement dynamics in the context of growth in a burgeoning regional industry. Although competition perspectives embedded in theories that explain ethnic succession assume that replacement/displacement dynamics are configured in particular ways with the likelihood of intergroup conflict, I argue that these frameworks offer limited utility for studying relations between Latinas/os and African Americans in the workplace.

Chapter 3 delves into the racialized language of the shop floor. In particular it examines the symbolic boundaries Latina/o workers construct vis-à-vis their African American counterparts through such designations of the latter as *moyos*. It traces the origins and usages of the term, locating it in a transnational field of ethnoracial meanings that reflect as well as produce negative boundaries with African Americans.

Chapter 4 links the strong symbolic boundaries that Latinas/os draw vis-à-vis African Americans to important social distinctions they perceive in the positions each group occupies within the workplace. That is, the strong and largely negatively valenced boundaries are intertwined with Latina/o workers' certainty that they are the most disadvantaged group at Swine's and that African Americans occupy a position of privilege. To explain my findings, I expand the concept of racial alienation by recognizing alternative sources of grievance that may motivate intergroup relations and that are context dependent, challenging scholars' preoccupation with job competition as the key source of intergroup conflict. By loosening the unnecessary analytic restrictions in the original formulation (Bobo and Hutchings 1996), racial alienation becomes a powerful part of the explanation for the social-relational dynamics at Swine's and for political configurations in the broader stratified system of belonging in the United States.

Chapter 5 delves in greater depth into the source of Latino/a workers' perception of themselves as the most oppressively exploited workers at Swine's. It argues that the vulnerabilities of "illegality," which objectively affect only migrants who lack work authorization, bleed onto the group as a whole—*hispanos*—for a variety of reasons. It further proposes that, while unauthorized migrants' vulnerabilities stem from their "deportability," as other scholars have argued, in the workplace their vulnerabilities operate through the mechanism of "disposability."

Chapter 6 considers how the composition of the authority structure—African American, white, or Latino/a—mediates the dynamics observed and described in the preceding chapters. It analyzes the widespread perception among Latina/o workers that an African American–dominated authority structure magnifies the "privileged" position of African American workers.

Chapter 7 turns to an examination of African American workers' perspectives on Latinas/os and immigrants. This chapter is dedicated to explaining my findings regarding the weaker and less negative boundaries that African American workers draw vis-à-vis their Latina/o counterparts. These findings are surprising given the conclusions put forth in recent research that relies on competition perspectives and interviews with (mostly) Latinas/os, namely that African Americans display more exclusionary attitudes and behavior toward Latinas/os in the South than do whites. In combination with an expanded construct of racial alienation, this chapter proposes that the concept of "linked fate"—the sense among members of a group that their individual fortunes are tied to those of the group as a whole—helps to account for the findings I put forth. Finally, in chapter 8, I summarize my findings and advance the concept of prismatic engagement as particularly useful to studying relations among subordinated groups encountering one another in a field of racial positions characterized by white dominance. I also take up the policy implications of these findings, and propose a set of reforms that are urgently needed to improve the lives of all workers on—and off—the line.

CHAPTER 2

All Roads Lead from Olancho to Swine's

The Making of A Latino/a Working Class in The American South

"I never imagined I'd end up here in this countryside breaking my back working a knife job. I'm from Honduras, from a place called San Nicolás de Copán. I was there until the age of five, when I was taken to Cortés department. My mother left me in the care of my father, but he took me and a brother of mine to an orphanage because he was unable to care for us. I was there for three years, but I was lost without my father. He came to get me and my brother and we went to work with him on the streets, after the aunt who had been taking care of us died of cancer. I worked from the age of eleven and lived with my father until the age of sixteen. When I was fifteen, I started working at a Korean-owned factory. About four years later they made me a line supervisor. I went to live with my mother because it was closer to the factory. I worked there for seven years. I met a guy and went to live with him in Olancho. We had two kids and he came over here [to North Carolina]. I stayed in Olancho for four years, doing housework and raising children, until Ernesto was able to send for me. He sent me money every month. He worked at Swine's."

Cristina's narrative is one of hundreds of thousands that tell the arrival story of the new working class in maturing destinations for Latino/a migration all over the American South. Listening to these stories, sometimes I felt certain that little had changed from the time when Upton Sinclair recorded the despairing tales of Lithuanian immigrants who came to work in Chicago's packinghouses at the turn of the twentieth century. In both scenarios, there was calamity upon calamity: the forward strides were barely perceptible and the setbacks continual. Cristina's mother, overwhelmed with other children and a new spouse, had left Cristina and one of her brothers in the care of her father when she was little, a period in her life she vividly remembers. For years, she and her brother lived in Catholic and Evangelical children's homes because her father, a street vendor, was too poor to support them. By the time she was twelve and living with her father again, she was working in restaurant kitchens and selling produce on street corners. She never had a lot of friends. She raised herself, she told me on several occasions, intimating at once her distance from and distrust of people and the unusualness of our budding friendship. She is enthralled by philosophical questions about the origins of life and the existence of God, and found my shop-floor explanation of human evolutionary theory irreverent and entertaining. "You say we came from monkeys?!" she would exclaim in awe, calling others over to come hear my strange stories. I learned some important lessons from Cristina, in terms of both understanding the questions about migrant incorporation and intergroup relations that I set out to research, and appreciating the dogged perseverance of the human spirit in the face of crushing defeats:

> We embarked on the journey one night in June 2002, and arrived in Guatemala around six in the morning. We stayed there for three days and exchanged money. To get to the border, we had ridden a bus, and we crossed into Guatemala via taxis. We stayed in "hotels" [meaning, informal waystations]. From there we went by bus to the border with Mexico. For two days we slept on the floor in the home of some *indígenas* [indigenous people] in San Rafael. From there, we were moved in a small truck, which had a hole underneath it by the tires, and we entered through that hole, nineteen of us lying in a line. At checkpoints, the police banged on the tires. We had been warned not to breathe. We traveled this way from about four in the morning, arriving at Puebla around six in the evening. We were there two days, and then two by two we purchased tickets for a bus to DF [Distrito Federal, meaning, Mexico City]. We were in DF for three days, at a house, and left on buses for Durango around eight in the evening and arrived around eight in the morning. That same day we left for Chihuahua, close to the U.S. border, on a bus for another "hotel." We were there for one day, and then we were all taken together toward the border. After another day, we were taken by truck and dropped off in the mountains to walk. We traveled on foot, walking for about seven days. Leaving from Cananea near Agua Prieta, we crossed a mountain, descended, and crossed another on route to the desert and to Phoenix. We walked at night and rested during the day, until we arrived at a sierra, a few homes in the desert. Three vans arrived to pick us up. My shoes were shredded. The vans were small and people were crowded into them. As we got out, our feet were asleep, tingling. I came with my brother-in-law. In Phoenix, we showered and changed clothes. Another van came and took us to Los Angeles at around one in the morning. There were fifty-two of us there, as our original group of nineteen had joined up with others in the desert, and other migrants had already been waiting in this trailer for several days. Around eleven in the morning, we were eating breakfast in the trailer home when masked gunmen arrived, holding us hostage until they received payment.

Cristina's story bears elements that are especially harrowing, though not unlike the stories of other migrants from Latin America. Her retelling of the hardships she faced on her winding, clandestine travels to the United States, though, was peppered with snippets of what I had already come to know by the time I sat down with her for an interview about a year after we met: her characteristic humor in even the direst of circumstances.

At the beginning of her bus ride from Mexico City to Durango, she had surmised that the police officer who boarded the bus to conduct inspections had taken pity on her because he refused the bribe she had been instructed by coyotes to discreetly fold into her identification papers. Thinking herself lucky at that moment, the man sitting next to her asked where she was from. "From the DF," she replied to the man, just as she had to the officer. "And going to Durango." After telling her that she did not sound Mexican, her seatmate said to her that perhaps he should have asked where in Central America she was from. He guessed Nicaragua, Guatemala, and finally Honduras. "How did you know?" she asked him. "I saw you hiding money in different places. And look who I am," the man said to her, showing her his police badge. "Are you going to turn me in?" she asked him nervously. "No," the man said, "I'm on vacation!" He then warned her that another police checkpoint was coming up, and that she should pretend to be sleeping so as to avoid risking detention or a fleecing, advice she promptly followed. Once the officers left the bus, he told Cristina it was safe to wake up. The next bus (from Durango to Cananea, where they would begin their treacherous march by foot) was filled almost entirely by transit migrants, and Cristina did have to pay up, as did all the others. Even so, she recalled with a chuckle, when a policewoman boarded the bus and asked where she was going, she was fortunate to have remembered her destination: Cananea. Another migrant had a lapse in memory and responded, "to Canada," to which the policewoman barked, "You can't even lie! Give me 300 pesos."

In these "lighthearted" details, mixed in with the severity of all she had endured, Christina's story revealed threads that were repeated in the stories of other migrants, especially women, who embarked on the migration journey with the hopes of earning enough money to provide for their families. Sometimes they were joining spouses who had already settled in the United States, and sometimes they were setting off on their own with the assistance of the transnational social networks in which they were embedded. Whether they came to reunite with spouses, like

Cristina, or were drawn by pioneering relatives and friends, like Cristina's husband, Ernesto, all of their stories culminated at Swine's. At Swine's, just as in the broader agro-industrial complex of the American South, Latinas/os have been incorporated as the premier labor force since the turn of the twenty-first century, ensuring that these labor-intensive industries have an abundant, steady, willing supply of hands.

This chapter frames the macro-level social and economic contexts in which this remarkable transformation of the South has taken place, preparing readers for understanding the middle-level intergroup relations between Latinas/os and African Americans discussed in subsequent chapters. The first section of this chapter describes general trends in Latino/a migration to new destinations and the more specific dynamics of Central American migration to the catchment area surrounding Swine's. This discussion draws special attention to the experiences of pioneer migrants and women as part of what some scholars refer to as the Latinization of the American South, and of the Southern agro-industrial complex in particular (Mohl 2005). I discuss both these migrants' motivations for leaving their communities of origin and their labor market experiences following their settlement in the United States. The second section draws the reader into the belly of the beast—Swine's—the twenty-first-century slaughterhouse in which this book is set. It describes major features of the plant, including its composition, and portrays the workday in the Loin Boning and Packing Department. The third section traces the transformation of Swine Inc.'s workforce from the early 1970s to the present. It highlights how struggles between capital's imperative to ensure an abundant and compliant workforce and episodes of resistance to labor subordination intersect with human resource policies and sociopolitical regimes dealing with unauthorized migration to engender the transformation of the Swine's labor force from predominantly African American to predominantly Latina/o. The final section considers the implications of the compositional dynamics at Swine's not only for bridging supply and demand–side accounts of migration, but for extending theories of "ethnic succession" in labor markets and recognizing their limited utility for explaining intergroup relations.

LATINO/A MIGRATION TRENDS IN NEW DESTINATIONS

Especially since the early 1990s, Latin American migrants have been drawn to nontraditional destinations in the Midwest and South: cities, towns, and rural locales with little to no recollection of experience with Latino/a newcomers. In general, these new migrant streams are composed primarily of Mexicans, but particular areas have attracted significant numbers of Guatemalans, Hondurans, Salvadorans, and other Central Americans as well as Haitian, Hmong, and Somali refugees. While the migration of these latter groups has to some degree been a response to recent political events or natural disasters in their countries of origin, Mexican migration to the United States has a long history that is divisible into several eras characterized by the shifting context of U.S. immigration law and its enforcement, and employer demand for cheap labor.[1]

Several factors explain this new geography of Mexican migration to the United States. The legalization programs of the Immigration Reform and Control Act of 1986 (IRCA) regularized the status of several million Mexicans. Many legalized migrants left traditional settlement areas in the Southwest and California and made their way East and South in search of new opportunity structures. The California recession and a rise in nativist hostility in the early to mid-1990s created inhospitable social, economic, and political conditions in traditional destinations and intensified this migration to new destinations (Light 2006).

Economic restructuring in the Southeast and the rise of the manufacturing, construction, and meat processing industries drew Mexican migrants to this area as well (Mohl 2005). By 2000, 21 percent of Mexican immigrants in the country were living in non-gateway states, and of those who arrived in the last five years (between 1995 and 2000), only 35 percent went to California, compared to 63 percent of those who arrived between 1985 and 1990 (Durand, Massey, and Capoferro 2005, 13). Thus, both the diversity of destinations, and the percentage of Mexican immigrants located in new destinations, has grown.

North Carolina is one of these new destinations. The Latino/a population there grew dramatically between 1990 and 2004, increasing almost sevenfold by official U.S. Census counts from 76,726 to 506,206, and growing to at least 7 percent of the state's population (Kasarda and Johnson 2006). Mexican migrants have been settling in North Carolina at least since the early 1980s to work in agriculture. By the mid-1980s they had begun moving into poultry processing and meatpacking, and later construction, manufacturing, landscaping, and restaurant and hospitality trades (Griffith 2005). The reasons for this growth are many, but the most important factors contributing to migration during the late 1980s and early 1990s included the growth of food processing, construction, and furniture manufacturing industries, the increase in legal immigrants with knowledge of North Carolina serving as conduits to North Carolina jobs and the post-IRCA mobility attained by many migrants previously settled in traditional gateway states, growing links between labor contractors and *raiteros* (transporters, especially of agricultural workers), and greater overlap between agricultural and rural industrial labor markets (Griffith 2005; Griffith 1995; Mohl 2005; Kochhar, Suro, and Tafoya 2005; Kandel and Parrado 2004; Parrado and Kandel 2008).

Of course, high Latino/a employment growth corresponded with this massive growth in the North Carolina Latino/a population (Kasarda and Johnson 2006). The Latino/a share of the workforce in the industries that are the focus of this study also grew dramatically over this period. Griffith (2005) notes that more poultry firms in North Carolina were hiring Mexican migrants in 1990 than in 1988, and those firms that hired in 1988 hired more in 1990 (Griffith 1993), trends that continued through the 1990s (Schwartzman 2013; Striffler 2005; Smith-Nonini 2003) and were apparent in the meat processing industry across new destinations beyond North Carolina (Parrado and Kandel 2008). Similarly, although their entry into the food service industry is more recent and their presence remains very uneven even among fast-food establishments located next to each other, Latinas/os are making significant inroads in employment in this industry.[2] Officially, the town of Perry, home to Swine's, is only slightly more than 5 percent "Hispanic," but the county-level "Hispanic population" is greater than 15 percent, and both of these figures are surely underestimates. At both the county and town levels, whites are the majority, though African Americans form a much larger minority in Perry at more than 40 percent, and occupy a more intermediate position at the county level. In part because of the more similar class distributions of African Americans and Latinas/os—their greater likelihood of meeting in the workplace as lower-wage, "low-skilled" workers—and African Americans' spatial concentration in the downtown residential and commercial areas, Latinas/os sense a more significant presence of African Americans relative to whites in the area.

THE PIONEERS

Domingo is from southern Veracruz, Mexico, an agricultural and livestock-raising area, where he labored in the fields ever since he was a child. In Veracruz, he met a man who had regularized his status through

IRCA and routinely traveled between the United States and Mexico, contracting workers to labor in the animal processing industry. This man recruited Domingo in 1992 in exchange for a $1,500 fee, and Domingo arrived directly to the town of Fall River, North Carolina. He took up work at the Watts Farms turkey processing plant, then after working there for several years, he moved on to the Pig Corporation plant in Davis, where they were hiring unauthorized workers freely at the time. After about two years, however, he was fired when his papers "*salieron malos*" (turned out bad). In 2000, he returned to Mexico thinking he would stay, but came back to the United States four years later in 2004. He had married a Mexican woman in North Carolina in 1995, and when the two returned to Mexico they "had problems," so they decided to go to North Carolina (but still ended up splitting up later). Upon returning, he and his wife took jobs at a Tasty Bird chicken processing plant in Fox Spring, North Carolina, on the night shift. It was hard, though, to have both of them on the third shift when their three kids needed looking after. So he worked in construction for two or three years, and watched the kids while his wife was at work at Tasty Bird. At this point, construction work suffered a sharp decline, the company he had been working for went into bankruptcy, and he needed to look for work. His search spanned the entire southeastern region, and included applications at Fresh Birds in Linden, Holden Farms in Hensley, and Swine's in Perry, all processing plants. Swine's called first, and he began working there in 2009. He has eight siblings, and all have spent some time in North Carolina, but only a sister and two brothers remain. When Domingo worked at the Davis hog processing plant, union organizers were reaching out to workers in the parking lots. In fact, he was at Watts Farms in October 1994, when the union won its second representation election, six years after a wildcat strike and representation election that followed it, which failed as a result of unfair labor practices. Perhaps if the New South ever came to reckon with its history, it would acknowledge its indebtedness to men like Domingo who have worked for most of the last twenty years in North Carolina's burgeoning agro-industry.

With little doubt, Mexican men blazed the trail to the American Southeast, with Central American men slowly becoming integrated into this migration circuit in the late 1980s and early 1990s. In North Carolina in 2010, there was approximately one foreign-born Central American migrant for every four Mexican migrants, and the statewide Central American population surpassed eighty thousand. Because the Central American population residing in North Carolina—comprised primarily of Hondurans, Salvadorans, and Guatemalans—is concentrated in the multicounty catchment area that surrounds Swine's, their proportion of the Latina/o population relative to Mexicans in this area is substantially higher, especially when agricultural workers, who are predominantly Mexican, are excluded (American Community Survey 2010).[3] In time, the Honduran presence came to dominate among Latinas/os in this region of North Carolina, far outnumbering the Salvadorans and even contesting the Mexican majority in certain workplaces.

In 1997, when Cristina's brother-in-law Heriberto applied for a job at Swine's, following several cousins who pioneered the early stage of Honduran migration to Clark County in the late 1980s and early 1990s, the Human Resources manager asked him to list nine nonconsecutive numbers off the top of his head. He could have a job under his own name if the number wasn't already on file for another employee. It was a time when work authorization requirements were lax and easily circumvented by Human Resources personnel and unauthorized migrants alike. Heriberto estimates that when he started to work on the Cut Floor, Latinas/os were already close to 70 percent of the workforce, but there was still a substantial minority of African Americans in the department. He is confident that at that time, Latinas/os were given preferential treatment in hiring, owing to both their larger share of the applicant pool and the systematic, disproportionate hiring of Latinas/os relative to others in the applicant pool, a process that he says paralleled the efforts of supervisors to speed up the disassembly lines.[4] Because Human Resources informally established separate application days for Spanish speakers, the disproportionate hiring of Latinas/os might not have been immediately evident to all who applied. From the late 1990s onward, a Puerto Rican woman named Myrna functioned as assistant Human Resources manager. In combination with her Honduran husband, and aided by the operation of migrant social networks, she succeeded in recruiting a multistatus, heavily Honduran labor force. Those Latinas/os who obtained employment despite or because of the presentation of documents known to be false showed their appreciation to Myrna with both generous and humble gifts.

FORCES PUSH HONDURANS, THEIR FEET IN THE DOOR, FURTHER TOWARD SWINE'S

As the saying doesn't go, company loves misery. Whoever said nature doesn't discriminate was wrong. If Mr. Samuels, founder of the Swine

Packing Company, is one of nature's noblemen, as the late U.S. Senator Jesse Helms once proclaimed, then nature is squarely on the nobleman's side; Hurricane Mitch brought a lot of misery to Honduras and parts of El Salvador, and the "lengthened shadow" of nature's nobleman—the Swine Packing Company—got plenty more Hondurans in return. Along with Honduras's entire Atlantic coast, Mitch devastated the central and south zones, leaving in its wake nearly 6,000 fatalities, 12,000 injured, 8,000 disappeared, and 285,000 homeless. In addition to the severe flooding in all eighteen departments, 60 percent of the transportation infrastructure was damaged, a quarter of all educational facilities were destroyed, and 70 percent of crops were ruined (Secretaría de Salud de Honduras, date unknown). Records kept by Casas del Migrante, a hospitality house for journeying migrants in Tecun Uman, Guatemala, and Ocotepeque, Honduras, show the enormous acceleration in Honduran out-migration following Mitch (Pastoral Social/Caritas 2003). A 2006 study estimated the proportion of Honduran households that included an emigrant as 11.3 percent (Flores Fonseca 2008b), perhaps reflecting the accelerated out-migration following Hurricane Mitch in 1998, and especially after 2000, when Honduras also suffered several droughts and declines in the price of coffee exports. The 2001 Honduras census estimated that at the national level, 3.34 percent of households included someone who had migrated internationally in the three preceding years, largely as a result of Hurricane Mitch.

Colón and Olancho, the two origin departments most prominent among Hondurans in North Carolina, were hard hit by the hurricane. They would become among the top five migrant-sending departments during this period, and 6.28 percent of households included someone who had migrated between 1998 and 2001. Some *municipios* (municipalities) in Olancho that had not been directly and seriously affected by Hurricane Mitch—for instance Santa María de Real, Silca, and San Francisco de Becerra—already had been strong migrant-sending areas before the hurricane. More than once, I heard Hondurans say that "all of" Silca was in North Carolina. If this was an exaggeration, it nonetheless reflected some grain of truth. By 2001, between 10 and 22 percent of households in these *municipios* were estimated to include an international migrant (Flores Fonseca 2008a). A study of migration and remittances in the four most prominent migrant-sending *municipios* in Olancho (Juticalpa, Catacamas, Santa María del Real, and San Francisco Becerra) found that 28 percent of households included a current international migrant, and that more than half of these current migrants had left after 2000. Among the current resident population of these *municipios*, 11.4 percent (6,306 persons) had some international migration experience. Of those individuals with migration experience whose destination had been the United States, 17 percent never made it past Mexico. While about two-thirds of "return migrants" stated that their return was voluntary or planned, 30 percent admitted to having been deported.[5]

Many Hondurans in North Carolina come from Olancho, the largest department in the country—larger than the entire country of El Salvador, Honduras's neighbor to the southwest. It is an extremely rural zone that stands in the national imagination as a bastion of "the old ways"— like kindness to your fellow humans and the subordination of women to men—and of lawlessness—Olancho is reportedly one of the most violent regions in a country that has close to the highest murder rate in the world (86/100,000 compared to 5/100,000 in the United States) (Pressly 2012; Frank 2012; Flores Fonseca 2008a).[6] Along with the Afro-indigenous Garifuna, West Indians, and other Honduran workers from the interior, Olanchanos made up an important source of labor for banana companies along the north coast in the twentieth century (Euraque 2003; Flores Fonseca 2008a). Olancho, the Honduran department with the richest natural resources (Flores Fonseca 2008a), has vast but dwindling pine and mahogany forests. Illegal logging operations flourish in the region, and while this wood ends up on the shelves and showrooms of European and U.S. retailers such as Home Depot, Macy's, and Babies R Us, communities like those in Salamá are left with dried-up riverbeds that destroy local economic sustainability and perhaps add to population pressures. These communities' resistance to the barefaced theft of profits by the underground timber trade and the environmental devastation that accompanies it is met with violent repression from timber companies and the Honduran state itself (Environmental Investigation Agency 2005).[7]

In the *longue dureé* of global capitalism's maturation, Honduras has played a key role as a staging ground for U.S. hegemony in Latin America. First as the original "Banana Republic," resulting from nearly two hundred years of domination by U.S. fruit companies, then as the "Pentagon Republic," resulting from U.S. suppression of rebellious movements in El Salvador, Nicaragua, and other Central American countries, Honduras has been pillaged and puppeteered by the usurious hand of global capitalism (Euraque 1996; Chomsky 1985). Reflecting the recent times of enormous dependence on the financial contributions of migrants, Honduras has been referred to as a "Remittance Republic" (Pine 2008).

In addition to Olancho, many North Carolina Hondurans are from the department of Colón, along the Atlantic coast to the north, which was also devastated by Hurricane Mitch in 1998. Few people I worked with at Swine's identified as Garifuna, but Colón is home to the largest Garifuna populations in the diaspora. From the late nineteenth century through much of the twentieth, Colón was ground zero for the banana plantation economy that made an empire of the United Fruit Company (Laínez and Meza 1973; Bourgois 2003). Since the later 1900s, Colón has also become an important site for the production of African palms and the extraction of palm oil. As elsewhere, the expansion of African palm cultivation has intensified land pressures and has led to conflicts between landless peasant families and the local corporate oligarchs who own much of the productive land along the north coast (Malkin 2011). Now in the early twenty-first century, the north coast of Honduras has also become a vital hub for the sale, transfer, and processing of cocaine destined for Mexican and U.S. markets (United Nations Office on Drugs and Crime 2011).

MOLDING THE PREMIER AGRO-INDUSTRIAL LABOR FORCE: LATINAS AT SWINE'S

Far less is known about the experiences of Latina migrants than about the experiences of their male pioneer counterparts. For that reason, the next section devotes attention to describing their decisions to migrate and their work experiences before and after migration. While Latino men initiated the early phase of migration into new settlement areas in the United States, women have become a substantial proportion of migrants, especially since 2000. Critically, Latinas have become fully incorporated into the agro-industrial complex of the American South, forming a vital share of the workforce in the animal production and processing industries.

Many of the Latina/o migrants working at Swine's had been incorporated into the circuit of global capitalism well before they left Honduras, Mexico, or El Salvador. Often they were employed in export agriculture on the north coast or as maquiladora workers in Choloma, in Cortés department. For most of them, the long and painstaking crossing through deserts, rivers, and mountains was only the latest in a series of uprootings, but by far the most costly in physical, emotional, and economic terms. Traversing three international borders spanning three thousand miles usually took Honduran migrants at least a month and cost $6,000 to $8,000, payment for a coyote (Sladkova 2010). In their retellings of their migration stories, I found it surprising that a number of the women had made split-second decisions to leave, frequently as a result of some happenstance that made imminent exit possible. A few were trapped in abusive relationships and felt that their only hope was to leave—an intimate sort of exile—which others studying Honduran migration have also documented (Schmalzbauer 2005). As Sarah Mahler (1995) found among her Salvadoran respondents in Long Island, and Jacqueline Hagan (2008) found among her Mexican and Central American migrant respondents, most if not all of the workers I interviewed gave sobering accounts of their migrant experience, from the actual journey to their years living and working in the United States. They were ambivalent and battle-weary stories of fighters who had weathered suffering and disappointment but were still standing in the closing rounds. They assessed their lives in terms of modest gains achieved through almost unbearable sacrifice, not in terms of feeling upwardly mobile here or doing very well compared to back there. These latter representations are the romanticized distortions of well-meaning sympathizers who fetishize the migrant experience and equate agency with heroism, who confuse subjugation born of compulsion and coercion with collective martyrdom.

Their usually lengthy and diverse work histories prepared them as much as possible for the First World exploitation they would be introduced to up North, and their experiences, sometimes first in U.S. textiles firms, and then often in animal farms and poultry production, molded them into the premier agro-industrial labor force at the dawn of the twenty-first century. In some sense, the trajectory of their work histories in the United States seems to slant upward, from employment in declining industries or animal production farms to poultry processing to hog processing. Hog processing pays far more than work in other growing or stable industries such as poultry processing or animal production, or in declining or stable industries such as textiles or canneries. And unlike the latter, hog processing is not seasonal work. And yet casting this trajectory as "upward mobility" seems like a gross misrepresentation. The largest departments at Swine's, such as Loin Boning and Packing, Cut Floor, and Kill Floor, have around two hundred workers each, but only two or three crew leaders, one or two supervisors, and one superintendent each, at most. Most workers will therefore never have even a remote chance to move up in the authority structure. At best, some workers might obtain higher-paying jobs within the department. A few men with mechanical skills might eventually obtain a transfer to the Maintenance Department, but this avenue is highly unlikely for most men, and all but closed off to women.

Like many Latinas/os who live in new destination states, some Latinas at Swine's spent a number of years in traditional settlement states such as Texas or California before settling in North Carolina. Such is the case for Carina and Leticia, sisters from Honduras who arrived in the United States before Hurricane Mitch and were subsequently able to obtain Temporary Protected Status. Carina reflected:

> We are from the beautiful city of Sabá, in Colón. I worked in cosmetology and had a beauty salon. Honduras is a poor country, and that's what makes us immigrate to this country. With the illusion of betterment, we think of coming for two or three years. We come here mistakenly believing that we will return soon. And once we get to this country, we come to the grand realization that this is not the country of immediate betterment, like one thinks when they're in their country. I lived a peaceful life. I don't even know in what moment I decided to come here. I think if I were there, I would be better off than I am here. I came here because a friend of my sister's [Leticia] arrived to pick her up [to migrate], and she didn't have the courage to leave, so she said to me, "You go," and I did. This friend I went with was pregnant, and we got nabbed [by authorities] three times. A fourth time I was deported when I was already in California. But I persisted, thinking I was already here, and I had to continue. My sister was younger. She didn't have the courage to come. It was 1993, and I was about twenty-four years old.
>
> I got to California, where I stayed with some pastor friends. I was there almost two years, and then I moved to New York, Florida, Colorado, and back to California. When I would be out of work, I would move, looking to improve life for me and my son. When I first got here, I worked at a Victoria's Secret factory, then at a beauty salon. In Colorado I did housekeeping in resort towns, and in New York I worked in housekeeping at a Marriott. I moved to North Carolina after Leticia married and moved here. I've been working at Swine's for two years.

Carina's sister Leticia, initially scared to go through with her migration plans, later followed her sister—and two brothers already in Florida—to the United States with a cousin. She arrived in Houston and worked for much of the next ten years as a nanny before moving to North Carolina when she got married in 2008. Before her international migration journey, Leticia had already migrated internally to an export processing zone for work. Unlike Cristina, Leticia says, "Ever since I could think, I dreamed of coming over here. I dreamed of being on the beaches in

Miami." Of course, now that she is here, she recalls this flight of fancy with irony:

> I left Colón to work in Cortés department, in the *maquilas,* which are cloth-ing factories. They made Levi's. That's what I worked in, a factory for export to the United States. There are many in Choloma. I went with a cousin. There I had the experience of working among many people and of seeing what a factory was like. I inspected the dress pants that Levi's brings over here. The salary was an equivalent of $50 per week. Only there, they don't mistreat you like they do here as an *hispano*! Because there is betterment here, but there is also a lot of discrimination in terms of race. We *hispanos* are often treated—especially in the company we are working for, Swine's— very poorly.

For other women, their initial period of residence in traditional gate-way states was relatively brief, after which better job opportunities and lower costs of living, along with expanding social networks, pulled them toward North Carolina. This was the case for Leslie, a woman who exudes a kind, grandmotherly aura beyond her actual age or tem-perament. She is from the town of Ilanga in Colón, Honduras, and is among the Latina/o migrants at Swine's with the longest tenure in the United States. Like Leticia and Cristina, her labor market experiences span the global production regime characteristic of late capitalism, cul-minating with her insertion into the agro-industrial labor market of North Carolina:

> My husband came to Houston in 1991, and I came three years later. I worked in garment factories since I already knew how to sew, having studied it in Honduras. We moved to North Carolina, and I worked at Textile Inc. in Kerr Hill for a year at $4.50 an hour. Then I worked in Boyd at a pickle plant. But that is paid by production, and since it is seasonal, in October or November they lay you off. Then I worked at another garment factory in Linden for about eight months. Then I became pregnant, and after having my son I returned to the pickle plant, since around May they started hiring again. Then I worked at Hansen Farms with turkeys. They bring the eggs from the farms and clean them with a machine. Low-paid, too, it was like $6 an hour, but I worked a lot of hours, like ten hours. Then around 1999 or 2000 I applied to work with hogs at Hansen Farms, since it pays a little more. I cared for the little *marranos* for seven months, fed them, gave them medications when they were sick, helped the sows give birth.

But most of the people I got to know at Swine's—especially the Hon-durans—embarked on their journey with North Carolina as their desti-nation, either to reunite with husbands who had already migrated, like Cristina, or as single women who usually had siblings or other family members here (Lichter and Johnson 2009; Massey et al. 1987). Luz is from Comayagua and has been in North Carolina for eight years. She left behind four children, and the pain of separation was almost unbearable at first. Her children are grown up by now, and they have no intention to travel to El Norte unless they get papers one day, she told me. It has become way too dangerous, and besides, she is thinking of going back soon. If she ever returned to Honduras, she swears she would never come back here. Although it is *bonito* over here, you live in a cage of gold, she said, paraphrasing a famous song by Los Tigres del Norte about the tribulations of unauthorized migrants. "The police are always bothering us." Scholars studying Latino/a migrant incorporation in other new destinations have also documented migrants' increasing sense of social isolation in the current sociopolitical climate, which is hostile to unauthorized migrants, and their feelings of being trapped in a gilded cage (Schultz 2008).

Luz studied cosmetology in Honduras, but she never had enough money to open a business, so she worked as a waitress. She never made enough money at that to support her kids and send them to school, either, so she decided to leave. Upon her arrival in Phoenix, she immediately headed for Perry, where her sister has been living for sixteen years; she also works at Swine's. Luz's analogy of the cage of gold made me think of the situation of Olga, another Honduran woman who worked at Swine's bagging loins and bellies. Olga left her teenage daughters behind in Honduras, and they don't want her to come back. When I asked why—"Don't they miss you?"—she grazed her thumb against the inside of her index and middle fingers, the expression on her face disturbingly flat. *Money*—the money she sends back home. Cristina's son, who they affectionately call Bubu, vowed to grow out his hair until he saw his father again. It has been thirteen years now, and the boy's scraggly hair flows down his chest in home videos brought back by traveling relatives.[8] I found the stoic resolve in these mothers searing, even unsettling. Their steely composure in the face of the painful decisions they made to separate from family, especially their children, and the heartbreaking consequences their departure frequently had for those left behind, have been captured poignantly by others (Nazario 2006; Schmalzbauer 2005; Menjívar and Abrego 2009).

Some women had wished to continue their education in Honduras, but, unable to afford it, had moved into the labor force. Under other conditions, they might have remained part of Honduras's white-collar working class. While they were usually able to find work, their pay was meager,[9] and some women refused to submit to the sexual exploitation that they said was expected of them. Such was the case for Reina. Her brothers already resided in North Carolina and had Temporary Protected Status, but it was only when an aunt came by her house before departing for El Norte (to bid farewells) that Reina decided in that moment to leave with her:

I'm from the coast of Colón, Honduras. I had been studying to be a secretary, and wanted to go to university but didn't have money to keep studying. I found work but it paid very little. That's why I had to come here. You can find work there but sometimes only through political connections. And sometimes the politicians offer you a job but they want you to give what you shouldn't have to in order to get the job [sexual favors]. That's why sometimes you decide it's better to come here. There's a lot of corruption, and they want to take advantage of young people in return for a job, which is why many young people prefer to come here. So I worked briefly, but it didn't pay well. And they were going to get me a government job, but, like I said, they want you to pay them with something else, to sleep with them. I'm not used to that. I preferred to come here, and not pay them with what they want.

I came in 2001. It hadn't occurred to me to come here. I had been working, and being single, one can make it. But an aunt of mine was coming, and she was saying goodbye to me and asked me to leave with her. I hadn't thought about coming here, but since I already had two brothers here, I asked if they would help me pay for the coyote and they said yes. So it was all of a sudden. It wasn't planned. One of my brothers worked in sanitation at Swine's, and a friend of his who had been his coyote brought me. It only took us fifteen days. It was very hard. Because sometimes you come venturing through all of Guatemala and Mexico. The crossings are hardest in Mexico because sometimes they just dump you in the hills. I hear it used to be easier, but not anymore. My advantage was that the coyote was a relative, so he protected me. When he had to send a group walking through the *monte*, he sent me separately by car. Other parts we traveled by truck, crawling through a hole beneath it and laying one on top of the other. Since I was family, they took care of me, and that's why I didn't suffer a lot. From Mexico, some of the groups crossed into the United States either by river or by desert. At the time I came, there was the advantage that when you passed through immigration they gave you "permission." So I passed with a little girl, pretending that she was my niece. Because when you came with minors, they gave you permission to enter for like ten days, and then you had to present to court, but since you're scared to, you don't show up. I went by bus to San Antonio and my brother sent for me.

Within four months of her arrival, Reina began working at a North Carolina chicken processing plant, where her relatives were employed at the time:

I worked at a *pollera* [chicken processing plant] in Hensley for almost four years. That was my first job here. My sister-in-law worked there, and she and my brother have TPS. She told me that they hire people there with a different name. So I got papers. When you come here, you don't know about any of that. You come here thinking you will work with your name just like in Honduras. You arrive ignorant of all that. But once you get here, you are disabused of such ignorance. If you don't have papers, you have to work with other identities. So they got me papers, and I worked at Holden Farms. My sister-in-law left the job, and since I didn't have a driver's license, I decided to leave there and come work here, when it was Hog Ventures Inc. I got other papers to come work here. Because at Hensley Farms they don't ask for ID or any of that, just a social security number and name. Not here; here they ask for ID, birth certificate. Over there, they just want to make sure it's a real number, they're more *chuecos* [crooked]. Here your papers have to be more correct. Now it's gotten much harder, not only papers that are correct, they check the papers. When I first got a job here, I had to stand in line all night to apply, and I had to do that two times before I got a slot. I worked for two years, bagging Japanese loins. It's really hard, and you're beat by the end of the day. I left the job to have my daughter, and came back to work five months later. They hired me back because Josué [her husband, who works on the boning line] spoke to Myrna, whom he gets along with, and because George [the superintendent of the Loin Boning and Packing Department] knew me and agreed to take me back.

Around 2000, Honduran women began arriving to North Carolina in greater numbers, reflecting diminished employment prospects in Honduras following the devastation of Hurricane Mitch and their male partners' transition from being temporary to semipermanent migrants, along with the more general trend toward diversification of Latino/a migrant destinations (Pastoral Social/Caritas 2003). For many Hondurans (and Salvadorans), the extension of Temporary Protected Status following Hurricane Mitch in 1998 further eroded the fixed timeframe migrants had initially proposed to themselves, even as it represented at best a "liminal legality" rather than an avenue to permanent residency (Menjívar 2006; Coutin 2003). As Heriberto explained it, many men like him arrived in the mid- to late 1990s with the intention of working, saving, sending money home, and returning to Honduras in two years, a short-term orientation shared by most labor migrants. Network members who had successfully migrated committed to informally sponsoring another family member, and in this way five of Ernesto and Heriberto's other brothers have also spent time in North Carolina. As the two-year timeframe elapsed, they became anxious and began to send for their spouses, initially with the idea that an additional earner would speed up their return to Honduras.

Women then became integrated into the chain migration network, increasing female migration by sponsoring sisters, cousins, and friends (Hagan 1994). Because they found plentiful employment opportunities in the animal farms and processing plants, women could be full members of the network, paying back family members who had fronted the fee for their journey. As the years passed, some of these women who had left children behind with parents or in-laws sent for them as well. Later, as the undocumented journey became more perilous, securing employment became more difficult, U.S. costs of living rose, citizen children were born, families became reliant on remittances, and some people secured work authorization indefinitely, migrants' horizons for returning became less clear or disappeared altogether (Pastoral Social/ Caritas 2003). By 2009, at Swine's, women made up close to half of the workers in the Cut Floor and Loin Boning and Packing Departments, and an even higher share in Bacon Slice, Dry Salt, and Microwavery. The next section brings the reader into the world of Swine's, a world that quite literally consumes the lives of its workers.

THE HEART OF HOG COUNTRY, THE BELLY OF THE BEAST

Perry is the seat of Clark County in North Carolina. This region is the heart of hog country, where three of the top five hog producers in the United States own or contract with more than 1,800 farms throughout the state. It is a key region for Pig Corporation, a vertically integrated company that is both the world's largest producer of hogs and the world's largest processor of pork, singlehandedly controlling 72 percent of the slaughter capacity in the south Atlantic region. According to the North Carolina Employment Security Commission, agricultural production, animal production, and food manufacturing accounted for more than 30 percent of the average annual private industry employment in the county in 2009, up from 20.5 percent in 1990. In nearby Garnett County, food manufacturing by itself accounted for close to 30 percent of all private-industry employment in 2009, and nearly half of all private-industry jobs were in agricultural production, animal production, or food manufacturing. Indeed, several hundred yards from any road in this multicounty region, on either side and surrounded by fields of corn or tobacco, you will see clusters of simple silver or blue rectangular structures that crowd hogs, turkeys, or chickens. At any given hog farm, a handful of workers are employed to tend to the hogs, feeding the animals and cleaning their enclosures, giving injections, snipping testicles, and helping sows deliver their piglets. Many meatpacking workers have worked at these farms and speak affectionately of their porcine charges, recalling cradling them like babies, or sorrowfully, recalling their aversion to performing the cruel tasks required of them.

Inside Swine's, A Twenty-First-Century Meatpacking Plant

On what is now the main road into town but was once a cow pasture, flanked by a large pawnshop (prominently advertising guns) and a McDonald's, is Swine's. You can smell Swine's before you see it. Starting out in 1950 as a small, family-owned slaughterhouse, it grew to 6,000 daily-kill capacity by 2000, when it was sold to Hog Ventures, which expanded the facility by adding a new Cut Floor and redesigning the Kill Floor to slaughter hogs using CO_2 gas chambers, raising the daily slaughter capacity to 8,500. In 2006, Pig Corporation acquired Hog Ventures and with it Swine's, and the plant now slaughters and processes 10,500 hogs a day, employing between 1,200 and 1,500 workers, more than double the number of workers employed by the factory in 1974, and about 30 percent more than were employed in the mid-1990s. Throughout the 1990s, when the Swine's workforce nearly doubled, the Latino/a share grew to be the majority among workers. By way of comparison, the largest hog processing plant in the world slaughters an average of 28,000 hogs a day and employs 3,500 people, so Swine's is a very respectably sized operation.

It is a full-scale production facility, from slaughter to "further processing" of case-ready pork and precooked products, with a significant share of fresh pork product for export to China and Japan. Departments central to the basic production process are the Kill Floor, Cut Floor, Loin Boning, Belly Conversion, and Hamboning Departments, and further processing includes the Smokehouse, Bacon Slice, Dry Salt, Pork Chop, Microwavery, and Marination Departments. Different smells emanate from these departments: pure shit on the Kill Floor, peppercorn or garlic-and-herb seasoning in Marination, a sweet smoky scent around Bacon Slice. Sometimes the overwhelming smell is neither the slightly pungent scent of cold blood and fresh meat nor the foul, warm pestilence of feces, but rather the dizzying and taste-bud-saturating bleachlike odor of the chemicals used to clean and sanitize the lines every night. The further processing and Hamboning departments work in two shifts, with the second shift in departments such as Dry Salt and Microwavery periodically shutting down according to swings in projected demand. Basic production departments work in one shift that begins at six in the morning and, in the case of the Loin Boning, can extend until nine at night or later. Thus, whereas one side of the plant—the further processing departments—is characterized by instability and even insufficient hours, the other side of the plant—the core production departments—is characterized by an unwavering excess of hours. Indeed, the departments and shifts that make up Swine's combine a patchwork of precarity and rewards that make it difficult to define which are the "good" versus "bad" jobs (Kalleberg 2011).

Although I lack precise figures, a certain level of segregation was evident within the plant across departments when I worked there between August 2009 and December 2010, with African Americans concentrated in further processing departments and in later shifts, and Latinas/os representing a preponderant majority in the central production departments, especially in Loin Boning.[10] In core production departments such as Kill Floor, Cut Floor, and Loin Boning, Latinas/os made up between 65 and 80 percent of the workforce, but in further processing departments such as Marination, these figures were reversed, with African Americans making up the majority.[11] Working conditions ranged from difficult and uncomfortable in certain departments, and insecure if the department was working less than forty hours a week, to brutal and despairing in other departments, and unbearable if the department was working seventy-five hours a week. Marination on the afternoon shift where I worked for the first seven months resembled the first set of conditions—it was "the supermarket" of the factory, as one Black worker referred to it, given that the tasks might involve pricing, labeling, and seasoning. Loin Boning, where I worked for the last nine months of my fieldwork, resembled the second set of conditions—it was "the real world," as the African American department superintendent referred to it when I told him of my desire to transfer there. Working conditions there were so severe that one Honduran worker (Luz's sister) I consulted about my impending transfer told me I would "regret life," and upon experiencing the conditions firsthand, I could only describe them as wage slavery. In fact, despite the relative difference in working conditions between Marination and Loin Boning, in both departments some workers—African American *and* Latina/o—referred to being treated like slaves, sometimes admonishing crew leaders for acting like "slave drivers." Still, I came to understand that once workers crossed an uncertain threshold and realized they could survive in "the supermarket" or in "the real world," some also found pride and a measure of enjoyment in their work. At times humor, especially of a sexual nature, could bridge boundaries and make working downright fun.

Life Working on the Line

The hog is the hero of Clark County, Cristina's brother-in-law Heriberto concludes, as it is the raw material responsible for the area's economic development over the last twenty years. The town of Perry pays homage to its local hero in dozens of colorfully decorated sculptures of the beast that adorn storefronts and public buildings throughout the historic downtown. The hog may be the hero of Clark County, but *el hispano* is the human engine that in the 1990s put in motion rural growth through agro-industrial development anchored in cash crop production, animal farming, and processing plants. At Swine's, cynical workers echo their perception of the relative worth of hogs and humans, to the company and to government inspectors. From time to time, an aggrieved worker will remark bitterly about how "they" care more about the *marranos* than about "us."[12] When production on the kill floor is shut down for hours because a hog was trampled by others on its death walk, workers can't help feeling bitter. After all, the animal was slated for slaughter—who would stop production for hours if a worker were injured, except for the time it took to sanitize the lines? Even when Giovanni, who sorts and bags riblets, lost his son Milton, a boning line worker, in a terrible car accident, few who wanted to attend his evening funeral service were allowed to leave work without penalty. Production was not suspended after a maintenance worker suffocated to death on methane fumes as he filled a wastewater tank with hog sludge. Production didn't even cease after a Kill Floor supervisor dropped dead in the middle of the workday, probably from a heart attack. The mission of production is a stampede of bulls that in the last instance does not recognize status distinctions. Supervisors make it clear to workers that production is not to be interrupted by such human needs as going to the bathroom. In fact, supervisors routinely threaten to replace workers with others who will submit entirely to their labor discipline in the service of ceaseless production.

It was eight at night in mid-April 2010 when our African American floor supervisor Michael called the packing workers to huddle around the staircase leading up to the supervisors' office for an impromptu and ill-timed threat session. We were fourteen hours into our shift, which had begun before sunrise and would end well past nightfall. Only a month into my transfer to Loin Boning and Packing from Marination, six of my fingers had gone numb from the incessant clenching and shaking associated with bagging heavy loins into torturously small bags over such a long workday. The discomfort and desperation caused by numbness and tingling in my fingers, which lasted for several months, was matched by intense pain and tenderness in my hand muscles that made it nearly impossible to turn a doorknob, and by sharp back pain that soured my spirit. But at least my fingernails hadn't fallen off, as had happened to Natalia, a Honduran woman I sometimes worked with on the loin bagging line. Natalia had also experienced the numbness and tingling in her fingers—a doctor later diagnosed me as having occupationally induced carpal tunnel syndrome—which she said had eventually subsided, but only after about eight months. Other workers told me the pain, numbness, and tingling would never go away, much to my despair.

Michael's voice boomed as he towered over us midway up the stairs. He shouted at us for going to the bathroom outside of designated break times (which amounted to less than an hour a day), and for coming back to the floor "late" from breaks. "When we say 'break,' y'all go to break! And when we're out there and we scream 'Boning,' you go back to work!" Going to the bathroom was a constant tug-of-war between workers and supervisors. Periodically, supervisors would institute a variety of rules for bathroom usage: Get the attention of a crew leader and wait for him to bring a replacement to your line position. Write your name on a clipboard with time out and time in from break. Workers pushed back against such rules because they violated their sense of basic human dignity, and followed their own informal arrangement whereby they took turns going to the bathroom, leaving others to cover their spots on the line, or ensuring that those left behind could pick up the slack while they were away. But when supervisors insisted upon their own rules, workers were forced to abide by them or risk suspension or termination. Most workers did submit to this most intimate mode of labor control, even to the point of wetting, shitting, or bleeding on themselves on the line. And now here was Michael, berating us about going to the bathroom outside of our negligible break times, *fourteen hours* into our shift.

He announced a new food safety policy that would begin in May, whereby any and all meat that fell on the floor would be thrown out as opposed to the current practice of assigning "product reconditioners" who would pick it up, wash it down with water, and return it to the line. As was typical of "food safety" policies, these would usually be applied at the discretion of supervisors, and always via threats of punishment. "We're going to pay attention to see who cares and who doesn't care, and we'll be happy to fire people and get a whole new group of workers in here!" I had been translating for Natalia because the Puerto Rican supervisor's (Luis) translation was inaudible. "I can't believe they talk to you this way after a day like this, after we kill ourselves here! What a thank you," I said to Natalia, who just shook her head in resignation, accustomed to such gratuitous menacing.

I thought that, having worked in another department at the plant for seven months before transferring to Loin Boning, I would be well prepared for the change.[13] I knew the hours would be longer and the work more arduous, but nothing prepared me for the intense, oppressive exploitation I endured: Not the cautionary remarks from the Loin Boning superintendent, George, who looked at me dubiously when I told him I was requesting a transfer to his department: "This over here is the real world." Not even the dire warnings of the Loin Boning worker who told me I would "regret life" and wondered aloud why in the world I would be asking to transfer there.[14]

The physically demanding nature of the work in departments such as Loin Boning was made harder to bear by the line speeds, volume of work, and extremely long hours, and withstanding this was made more difficult by the incessant surveillance, rushing, reprimands, and threats from supervisors. Not even breaks offered workers a chance to really relax, given that they were so short and that supervisors usually patrolled break areas and shouted for people to go back on the lines even before time was up. Worker-friends such as Leticia and Natalia, with whom I discussed my research, insisted that my story recount the blistering humiliations they faced on a daily basis at work. For Leticia, Natalia, and many others, this is what they said hurt the most.[15] But oppressive labor discipline regimes did not begin with Latino/a workers at Swine's. Rather, Swine's has a long history of struggles between workers and management, one that is intertwined with the changing composition of the workforce since the early 1970s.

LABOR UNREST, LABOR DISCIPLINE, AND THE SHIFTING ETHNORACIAL COMPOSITION OF SWINE'S

The Early Years

Horace A. Samuels Sr. was one of "nature's noblemen," at least according to the late great segregationist Senator Jesse Helms. This tribute was conveyed in President of Chester University Dr. David B. Jenkins's introduction of Laura Bosworth, Samuels Sr.'s daughter and chairman and CEO of the Swine Packing Company, when she was the guest of honor at the 1990 meeting of the Fortune Fellows (Fortune Fellows 1990). Samuels had turned a cow pasture into a steady meatpacking operation in the early 1950s, finding in Perry an ideal place to relocate and expand the business he had started in Pennsylvania. In the summer of 1973, nature's nobleman, incensed at the rising tide of unionism, delivered a stern warning to the rebellious workers at Swine's: "We do not want a union in this company, and we are not going to have one." Considering that Swine's had illegally banned the distribution of union literature on company premises, subjected employees to interrogation about union activities, led workers to believe that union activities were under surveillance, and illegally fired workers who were union activists, the National Labor Relations Board would later order Swine's—and in particular nature's nobleman—to cease and desist its unfair labor practices and reinstate its striking employees.

In 1974, forty-four workers at this plant, mostly young African American men, went on strike to protest unfair labor practices by the company, which included harassment and termination of workers involved in union organizing activities. The Amalgamated Meat Cutters, now the United Food and Commercial Workers, had initiated an organizing campaign at the plant that the company owner and plant management vehemently opposed and went to illegal means to quash by spying on, interrogating, and firing union activist-workers. Gary, a shy and mild-mannered sixty-three-year-old African American man who has worked a knife job since he began to work at Swine's in 1973 after returning from the Vietnam War, says one day a worker instructed him and his coworkers: "Y'all follow us at break time." At the moment, he didn't know exactly what was going on. Gary, eager to follow in the footsteps of his father, who had worked at Swine's for three years before falling ill, had tried to get a job at Swine's for four or five months, but so many people were applying that he couldn't, despite his persistence. After almost giving up, he was finally hired on what he had decided was his last attempt. He thought to himself, "I had a hard enough time trying to get here. I'm not going out for nothing!" He asked one of the guys what was going on, and was told they were going on strike. Gary replied, "I just got here. I can't afford to be going on a strike." Several workers who had walked out without knowing it was a strike were allowed back in, but it took almost three years for the strikers who were locked out by Swine's management to be reinstated to their jobs, and fourteen years before they received their back pay settlement. The organizing campaign failed, and even now a man Gary sees at church, who was fired from Swine's during the campaign, reproaches him, "If it weren't for you, we would've got that thing [the union] in there!"

When Gary started working at Swine's, almost all of the workers were local African Americans, with only "one or two whites." After the strike, more whites were hired as replacements for Black strikers and Black union activists who were bullied by supervisors and forced out. Gary says union sympathizers' work was scrutinized by supervisors to a degree that others' work was not, and union supporters were designated to do some of the toughest jobs. But management's strategy of bringing in white replacements didn't work out "because they didn't want to work that hard." Gary chuckles as he remembers one worker, an "Indian preacher," who would tell white workers, "That's a nigger's job, you ain't supposed to do that!" Gary says the preacher "would get a kick out of" seeing the white workers squirm, and that some of them "would leave right then."

After a period of apparent quiescence, organized labor resurfaced in a region that had long eluded it. The United Food and Commercial Workers initiated an organizing campaign at Swine's in 1993, which culminated in a narrow election victory for the union in the summer of that year. Among the concerns raised by union officials regarding working conditions at the plant was an outbreak of brucellosis that had caused close to fifty workers out of the total workforce of 650 to fall ill between 1990 and 1993. Around this same time—the late 1980s and early 1990s—workers in a number of other food processing plants in North Carolina were waging their own battles for dignity at work, and unions took notice. From walkouts by the mostly Mayan workers at a Hensley Farms poultry processing plant in Harpers, to the wildcat strikes by the mostly African American workers at a Watts Farms turkey processing plant in Wattsville, and most famously the fifteen-year campaign to organize Pig Corporation workers at the Davis plant, this was a period of some agitation by labor across the industry (Fink 2003; Wright 1988). The workers at Watts who walked out in 1988 demanded to speak to the CEO of Watts Farms, Elliott Carson, son of Bob Carson, an early poultry producer in the region and a powerful enemy of unions (Wolcott 1976). Carson finally stepped outside to see the workers, who—incensed at a rumor about Carson referring to them as "Black slaves"—shouted at him defiantly, "We are not your Black slaves!"

In a stunning twist, the union win at Swine's was overturned by order of a 1995 U.S. appellate court ruling against the National Labor Relations Board over its determination of the proper collective bargaining unit. At that very moment of great disappointment and worker frustration, just as the Fourth Circuit Court of Appeals dealt a crushing blow to workers at Swine's who thought they had won the hard fight for union representation, denying enforcement of the NLRB's bargaining order, a dramatic transformation was under way. Probably not by coincidence, the shift in the racial/ethnic composition of Swine's workforce began to accelerate. Latino/a migrants, at first mostly men and increasingly from Honduras, began to fill more and more positions throughout the plant. Court records suggest an idea of the minority position Latino/a migrants occupied at Swine's in 1995. Among the reasons cited by Swine's for their refusal to bargain with the UFCW following the union's narrow victory in an NLRB-certified election was the alleged failure to accommodate Spanish-speaking workers. One might conjecture that at this time, between 1993 and 1995, Latino/a migrants would therefore represent as yet a minority of the nearly nine hundred workers by then employed at the plant. And of course, since *the company* brought up the issue of accommodation for Spanish speakers, one would suppose that this was because they believed these workers would vote against union representation. Gary pinpoints the mid-1990s as the time Latinas/os began to work at Swine's in noticeable numbers, recalling the recent fifteen-year anniversary several longtime Latino/a workers commemorated with stickers on their hard hats. When I ask Gary why so many Latinas/os started coming into the plant at that time, he said, without hesitation, "to keep the union out and make sure it didn't come back in!"[16]

Enforcement and Labor Discipline

The past has a funny way of living on in the present. As fate would have it, Billy, one of forty-four workers who walked out on strike in 1974, and fumed about other workers who didn't, is now a crew leader on the boning line and disliked by workers for his gruff demeanor. Worse, Billy—an American Indian who is usually identified as white by workers, and whose brother is a Smokehouse supervisor—recently reminded a boning line worker he supervises that she is a "wetback" and must therefore do as he demands. Despite her protestations and those of her husband, who also works on the boning lines, Billy was not reprimanded. Questioned by Human Resources staff about the incident, Rocío, a Puerto Rican loin trimmer who is thought to receive relatively more favorable treatment from supervisors because they find her attractive (and perhaps because she is a citizen), would not confirm Elsa and her husband's allegations, and Ileana, an unauthorized Honduran whizard knife worker with limited English ability, claimed she only understood bits of the discussion. James Jefferies, who in 1974 was a Cut Floor supervisor involved in the intimidation and persecution of union activist-workers that eventually resulted in court orders for restitution and the reinstatement of strikers, is now director of operations at Swine's. He is an older white man who occasionally makes the rounds on the production floor and is still called on to quell insubordinate workers with the casual threat of replacement.

When the company strategically elected to enlist in the federal E-Verify program in 2008, which compares employees' I-9 form employment eligibility information to data from the Social Security Administration to confirm employment eligibility, Renata Chatuye, a Honduran Garifuna who had previously lived outside New York City, was hired as an assistant manager in Human Resources. Myrna was given the job of recruiter, handling the initial interface with prospective employees. It was around this time when hiring personnel began informing prospective applicants that they would no longer accept *papeles de puertorriqueños* (Puerto Rican identification documents); they would need to present *papeles de chicanos* (Chicano identification documents) instead. This bizarre condition was perhaps intended to create a more credible paper trail of the workforce, which had increasingly become "Puerto Rican." Upon finding out I was Puerto Rican, it was not unusual for a Honduran coworker to tell me excitedly that he too was from Bayamón or Río Piedras or Cayey (towns in Puerto Rico), a ploy that confused me immensely at first. Intended to project compliance with federal laws on employment authorization and therefore deter ICE raids of the sort the company had faced (or collaborated with) at other plants, and which increasingly were being deployed as a strong-arm "interior enforce-ment" tactic under the George W. Bush administration, participation in the E-Verify program has had a chilling effect on the hiring of unauthor-ized workers, while the looming threat of the Obama administration's "silent raids" (i.e., employer audits) has had a paralyzing effect on their conditions of existence at work.

The dwindling numbers of unauthorized workers currently employed increasingly face the prospect of being fired or forced to resign upon the "discovery" that their documents are in question. By 2011, Myrna's discretion had been limited to the point where she feared losing her job if she wasn't careful about hiring unauthorized workers, as she explained to Ileana, a relative of Cristina's husband, Ernesto, with whom she had developed a close relationship since Ileana was hired three years ago, to the point of calling Ileana her daughter. She told me how a recruiter for hog farm labor recently told her that work authorization is being seri-ously verified even for those jobs:

> The interviewer knows. My mother [Myrna] knows if you are who you say you are once she interviews you. And with a heavy heart, even though she would like to [hire you], she can't because the company said no more. She says that the ones who managed to get in should take care of their jobs. At this point she risks her job, and she's not going to risk her job for someone else. When I started to work here she still could, but not any more. From what I have heard, once you lose this job most people leave, because there is no longer any work to be found. Before people emigrated from there to here, but now we have to emigrate from here to there!

Human Resources managers instituted a piecemeal purging of unau-thorized workers that would not risk disruptions to production, as would occur in the event of a sudden sweep by government authorities. The climate of fear this state of affairs creates has the added bonus for management that they can effectively dissuade unauthorized workers from rocking the boat in any way, whether by protesting working con-ditions or seeking medical attention for their injuries. Their best, and increasingly only, prospect for employment hanging by a thread, these workers get by as well as they can, and management squeezes every pos-sible bit of labor effort from them until the day when they are "forced" to admit that their papers are in question. Every few weeks, one or two workers in each department throughout the plant are let go in this way. Some abandon their jobs on the spot when they are told Human Resources wants to speak with them, assuming the worst, even the possibility that police or ICE are waiting for them, which is exactly how Cristina would be ambushed, as detailed in chapter 5. Others are informed that their wages will be garnished to recover a debt or to pay child support (when a judgment has been issued against the social security number they are identified with), forcing them to leave their jobs or continue to relinquish their wages to cover the real social security number owner's debts, which some workers feel they have no choice but to do. Workers purged in these ways frequently are robbed of their pensions, accrued vacation time, and attendance bonuses. The sobbing but otherwise unmarked farewells of workers who poured their blood, sweat, and tears into this work for years—like Cristina, Adriana, and Luna—are a testament to the ultimate dispensability of all labor, no matter how perfectly exploitable.

Ethnic Succession in Reverse?

A noticeable shift in the composition of new hires followed these more stringent enforcement measures, and certainly by March 2010 a majority of new hires were African American, older and more established Latinas/os and young second-generation Latinas/os, and whites or Coharies (a group of Native Americans). The heyday of this cycle of ethnic succession was over, and the pendulum began to swing, if only briefly, in the opposite direction, a phenomenon that has been documented at other food processing facilities following raids and government investigation, for instance at Faircloth Farms, a poultry processing company with operations in North Carolina. The plant's appetite for workers was apparent during several months from July 2009 to approximately October 2009, when applications were taken directly by plant officials instead of via the usual (longer) screening process that began at the local unemployment office. Throughout this period, dozens of job seekers—me included—gathered in a line outside the factory gate for an overnight wait for a chance at a job at Swine's. Plastic numbers were handed out by a guard every day at four in the morning to the first twenty people in line for a nine o'clock interview with Myrna, who decided usually on the spot who would get hired.

In June 2010 the company circulated by word of mouth a new policy on hiring that could have no effect other than restricting the supply of potential workers, and make current workers think long and hard about leaving their jobs: the company would no longer employ rehires or people with criminal records. Only a year before, the plant had no such blanket restrictions. Remarkably, Myrna deployed the new no-rehire policy preemptively to dissuade some prospective workers from even applying. At a baby shower held for Julio, Cristina's brother-in-law who works on the boning line, and his wife, I listened as Myrna recounted to Susie, the one African American worker in attendance, that she had advised Shameela, an African American worker in the boning department, that her son should not apply for a job at Swine's. Shameela had approached Myrna about getting her son a job. Despite the fact that there are afternoon shifts at the plant, and some departments that rarely work more than eight hours, Myrna told Shameela that if her son was in school at the community college, it would be difficult for him to commit to the job, and that since there was no longer a chance of being rehired in the future, he was better off "keeping that door open." Whatever other motives behind the implementation of such policies, in so arbitrarily limiting the supply of eligible applicants, the company would be poised to clamor for the kinds of workers it had the most taste for: immigrants.

And so in January 2011, one month after I left the job, Latina/o and African American workers at Swine's were blindsided by the sudden commencement of a new cycle of ethnic succession, this time involving recruiting Haitian refugees who had resettled in Florida and Virginia. Ileana said that some of the Haitians showed Myrna videos of the harsh conditions they left behind, with families living under tarps, to underscore their desperate situation. Over this period of slow but steady upheaval, adjustments to the labor discipline regime ensured no slack in the extraction of workers' efforts. In October 2010, the African American superintendent of Loin Boning was forced out and a friend of the Human Resources manager, an energetic white man plucked from the ranks of management at Berkshire Chicken, brought the exploitation to a new level, timing workers with a stopwatch to establish per-minute standards that sped up the labor process significantly, and instituting unlawful prohibitions on bathroom breaks that resulted in workers—including a Haitian new hire—soiling themselves on the line.

SCALING UP THE DYNAMICS AT SWINE'S: EXPLAINING MIGRATION AND COMPOSITIONAL CHANGE

Migration Explained: Demand- and Supply-Side Arguments

Responding critically to the growing trend among prominent migration scholars toward emphasizing supply-side explanations for migration, in particular the role of social networks in sustaining and promoting migration independently of demand-side factors (Light 2006; Light 2004; Light et al. 2002), some researchers have called for renewed attention to demand-side explanations, especially employer recruitment preferences and practices (Izcara Palacios 2010; Champlin and Hake 2006; Krissman 2005). Indeed, analysis of trends in migration from Mexico to the United States shows the dramatic effect the recent U.S. economic recession has had on migration rates (Passel, Cohn, and González-Barrera 2012). In the context of a slumping U.S. economy, and possibly in conjunction with the increasingly hostile anti-immigrant policies and the vastly heightened workplace enforcement measures that have severely curtailed unauthorized migrants' employment opportunities, net migration rates from Mexico have ground to a halt (Passel, Cohn, and González-Barrera 2012). Such susceptibility to a vastly transformed economic-legal-political field offers a sharp rebuke to the excessively supply-oriented accounts of migration. Just as the people and places in Southern communities Latino/a migrants have settled into are the inheritors of historical events that shaped their present circumstances, so too are Latin American migrants the progeny of a series of historical events that primed them to become international labor migrants and groomed them to be an abundant and reliable labor force for the region's agro-industrial complex at the dawn of the twenty-first century.

At Swine's, these legacies converge. Researchers have conceptualized the dynamics involved in such convergence as a model of "ethnic succession," which explains the process of compositional change at different levels (e.g., factory, occupation, industry) by accounting for the ordering of preferences of both employers and workers (Waldinger 1997). Interviews with area employers and workers in 2000 and 2001 confirm a preference for "Hispanic" workers in the animal processing industries (Leiter, Hossfeld, and Tomaskovic-Devey 2001; Smith-Nonini 2003; Schwartzman 2013), much as researchers have documented for other regions and industries where the ethnoracial composition of the labor force has shifted. Even so, employers are usually careful to maintain that they can only hire based on the pool of applicants they have, thus couching their preferences as insignificant factors against the impersonal and in any case external conditions of supply (Leiter, Hossfeld, and Tomaskovic-Devey 2001). However much causal weight we attach to employers' preferences, the ability to enact these preferences is situated within a structure of opportunity shaped by the legal and political environment that either facilitates or inhibits action according to those preferences. This opportunity structure is in turn also influenced by the firm-level policies crafted by employers to maximize the potential for hiring that reflects their preferences at a given time.

Contributing to research that shows ethnic succession to be a process actively directed by management (Stuesse and Helton 2013; López-Sanders 2009), and not simply the cumulative effect of migrant social networks operating in the context of passive employer preferences, this timeline of events shows how human resources managers at the corporate level have at times intentionally created the conditions for labor shortages that justify their recruitment of immigrant labor, in the latest case via government refugee resettlement programs.[17] Faced with a severed pipeline for supplying their ideal, unauthorized workers—the result of "voluntary" or "involuntary" subjection to heightened workplace enforcement measures—industry agents still managed to mold the local labor market conditions to suit their preferences for vulnerable workers. More broadly, this sequence of events shows how the process of ethnic succession is adapted in the shifting sociopolitical context of laws targeting unauthorized migrants. Hence, I account for formal, semiformal, and informal organizational policies and practices, as well as federal, state, and local policies and practices that shape the structure of opportunity.

Compositional Change Explained: The Ethnic Succession Model

The ethnic succession model of labor market incorporation emphasizes the *collective* nature of groups' search for economic opportunities, and supports the notion that immigrants and natives are often likely to be in a "complementary," as opposed to directly competitive, relationship to each other (Waldinger 1996). Still, scholars who draw on this model to account for compositional change at different levels—workplaces, occupations, industries—often seek to identify whether these changes were brought about by the replacement or displacement of incumbent workers (Moore 2010). It is thought that when ethnic succession is driven by displacement dynamics, intergroup conflict is likely to be highest. In contrast, it is thought that when compositional change is driven by replacement dynamics, intergroup conflict is likely to be low. Studies have applied the general logic of the ethnic succession model to analyzing the impact of migrants on the composition of labor markets in the U.S. South and drawing inferences as to the quality of relations between (usually) African Americans and Latinas/os.

Though conclusions about the extent to which Latino/a migrants "displace" or "replace" native-born whites and African Americans are not in any way definitive, studies have tended to interpret the evidence as supporting replacement (Griffith 1995; Griffith 2005; Skaggs, Tomaskovic-Devey, and Leiter 2000; Rosenfield and Tienda 1999; Kandel and Parrado 2004).[18] Just as Mark Grey (2000) found among Mexican poultry workers in Iowa, David Griffith (2005) found that African American poultry workers in the U.S. South saw this work as "seasonal," moving in and out of the poultry workforce for various reasons, including injuries, problems at work, and checking out other jobs. In an earlier period, prior to extensive Mexican in-migration, these workers moved in and out of poultry work rather freely, aware that regaining their employment would be fairly easy. Griffith argues that as Mexicans started entering poultry processing in the late 1980s, it became harder for African Americans to exit and enter the poultry labor force in this manner, since more and more Mexican workers were being hired to fill their positions, fueling ethnic succession and freezing them out (Zúñiga and Hernández-León 2005). Although poultry processing work has high turnover rates, it is not, at least nowadays, considered "seasonal work," as these scholars suggest. Nevertheless, Griffith's findings suggest a pattern of displacement through replacement. Echoing the findings of others (Cravey 1997; Kandel and Parrado 2004; Striffler 2005; Marrow 2007), such compositional change, ambiguously attributable to displacement or replacement, is taking place outside of workplaces as well, in trailer parks and neighborhoods.

Kandel and Parrado (2004, 265) are equally uncertain about the pattern of ethnic succession unfolding in the poultry processing industry in the South, specifically in Duplin County, North Carolina, and Accomack County, Virginia, where large Carolina Turkeys, Tyson, and Perdue plants are located. According to the U.S. Department of Commerce, there was a significant compositional shift in the meat processing industry between 1980 and 2000: whites dropped from close to 70 percent to slightly over 30 percent, Blacks increased from 30 percent to 50 percent, and Hispanics went from about 1 percent to 17 percent. However, noting that Latinas/os tend to be undercounted as per the National Agricultural Workers Survey findings, William Kandel and Emilio Parrado say that "Hispanics may be replacing non-Hispanic whites, which, assuming the latter are moving into higher-paying jobs, leaves everyone better off. Non-Hispanic Blacks may also be leaving the poultry industry in absolute numbers, but their increasing proportion suggests that immigrants may be competing for the same low-skill jobs" (2004, 265). National estimates of the poultry processing workforce composition are 50 percent Black, 40 percent white, and 10 percent Hispanic, but in North Carolina the Hispanic proportion is greater, and Kandel and Parrado note a level of 65 percent in one plant (2004, 269). Whites tend to occupy managerial positions, as well as some Blacks, and Hispanics tend to be in manual positions.

Sheryl Skaggs, Donald Tomaskovic-Devey, and Jeffrey Leiter (2000) used EEOC data from 1993 to 1997 to study the distribution by race/ethnicity across occupations within industries. These scholars interpreted the data as showing primarily replacement of African American or white workers who were leaving the worst jobs in the top ten industries by Latino/a employment, including in meat products, knitting mills, and household furniture manufacturing, the top three industries Latinas/os were entering. They considered the possibility that African Americans and whites were moving up within these industries or moving on to (presumably) better employment opportunities. On the other hand, they suggested a pattern of clear displacement of African Americans in the poultry and eggs and miscellaneous plastic products industries. Although the authors suggest that such findings point to industries where ethnic conflict might be more serious, their findings are only somewhat suggestive, and are subject to the limitations discussed above for the ethnic succession model.

Although it is not my objective to determine the precise mechanism that best explains compositional change at Swine's, the evidence I present suggests that replacement and displacement tend to co-occur, and are difficult to untangle. First, the scale of agro-industrial development in this region, which expanded significantly in the 1990s, required an abundant and growing supply of labor. Indeed, some argue that immigration was a crucial element of the industrial strategy pursued by meatpacking firms, which was based on plant (re)location to rural areas outside the historic centers of meatpacking (Champlin and Hoke 2006). While the baseline level of development of the agro-industrial complex in the early 1990s may have barely been able to subsist with only local native-born labor, particularly in the context of rising educational levels and employment prospects among African Americans, who constituted the majority of the incumbent labor force, it is doubtful that the vast expansion of these industries that began in the 1990s would have been possible without the massive growth in the rural labor force through Latino/a immigration. If this were the case, we could see dynamics of both displacement and replacement in the growth of the Latino/a share of the workforce in the context of expansion. Alternatively, if industry expansion paralleled growth in better employment opportunities for African Americans in other areas of the labor market, then we could see ethnic succession more characteristic of growth and replacement, or if it did not, we could see ethnic succession more characteristic of growth and displacement. These assessments take an aggregate perspective, looking at compositional change across whole industries or occupations as a function of demographic and economic shifts in the broader labor market.

At the micro level of succession at Swine's, we can see that it is not simply a matter of immigrants filling labor shortages as industries expand, or as incumbent groups leave for better jobs elsewhere (ethnic succession through growth and replacement), but rather a complicated story with multiple feedbacks that revolves around how capital satisfies as well as creates the demand for super-exploitable workers in a shifting sociopolitical environment.[19] Proving whether ethnic succession via replacement or displacement is the case is not my ultimate objective. Rather, my goal is to shed light on the social relational dimensions of dramatic demographic restructuring in workplaces as it unfolds in order to better understand how Latino/a migrants are becoming incorporated in the U.S. South. The ethnic succession model, focused as it is on the operation of migrant social networks and the closure (i.e., exclusionary boundary drawing) they ensure for some migrant groups as well as employer preferences in the ordering of a labor queue, is limited by its built-in assumptions about the relationship between compositional change and intergroup relations. Understanding social relations between Latino/a migrants and African Americans requires attention to the meaning-making dimensions of real and imagined encounters around group boundaries. Further, the evidence I present suggests an important consideration that is missing from studies of ethnic succession, and which has crucial implications for intergroup relations. The conditions that inform employer preferences for Latino/a migrants relative to native-born workers yield an "advantage" for them at the hiring interface that is simultaneously the basis for their "disadvantage" within the social organization of labor. Thus, I point to sources of grievance that pattern social relations among subordinate groups *beyond* "competition," the motivator that scholars typically highlight and which presumes displaced incumbent groups to be the aggrieved parties.

My argument is that the root of the problem is not competition from unauthorized migrants per se, but rather the tendency of capital to mine and magnify distinctions among workers. Employers often single out unauthorized migrants because they are an especially vulnerable population, but in their absence, employers will seek other group-based attributes on which to base distinctions among workers. Long before Latinas/os ever showed up at Swine's, management had tried to undermine a nascent collective consciousness among African American workers by bringing in white replacement workers. This strategy failed because at the time, meatpacking jobs there had become identified squarely as "nigger jobs" and white workers shunned or fled them. The native/non-native distinction that employers make is broader than authorization status, and the particular ethnoracial group identification that frequently signals being "from here" versus not produces different advantages and disadvantages for workers belonging to particular groups. In this sense, even Latino/a workers with legal permanent resident status or Temporary Protected Status experience the vulnerabilities in the workplace that are thought to afflict only unauthorized workers.

But it is important to recognize that these distinctions do not unequivocally favor one group over another, as I point out. In the case of Swine's, while it is possible that local African Americans saw shrinking opportunities for employment as Human Resources personnel favored the hiring of Latino/a migrants in the mid- to late 1990s ("displacement through replacement"), African Americans who remained employed at Swine's perhaps saw growing opportunities for some advancement at long last. And as the Latino/a majority established itself as the stable core of the production process at Swine's, Latinas/os began to sense that their own group position was the most subordinated of all, and that the African American minority that has continually replenished itself occupied a privileged position at Swine's at their expense. This view was shared by Latino/a migrant workers throughout agro-industrial workplaces in the region already by the early 2000s (Smith-Nonini 2003). That native-born workers would occupy a comparatively more favorable position in the workplace is not a surprising proposition. What is important in this story is how these perceptions become *racialized* by those who feel most aggrieved such that being Black is seen as a valuable resource and being *hispano* as a disadvantage regardless of authorization status. The ways in which Latina/o workers perceive their place in American society, discerned through their subordinate experience in the workplace vis-à-vis African Americans, and mediated by the two-way transparency of their white overseers, has critical implications for how Latino/a migrants become incorporated into a shifting racialized system of belonging that retains a core of white dominance. This latter point, that social relations among subordinated groups are structured through the refractory lens of white dominance, produces the qualities of what I refer to as prismatic engagement between Latinas/os and African Americans at Swine's. The following chapters delve into these dynamics.

CHAPTER 3

The Meanings of *Moyo*

*The Transnational Roots of Shop-Floor
Racial Talk*

Thomas, an older African American worker, and I were bagging a combo of one-piece ribs when we were joined by Rosa, a Salvadoran rib trimmer, and Vincent, a young African American. Thomas and I leaned into the combo to grab ribs to feed to our partners, who were holding long, narrow black bags they snatched out of a box thousands of times over. I was handing Vincent a rib when he laid into Rosa with his typical taunts, seeming a bit cruel even though he was joking, insensitively referencing her recent abandonment by her husband Jaime in a singsong tone: "Rosa, you need a new boyfriend, you gotta get you a new boyfriend, Rosa." As usual, it being prohibited but common on the floor, Rosa was gnawing on a piece of candy. "Look at her with all that caramel up in her teeth," Vincent said, proceeding with a dose of sexual innuendo. "No, I have a boyfriend—Michael," she said mischievously.

I smiled to myself as I recalled Rosa's comment one morning several months before at the rib trimming table regarding a romantic dream she had had about our African American floor supervisor Michael, in which the two of them shared an intimate moment on a beach. "Oh yeah? That makes sense," Vincent played along. "You must be doing something to him because he doesn't bother you." Vincent tried to tease Rosa about having a thing for Black men. "What's that word? *Bollo? Mollo?*" "*Moyo,*" Rosa and I blurted out at the same time. "That means nigger," Vincent said to Thomas.

"That means what now?" Thomas responded, perhaps taken aback by the slap of the familiar slur. Vincent repeated himself and elaborated: "It means nigger. I mean, because *negro* is Black but you say that and you think they calling you a nigger, but it just means Black. But *moyo*"—he paused to contemplate his explanation—"it's not like they're always saying it in a racist way, but it's more like slang, like nigger [nigga] sort of." "All right, well, now I know, when I hear it I'll know," Thomas said, nodding vigorously as he squatted to dig out racks of ribs from the combo to feed to Rosa. Vincent wasn't finished explaining the intricate meanings of *moyo*. "Yeah, and then you gotta look at the person and be, like, "Hmm, you and me, are we cool?" I guess like when someone calls you a *moyo*, you need to check the person out and see in what way are they saying that word." "Okay, now I know, I didn't know that," Thomas replied, not seeming especially interested in this shop-floor lesson. Rosa, who had been listening quietly to Vincent and Thomas's exchange, sealed the conversation with fitting irony, leveling at Vincent with perfect comedic timing, "Shut up, *moyo!*"

This chapter examines the categories, uses, and meanings of ethnoracial talk deployed by Latina/os to express symbolic boundaries vis-à-vis their African American counterparts. It situates the language used by Latinas/os to refer to American Blacks, and the underlying significance of blackness these categories convey, within both the broader ethnoracial panoramas of Mexico, Honduras, and El Salvador and the structured dynamic of an American workplace. In doing so, it shows how a transnational field of meanings develops that devalues blackness universally and yet locally, in a Southern meatpacking plant, associates being Black with privilege. The chapters that follow develop the crux of the story that is strung together in this book: that the ways in which Latina/o workers navigate boundaries vis-à-vis African Americans in the workplace is inextricably tied to their sense of group position within the social organization of labor and in American society beyond the workplace. In other words, such boundary making is intertwined with Latina/o migrants' perception that they are the most exploited workers at Swine's, with unique vulnerabilities that condition their lives on the line and outside the factory gates.

The first section of this chapter describes the structure and language of race in migrants' origin communities, drawing special attention to the contrasts between Latin American and U.S. racial systems generally and the panoramas of Honduras and El Salvador specifically. The principal commonality between Latin American and U.S. racial systems— white dominance and the devaluation of blackness—predisposes Latino/a migrants to view groups identified with blackness negatively in a broad sense. But the strong identification of Black Americans as *moyos*—a term that has evolved in the transnational space that migrants occupy—and the pejorative meanings that such a designation reflects and reinforces, are dynamics that unfold in ways that convey their uniquely American character. The second section of this chapter proposes an analytical framework for understanding language as a symbolic boundary that reveals crucial social distinctions between Latinas/os and African Americans. The third section focuses on the deployment of ethnoracial forms of identification on the shop floor at Swine's, drawing attention to the categories, uses, and meanings of such language. The last section discusses how native-born workers navigate and challenge Latinas/os' use of such language, while pointing out the rarity with which native-born workers refer to Latinas/os in ethnoracial terms.

MOYOLO, MAYATE, MOYOTE, MOYO: THE STRUCTURE AND LANGUAGE OF RACE IN MIGRANTS' ORIGIN COMMUNITIES

Although at a superficial level the *moyo* designation appears merely to refer to American Blacks, upon further consideration the term reveals much more about the "structure of feeling" (in the words of Raymond Williams [1977]) that governs relations between Latinas/os and African Americans. As Vincent explained it, depending on the context in which it is articulated, *moyo* can mean either the unambiguously racist "nigger" or the familiarly casual "nigga." Indeed, although in this opening encounter Vincent appropriated *moyo* in his playful banter with Rosa, while Rosa comically cast it back at him after he finished his discursion, at other times Vincent responded to this designation with far less flexibility.

This chapter closely examines the deployment of ethnoracial forms of identification on the shop floor in order to shed light on their significance for understanding relations between Latina/o and African American workers. It argues that language is a vitally revealing medium through which Latinas/os draw boundaries between African Americans and themselves, and that it has been woefully neglected in the literature on intergroup relations. The source of the particular designation of African Americans as *moyos* can be located in a transnational field of ethnoracial meanings in which migrants are embedded. In order to trace this source, it is necessary to begin with a discussion of the ethnoracial panoramas of Latino/a migrants' origin communities. This chapter argues that, while the racialized systems of stratification in Latino/a migrants' origin communities precondition them to view blackness negatively as a subordinate status, it is only in the U.S. context that such vaguely tangible predispositions take on the full-bodied form of meaningful relations between groups.

Vincent's consideration of how and why Latinas/os use the term *moyo* instead of the more direct "negro" designation invites a closer look at the categories and meanings that prevail in migrants' origin communities, and which inform those they elaborate in the United States. This chapter explores in greater detail the specific ethnoracial panoramas of Honduras (and to a lesser extent El Salvador and Mexico), given the scant scholarship on this context and the substantial contribution of Hondurans to the Latino/a agro-industrial labor force in the contemporary American South. The ethnoracial panoramas of Honduras and El

Salvador, in particular, present interesting contrasts that I will focus on in depth, drawing on insights gleaned from interviews and conversations with Latina/o workers. These analyses will be tied back to the central theme of this chapter: the categories and meanings that Latinas/os use to designate and define native-born groups, especially African Americans.

Racialized systems of stratification throughout Latin America and the Caribbean differ from the U.S. model in important ways. Scholars have pointed to their greater fluidity of racial categories, their more fine-grained differentiations, their blurrier boundaries, and their closer relationship to somatic, cultural, and class markers than to ancestry or hypodescent (Telles 2004; Bonilla-Silva and Glover 2004; Wade 1997). For its part, the historiography of race in Latin America and the Caribbean has had to unravel itself from the various nation-building projects that have shaped (mis)understandings of race and racial inequality in the region.

The racial ideology of *mestizaje* was prevalent in the modern history of Mexico and Central America, as political and intellectual elites fashioned a national imaginary that could cement solidarity in newly independent republics. This new mestizo identity was predicated on a fusion of Amerindian peoples and Europeans and effectively marginalized Indian and African identities, representing the former as bygone and erasing the presence of the latter altogether (Mollett 2006; Gould 1998; Wade 1997). In Spanish colonial times, the ambiguities of position within the socio-racial hierarchies of Latin America were more evident with respect to indigenous peoples than Africans, whose status at the bottom of the colonial order was hardly questioned. Indeed, whereas debates regarding the treatment of native Americans centered around legislating both their protection and their exploitation, the primary concern with Africans was ensuring control over them (Wade 1997, 27).

Certainly, both were oppressed and exploited—indeed, exterminated—but colonial authorities did make distinctions between indigenous peoples and Africans that are important in understanding present-day socio-racial hierarchies in the region. While Indians were not barred from intermarrying, there were "antimiscegenation" laws that restricted the marital options of Africans, though these of course fell by the wayside in practice. And whereas indigenous (Amerindian) groups have accessed state recognition of rights on the basis of unique categorical identification, the non-recognition of Black identities in Latin America has had the paradoxical effect of permitting popular alternatives to the most stigmatized statuses, while impeding redress based on claims to these identities. The devaluation of blackness was formalized in the early to mid-twentieth century, at the height of eugenicist thought and practice, when Central American republics institutionalized white supremacy in laws that barred the entry of Blacks and other groups considered undesirable for the nation or threatening to the livelihood of Honduran workers (Andrews 2004; Euraque 2003; England and Anderson 2004). In Honduras, scholars have argued that the elevation of the mythology surrounding the indigenous Lempira as representative of the nation—in the form of its currency—was a racial project aimed at solidifying Honduras as a mestizo nation and marginalizing the contributions of blackness (Euraque 2003).

Given their departure from U.S. racial categorical schemes, an issue in the study of racial systems in Latin America has been the question of how exactly to identify "Blacks." While some have argued (or implicitly assumed) that "Blacks" should be limited to those people who identify as such, other scholars argue that such a specification unduly constrains the study of blackness.[1] After all, the denial or suppression of blackness (and Blacks) has been a crucial element of many Latin American nation-building projects, and perhaps doing the former merely perpetuates this ideological erasure. But for all the differences between the Latin American and U.S. models, they all share racialized systems of stratification that converge around a core of white dominance.

Honduras counts several independent streams of Afro-descended people in its history, but only some of these are identified (by themselves and by others) as Black.[2] Among the various African and Afro-descended populations who arrived in Honduras between the sixteenth and the early twentieth centuries, some are socially recognized as Blacks while others are not. These include African slaves brought in in the mid-sixteenth century to replace the depleted population of indigenous slaves, many of whom had escaped by the 1600s and mixed with dispossessed indigenous peoples, poor whites, and free Blacks, and would come to be categorized by colonial authorities as a *casta* (e.g., racial categories of *ladino, mestizo, mulato, zambo*) depending on the particular combination. In fact, descendants of African slaves brought in in the 1600s, who escaped or otherwise found freedom and mixed with others, make up a substantial number of people in Olancho, the department from which many North Carolina Hondurans originate. Although these people would be classified as Black by U.S. standards, they do not identify as Black but rather as mestizo (Bueso, in Centeno 1997, cited in England and Anderson 2004, 7).

In the 1600s and 1700s, British settlers in the Bay of Honduras brought African slaves to the north coast, some of whom mixed with the Miskito Indians, and in the 1840s, Black freedmen from the Cayman Islands followed white Cayman Islanders to the Bay Islands of Honduras. A third major Afro-descended population are the Garifuna, whose origin story is described as the fusion of Carib Indians and Africans marooned on St. Vincent, later exiled to the Bay Islands by the British at the end of the eighteenth century. From there, Garifuna migrated to mainland Honduras, and to coastal areas from Belize to Nicaragua. In the early twentieth century they became an increasingly important part of the multinational fruit companies' labor force. The last major stream was comprised of West Indian Blacks brought in by multinational fruit companies to work on plantations in the early twentieth century, which sparked labor conflicts that nationalists fanned in support of racist immigration laws (England and Anderson 2004; Andrews 2004; Euraque 2003). Despite the fact that Honduran elites since the early twentieth century carefully crafted a nationalist narrative that depicted a Spanish-Amerindian mestizo nation, ethnoracial minority groups such as the transnational Afroindigenous Garifuna community have achieved some measure of supranational political voice in recent decades (England 2006).

In contrast, El Salvador stands out for the near-total absence of any mention of Africans, Blacks, or slaves in its historiography, despite the fact that such a wholesale absence did not exist in reality. If Honduras, at least in recent decades, has acknowledged indigeneity *and* blackness as partly constitutive of the national imagination, especially as these come together in the Afro-indigenous Garifuna (England 2006), the national imagination of El Salvador has been characterized by the erasure of indigenous peoples and the denial of a Black contribution altogether (Tilley 2005). Indeed, the near-complete absence of Blacks or blackness in Salvadoran historiography is usually justified by reference to the very small number of African slaves that were brought in during the colonial period. The popular idea that there are no Blacks in El Salvador is accompanied by a strong scorn for blackness itself. This sentiment was expressed clearly by Hernán, a short Salvadoran rib trimmer and former rebel fighter from Aguilares, who exclaimed one day, "If there had been Blacks in El Salvador, they would have all been killed during the war." A less dismal, but equally revealing, insight into the valorization of blackness was proffered by Claudia. She was affectionately referred to by her family as *Chele* (White), whereas her younger brother Antonio apparently grew up feeling disdained for his darkness. "*No me quieren porque soy negro!*" (They don't love me because I am Black!), he would frequently protest as a child. Their childhood experiences are not unlike those memorialized by the Mexican American writer Richard Rodríguez in his *Hunger of Memory* (1982), and by the Puerto Rican writer Piri Thomas in his *Down These Mean Streets* (1967). Ironically, then, given the supposed lack of a socially discernible group of Afro-descended people in El Salvador, Salvadorans nevertheless articulate a polarized racialization in which whiteness is positively valorized while blackness is negatively valorized. Perhaps because of the legacy of erasure and denial, Salvadoran workers asked to articulate aspects of their country's ethnoracial panorama provided vexing accounts. Sitting in her living room one evening, I asked Sara, a *tortuga* machine operator, why people say there are no Blacks in El Salvador. She explained:

> There are no *negros* because El Salvador is too small, and other countries are bigger so they can go there. Yes, there are *negros*, but they aren't born there, they aren't native to there. They come from other places. You see them. You're not surprised to see a *negro*. But it's not like in Honduras, where there are cities, departments, that are *morenos*. Where we're from, no. There are *indios*—that's what we call them, *indios*, which are the *indígenas* that dress in *refajos*, sandals, and *caites*.

On another occasion, I asked Sara how Salvadorans talk about blackness.

> That I recall, no one pays attention to whether there are or aren't Blacks, since there never are any. Yes, there are people who are *morena*, but not of the *negra* race. They're born that way, but it's not that they come from a *negra* race. Rather, there are *morenos*, people who are *morena* but not *negra*.

Claudia provided a similar perspective on the ethnoracial panorama of El Salvador, with added flair that conveyed in no uncertain terms the status of blackness and indigeneity in El Salvador:

> The thing is that in El Salvador there aren't any distinctions, because over there we don't have any other class. There aren't people who are *morena*. There aren't people who are white. I mean, there aren't *bolillos* or *negros*. In El Salvador you're going to see people just like us. I mean, if you go to Honduras, Honduras has a class like us, and a *negra* class. I mean, there are the Garifunas, what they call them. Not in El Salvador.

Recalling the work of Virginia Tilley (2005) on indigeneity in El Salvador, I asked Salvadoran machine operator Claudia about this group, which elicited a response that communicated Salvadorans' strong repudiation of both blackness and indigeneity:

> No, there aren't any. We don't admit any. *Ni indios ni negros.* We sent them to Honduras, and others to Guatemala and Mexico. In El Salvador we don't want them. . . . No, we don't want them! Then we're going to be speaking in dialects. We're not going to understand each other [laughing].

Honduran workers were far more likely to describe a complex ethnoracial panorama in their origin country than Salvadorans were, and they also noted important contrasts to the deployment of ethnoracial boundaries in Honduras versus the United States. Gerardo, a twenty-six-year-old rib sorter, contrasted the salience of bold ethnoracial boundaries in the American context to the situation in Honduras. Over breakfast one Saturday morning at a Waffle House, I asked him about the use of ethnoracial identifiers in Honduras.

> In general, it doesn't exist the way it does here, where you do separate them—the *moyos* from the *bolillos* and the *hispanos.* Over there if you want to specify 100 percent you say the *negro* or *moyolo,* but it's not so much to discriminate against them or to talk about them as *negros.* If you want to talk specifically about that person's race [then you specify], but otherwise it's not used as much. Like here, where you do have to separate them, to say specifically that a *moyo* said this or a *bolillo* said that.

His comments reveal several distinct features of racialization schemes in Honduras—and probably other Latin American countries—versus the United States. Gerardo distinguishes between the nearly compulsory identification of a person's race in speech in the American context, where races "have to be separated," to the situation in Honduras, where this explicit identification is considered optional, extra information, or used in special cases to uniquely identify someone. In fact, comments from Gerardo and other Hondurans reveal that strong ethnoracial identification is typically reserved specifically for the Garifuna (and smaller recognized minority groups), not for the broader Honduran population, some of whom are also Afro-descended. In this sense, when I asked Hondurans about their country's ethnoracial panorama, contrasting it to the United States, "where you have African Americans, whites, Latinos, et cetera," most singled out the Garifuna of the north Atlantic coast. If I asked about *negros* in Honduras, respondents would often answer that there are a lot of Garifuna, especially in the coastal region, downplaying distinctions among the heterogeneous non-Garifuna Honduran population. In fact, this understanding of who belongs to the category "Black" (i.e., ethnoracial minority groups such as the Garifuna) is also reflected in scholarly undertakings on the topic of blackness in Latin America and the Caribbean (e.g., Yelvington 2001). Even those scholars whose explicit focus is blackness in Latin America wrestle with identifying who is to be considered Black, beyond the officially recognized ethnic minorities (Lewis 2012; Torres and Whitten 1998).

Much as the anthropologist Laura Lewis (2012) experienced during her study of Black Mexico along the Costa Chica, asking Hondurans to describe the ethnoracial panoramas of their communities of origins was sometimes akin to pulling teeth, so much less stark did the ethnoracial group boundaries appear to them. My discussion with Cristina was a clear illustration of the difficulty Hondurans could have when asked to articulate it. Asked to describe the different groups in Honduras, she insisted people were just "Honduran" or whatever nationality they belonged to. Prodded further, she distinguished between Garifuna—whom she also referred to as *morenos* or *negros*—and "us," people "of the other color, not *negros*." Pressed to describe the "distinct groups" in Honduras, Cristina extolled the artful skills of *negritos* who easily peel coconuts by hand, and play music and dance *punta* on the beaches of the north coast.[3]

The association between Blacks and ethnic minorities was quite strong among Hondurans when asked about the ethnoracial panoramas of their origin country.[4] Talking with Carina, a Honduran boning line worker, about her experience working with Haitians, who began working at Swine's in growing numbers starting in January 2011, immediately sparked this connection for her. And, as was the case for Cristina, it also triggered a fondness for these groups that I did not find among other Latinas/os (Salvadorans and Mexicans). This fondness was the sort of benevolent racism typical of other Latin American (and Brazilian) contexts, where the music, dance, food, and perceived lifestyles and personality traits of Blacks are represented with a bemused objectification that is fraught with affection and disgust, intimacy and stigma, all at once. Carina observed:

> There are many dialects in my country as well. And Garifuna is the most predominant one. In La Ceiba and Trujillo, I had many friends. Because the *afroamericanos* over there are from there [note her adoption and transference to the Honduran ethnoracial panorama the American terminology for American Blacks]. So we feel equal, because we're from the same country. There isn't that racism, that hate, that discrimination. The department we're from [meaning she and her sister, Leticia], is one of the places with the most Garifuna. And there are other *razas negras* [Black races] that are not Garifuna. The *ingleses, misquitos, belices hondureños*. There are some very good things about them. Their food is delicious. And as Garifuna, many prefer to have *hispanos* as

friends. They'll say, "Look at that *negra,* she did this or that to me." And if you, as an *hispana,* rubbed her the wrong way, they'll say, "Look at that *india tal por cual*" [good-for-nothing Indian]. But you don't feel offended because they are your race, they're from your country and you're in your country. They're from another country but since they've been there for generations . . .⁵

Carina's sister Leticia schooled me on the proper etiquette for making ethnoracial identifications in Honduras, while also explaining how she came to learn of *moyo:*

> In school I had *morena* classmates. Because over there you don't call them *negros. Negros* is offensive. Same as here. So you call them *morenos.* Here, *negros* feel offended if you call them *negros.* Or *moyos.* In fact, I didn't know that word, *moyo.* Here is where I first heard that you call them *moyos.* Because in Honduras you say *morenos.* Or *mayates. Mayates, prietos.* But it's offensive.⁶

Unlike Carina, Cristina's in-law Ileana was under the impression that *mayate* is not a term that is poorly received by those who are identified as *morenos:*

> Over there [in Honduras], they [Blacks] don't get mad if you call them *mayate.* We had a *compañero* [classmate] and we called him *mayate,* and he would answer quickly. In other words, he wouldn't get mad. I think he liked it more when people called him *mayate* than when they called him by his name. Because when he would sign the yearbook, or write on his desk, he would write "El Mayate." In other words, it never bothered him. He was from Tela, from a place called Tornabé. And it didn't bother him.

Leticia was less sanguine than Cristina, her sister Carina, or Ileana about the social status of Blacks in Honduras:

> Racism is also practiced over there. In Sabá, where we're from, there were two *familias morenas,* and these were the Williamses and the Joneses. And all of the women married *hispanos.* But the same bad things were practiced—despising people because they are *negros.* I had a classmate who nobody wanted to share a seat with in class. Over there they eat a lot of coconut with seafood, and that emanates from their pores. She was a good friend of mine. She was Garifuna, she was the only one who sat with me. I didn't care that she smelled bad. You will also see many *hispanos* that are *morenos.* Discrimination, racism, also exist but not like over here where it's front and center. Over there we have only three groups: *hispanos, morenos,* and foreigners. There are people like you, they call them "*gringas de cerro*" [hill gringas].⁷ The children of an *hispano* and a *moreno* are called *mulato.*

While profoundly confused by my attempts to extract from her a list of categories used in Honduras, Cristina easily identified the primary designations for ethnoracial groups in the U.S. context. Like Carina, Cristina told me she first learned of *moyos* in North Carolina, and indicated that her brothers living in Minnesota had never heard of this designation. Cristina also understood that African Americans did not like being referred to as *moyos* but nevertheless believed the term to be benign. I asked her where she first heard *moyo* and why she thought African Americans did not like the term:

> When I got here, I heard about the *moyos* and the *bolillos*. But they get mad when they're called *moyos*. *Morenos* get mad when they're called *moyos*. Because I said something there at the factory. Vincent—with someone who spoke Spanish—asked me why I called him *moyo*, what did *moyo* mean. And I didn't know how to explain it. I just know that's what people call them. But I don't think it's bad. Because Heriberto [her brother-in-law] is *trigueño* [literally "wheat-colored," having light brown skin] and his brothers call him *moyo*. All his brothers call him that. "Where's the *moyo*?" "Is the *moyo* here?" And Heriberto doesn't get mad.[8]

Both Ileana and her husband Jorge concurred that *moyo* has its origins in the parlance of Mexican migrants, and that their adoption of this term happened only as a result of contact with Mexican migrants and other Latinas/os established in workplaces in the American South, such as Swine's. Jorge told me that "when we came here, we called them *morenos*. *Moyo* comes from the Mexicans. They say they [Blacks] are *moyos*, and they say the Americans are *bolillos*. More than anything we've picked up those words from the Mexicans. *Morenos* don't like to be called *moyo*. And Americans don't like to be called *bolillos*, either." Ileana agreed with this explanation, emphasizing her understanding that being referred to as *moyos* is hurtful to African Americans: "Truth is, I first heard that [*moyo*] at the plant. But that came from the Mexicans most of all, saying *moyo* and *bolillo*. More than anything, I heard it from the Mexicans; you start picking up words and they stick. But many Americans—*morenos* don't like being called *moyo*. They feel bad when they're called *moyo*."

The etymology of the term *moyo* is difficult to trace. One anthropologist documents the use of *moyo* among *morenos* in the southern Pacific coastal Mexican state of Guerrero, which has a concentration of Afro-Mexicans, as an insult referring to U.S. Blacks. Although the origin and meaning of the term are not entirely certain, scholars have suggested that *moyo* might derive from the Nahuatl *moyote*, which is a kind of black bug (Lewis 2012; Lewis 2000).[9] Why a term derived from Nahuatl would be used by Mexicans in Mexico to refer to U.S. Blacks but not to Black or *moreno* Mexicans in Mexico is perhaps odd. But its usage suggests that the term evolved in the American context, and was perhaps re-exported to the Mexican context by returned migrants, where it maintained its singular reference to American Blacks as opposed to Blacks more generally.[10] Hondurans and Salvadorans report not having heard the word until they learned it in the United States, some hearing it for the first time when they started working at Swine's, and they cannot say definitively where the word comes from or what it means, other than referring to U.S. Blacks, though most credit Mexicans as the source of the term. They are mostly ambivalent about or claim to be unaware of its pejorative connotations. But a few say they understand that African Americans do not like being referred to as *moyos,* and these individuals usually project far less negative views of American Blacks than other Latinas/os, and their more nuanced consideration of the symbolic functions of language reflects social boundaries between these groups that are less intensely racialized.

CONCEPTS FOR UNDERSTANDING THE IMPORTANCE OF SYMBOLIC BOUNDARY MAKING AND LANGUAGE IN A MATURING MIGRANT DESTINATION

The analysis in this chapter brings into sharp focus the typically implicit relationship between symbolic and social boundaries, foregrounding the ways in which conceptual distinctions and representational devices communicate social differences in status ossified as groups (Lamont and Molnar 2002; Emirbayer 1997; Somers 1994). I aim to situate the study of intergroup boundary-work in the most crucial social domain of both native-born workers' and Latin American labor migrants' lives: work. Social identity theorists have defined identities as "strategic social constructions created through interaction, with social and material consequences" (Howard 2000, 371). In this sense, language is crucial to the production of identities. This chapter, then, draws attention to the shop-floor language that produces *and* reflects ethnoracial boundaries between Latinas/os and African Americans in particular. It argues that understanding the identities that Latino/a migrants come to assume through their incorporation into American racial and class stratification systems requires attention to the ways in which language is deployed to express symbolically the socially significant distinctions that inhere in ethnoracial boundaries. Ethnoracial nomenclature, or ethnonymy, is a symbolic boundary that both reflects and magnifies social boundaries as groups perceive these. As such, attention to the forms, frequency, and contexts of ethnonymic expression reveals important information about the character of intergroup relations and the positions occupied by various groups in a given stratified system of belonging (Stephens 2003).

Studies of social relations in the context of the "new immigration" have not mined the symbolic functions of ethnoracial identification for what these can tell us about how putative groups project their collective understandings of other groups as well as their own. Although perhaps scholars cannot be faulted for taking for granted the social realness of groups often now called "Blacks" or "Hispanics," it is another thing to ignore the existence and implications of ethnoracial language used to designate and characterize these groups in organic contexts. Given the prevalence with which this talk appeared throughout my fieldwork, it is hard to believe that these kinds of designations did not manifest in other researchers' data, though perhaps the researchers did not interpret them as data worth noting. This is an enormous oversight, tantamount to taking for granted the designations of southern European immigrants in the early twentieth century as "guineas" and "dagos," or overlooking the inconsistent ways in which social and legal categorizations as "white" were applied to these and other groups, or accepting the "wetback" label as a neutral referent for Latino/a migrants. Scholars have shown the importance of understanding who gets classified as what, what these classifications mean, and how classification happens for comprehending "race" as a discourse that naturalizes more or less discrete human groups based on perceptions of difference, primarily related to physical appearance and ancestry, but also to attributions of mental abilities, personality traits, and cultural dispositions (Desmond and Emirbayer 2009; Loveman and Muñiz 2007; Roediger 2007 [1991]; Roediger 2005; Nobles 2000; Rodríguez 2000; Haney López 2006 [1996]; Shirley 2010). Language in the form of ethnoracial identification can hardly be considered a neutral arena of categories that are merely referential rather than representational.[11]

Rather than "vigilantly doubt the racial categories" they use, social scientists have instead been certain that they can write about "Hispanics" and footnote the rest of the ethnoracial categorical question (Almaguer 2003, 216).[12] In doing so, they have overlooked a rich source of data regarding the everyday symbolic manifestations of intergroup relations and the role these play in the incorporation process, given how racialization is neither unilateral nor uni-national (in the case of migrants). Attention to Latinas/os' self-identifications has mostly been limited to assessing the extent to which official pan-ethnic or pan-ethno-racial categories have been adopted (e.g., "Hispanic," "other"), or the salience of such categories in Latinas/os' ethnoracial self-identifications versus national or subnational identifications (Marrow 2011; Itzigsohn and Dore-Cabral 2000). These are important foci, but because studies tend to measure identification with official or formal categories, they miss the street-level dynamics by which group-based self- and other-understandings and categories are constructed, expressed, and contested, and the meanings these convey. It is these street-level dynamics that are most revealing about how groups see one another in the real-life contexts through which they encounter one another.

Yet perhaps "identities" is not the best way to think of what is being created through the uses and meanings of categorical signifiers that correspond to ethnoracial boundaries. After all, some critics argue that "identity" is made to mean too much, too little, or nothing at all by its excessive application. To these critics, "conceptualizing all affinities and affiliations, all forms of belonging, all experiences of commonality, connectedness, and cohesion, all self-understandings and self-identifications" as identity make the word lose analytical power (Brubaker and Cooper 2000, 2). Indeed, the sort of well-established group-ness that identity implies is not quite what is suggested in Latino/a migrants' efforts to distinguish other groups, namely American Blacks and whites, from themselves. Rather, the symbolic boundaries they communicate, partially informed by understandings they transport from their communities of origin, are tied to an *incipient* sense of their group position in the American context, anchored in the perception of their disadvantaged status in the workplace relative to other groups, yet still uncertain in the broader society. This uncertainty makes it critical to understand incorporation as a process, and relations between subordinate groups as prismatic engagement. The encounters between Latina/o migrants and African Americans on the line, operating in the shadows cast by whiteness, have everything to do with shaping the emergent racialized system of stratification in the twenty-first-century United States.

MOYOS, NEGROS, MORENOS: THE LANGUAGE OF BOUNDARIES BETWEEN LATINAS/OS AND AFRICAN AMERICANS ON THE SHOP FLOOR AT SWINE'S

This section focuses primarily on the ways in which Latina/o workers identify Blacks, and secondarily on the ways in which Blacks contribute to, make sense of, or challenge Latinas/os' identification of Blacks. Largely absent from this account is a counteranalysis of the ways in which Black workers identify Latinas/os. The reason for this absence, itself a meaningful finding, is straightforward: African American workers rarely talked about Latina/o workers in ethnoracial terms, meaning that they were far less likely to verbalize characterizations of Latinas/os as a group (e.g., "Hispanics are lazy," "Hispanics are hard workers"), to target Latinas/os as the source of their grievances (e.g., "Hispanics get preferential treatment," "Hispanics are taking our jobs"), or even to refer to them casually in such terms (e.g., "Tell that Hispanic to throw the meat on the line correctly").[13] On the infrequent occasions when I heard Black workers refer to Latinas/os in this way, this was usually in more or less neutral contexts, and the most common terms were "Hispanic," "Spanish," "Mexican" (often irrespective of national origin), and "Honduras" (as opposed to "Honduran"), in roughly that order. Perhaps one could argue that in a department such as Loin Boning and Packing, where out of approximately two hundred workers, 75 to 80 percent were Latina/o, ethnoracial identification would clarify little about who was being talked about, which might account for why, for instance, casual references of the sort mentioned above were less frequently made. But the same pattern held in the Marination Department where I worked for seven months, where out of approximately twenty-five workers, 80 percent were African American. In both departments, African American workers were far more likely to refer to individual Latinas/os using their names rather than by any group-based form of identification, and they were far less likely to express a categorical distinction of any sort through ethnoracial identification of the group.

On the other hand, Latinas/os in both departments frequently referred to Black workers, both individually and as a group, using terms of identification such as *moyo*, *negro*, and *moreno* rather than their names, although this was more pronounced in the Loin Boning Department. Ethnoracial identification of white workers was common as well. American whites, whether workers or supervisors, were usually referred to as *bolillos*, but because there were so few whites on the production floor, Latinas/os talked about them in any way far less frequently. Like other popular forms of identification, *bolillo* is a term that finds its origins among Mexican migrants. But unlike the meanings of *moyo*, which will be discussed in depth in this chapter, the literal meaning of *bolillo*—loaf of bread—is hardly imbued with negative associations, and its usage seems to have an ostensibly neutral valence. And, in a telling elision, white workers identified as *bolillos* were just as often referred to as *americanos,* a conflation of ethnoracial and national origins forms of identification that rarely occurred when speaking about African Americans. The significance of this last point will be discussed in a later chapter.

Moreover, negative imagery associated with blackness did not have its counterpoint when it came to ethnoracial depictions of white workers. An older Salvadoran worker affectionately known as "La Madrina" (The Godmother) occasionally referred to individual Black workers using creative racialized slurs. She had such a name for Janice, a middle-aged African American rib trimmer, who was generally despised by both Latina/o and African American workers for her selfish and sluggish work performance, but was usually avoided lest she unleash a cascade of anger in your direction. La Madrina referred to this woman, whose complexion was a deep brown, as "Hígado Quemado" (Burnt Liver). Such vivid depictions were part of La Madrina's repertoire of spitfire. Workers told story after story about how La Madrina, a ten-year veteran of the Loin Boning and Packing Department, had exploded in tantrums or made a new hire break down in tears. She was a fierce little old lady, and her age is probably the only reason nobody had ever punched her in the face. Rafael, a Honduran worker who had transferred to Swine's a year earlier after another plant he was working at closed down, confessed that he came close to doing so when he first started.[14]

Pejorative meanings were also attached to Blacks as a group in departments where they were the majority rather than the minority. In the Marination Department, Latinas/os sometimes used popular refrains to express these ideas, or simply stated some negative quality presumed to adhere to Blacks. One evening, the line was stopped while the machine that vacuum sealed our seasoned meat products was getting fixed. I chatted with Lydia, an older South American worker, who was annoyed at all the mishaps we had been having that night as we tried to run our product. *"Por eso es que no quiero tener un negro parado al lado mío, porque llegando o saliendo la joden"* (That's why I don't want a *negro* standing next to me, because coming or going they are going to fuck up). This was a saying her mother often repeated, she told me, and a refrain that is known throughout Latin America, including in Brazil (Telles 2004).

On another night soon after this incident, my Marination coworkers and I were reworking pallets of pork chops that had been weighed and boxed incorrectly by the Pork Chop Department. Per the instructions of

FIGURE 4. Partial view of the Marination Department, with a crew leader in the background.

Edrick, the Quality Assurance worker, we were to take each box off the pallet, open it, weigh every pork chop, sort them by weight, and repack them according to the correct weight range per pork chop for that box. Around the second or third pallet, my coworkers began to just weigh the boxes instead of each chop. Our African American crew leader, Clyde, had apparently told some workers to do it this way, even though he hadn't explained this "shortcut" to all of us. When I looked around and asked in frustration what was going on, Tina pulled me aside to explain. Clyde, who was chatting idly with a Quality Assurance supervisor, yelled out, "You don't got to explain anything to her. I do the explaining!" Looking over, I yelled back, "Except you *don't*, that's the problem!" Lydia tried to ask him what we were doing now, and

I snapped to her sarcastically, "Don't ask any questions, don't ask questions if you don't understand!" and cursed Clyde in Spanish. Later, we were back to weighing chops when the Quality Assurance person, Edrick, reappeared. The work suddenly stopped. Edrick had pulled reworked boxes and found chops that were both under and over the weight specifications. Our white supervisor, Joe, called a huddle about this latest blunder, and Larissa, Lydia, and I protested that there was a whole pallet where workers were told to just weigh the boxes. Who told us that, Joe asked? "Clyde, I guess," I said. "Everybody was doing it." Lydia was fuming. "This *negro* is dumb. Like my mother used to say, when have you seen a smart *negro*?"[15]

The ways in which Latina/o workers identify Blacks, individually and as a group, display subtle distinctions in meaning depending on context and tone, much as Vincent had grasped in the encounter that opened this chapter. But some patterns were clear. The three most common terms used to identify Blacks were *moyos, negros,* and *morenos,* in roughly that order of frequency. Salvadorans seemed more likely than Hondurans or Mexicans to use the term *negro* interchangeably with *moyo,* and *moreno* was less likely to be used in purely inflammatory remarks about Blacks. For example, although a statement to the effect of "*morenos* are treated better than *hispanos*" was not uncommon, I cannot recall a single instance where this term appeared alongside negative descriptors targeting Blacks, such as *moreno desgraciado* (good-for-nothing). On the other hand, phrases such as *la negra desgraciada* or *el moyo jodido* (fucking *moyo*) were much more likely to appear conjunctively, suggesting that these identifications permit a broader range of pejorative meanings.

Sometimes Cristina referred to Thomas by his name, carefully pronouncing it in English, but as often or more she referred to him as *el moyo* in negative contexts. Thomas frequently relied on Cristina to sharpen his knife, and after obliging, she would turn to me and say, "See, that fucking *moyo* has been here ten years and still doesn't know how to sharpen the knife." Or because Thomas had a habit of warming his hands in the *tortuga*'s hot-water stream, she'd complain that that was all that *moyo* did all day. In the most sweeping of condemnations, Cristina pointed to Thomas and said, "That *moyo* has made it ten years here because he doesn't work."

Claudia operated the *tortuga* with Denise, a middle-aged Black woman who had transferred from the Hamboning Department in June 2010. Claudia despised her and the two had frequent blowups when they weren't doing their best to ignore each other. Each time Claudia recounted an incident with Denise, she called her "that *moya pendeja*" (dumbass *moya*) or "*la negra hija de la gran puta*" (literally, "the Black daughter of the great whore"). Sara told me of problems she was having with Angeline, an older Black woman she worked with sometimes, calling her "*la negra desgraciada.*" One Saturday about thirteen months after I left the job at Swine's, I was sitting on the sofa with Sara at Claudia's house. I asked her how work had been that week, to which she replied caustically that it had been the same as always. I pressed her for specific information, saying, "What do you mean the same? Something happens there every day." "Something happens like what? Hmm? Like what? Like that I got into a fight with a *negra desgraciada*?" Sara asked me provocatively. "Well, yes, for example," I replied. "Oh, well then yes, I got into a fight with a *negra desgraciada*," she said in her characteristically blunt, but also inappropriately comical, style.

An underlying usage of these terms is important not because it directly expresses a value-laden meaning, but because its seemingly neutral ubiquity is itself significant. Latina/o workers regularly foregrounded a worker's blackness by referring to him or her as *el moyo* or *la moya* rather than by his or her name. When Aisha, a young African American woman who started to work in Loin Boning packing ribs, would go on one of her frequent bathroom breaks, workers would ask about her whereabouts: "And the *moya*?" (or, because she was young, "and the *moyita*?"). Even after Claudia had worked alongside Denise at the *tortuga* for more than nine months, Claudia never once referred to her by name, calling her instead *la moya* or *la negra*, a tendency probably aggravated by her explosive relationship with the woman. Even after working with Thomas for close to two years, Cristina frequently referred to him casually as *el moyo*. Even on one of the few occasions in which spontaneous positive assessments of a Black worker were expressed, their ethnoracial identification stood out. One afternoon I was bagging ribs with Elsa, a Salvadoran woman who normally worked upstairs in the box room and had moved to North Carolina from Dallas with her children after breaking up with her husband. As we chatted about her son wanting to go to college and her younger daughter not liking school, she spotted Jeremy nearby and said to me in a tone of affectionate admiration, "I love that *moyo*. That *moyo* is so nice."

My sense that the uses of *moyo*, and their frequency, were significant for understanding how Latinas/os view African Americans, the group they are most likely to encounter in the workplace, was confirmed by Ileana, who spontaneously singled out this issue in discussing her unusual relations with African American coworkers. Ileana is related to Cristina's husband, Ernesto, and was originally sponsored by friends in Virginia. She was brought to North Carolina by Ernesto's brother Julio when she couldn't find work, and now lives in a trailer with her new husband, Jorge, next to Cristina and Ernesto, in the same park as Julio, Heriberto, and several other brothers, and has worked at Swine's for almost three years. Recall that Ileana had an intimate relationship with Myrna, the Puerto Rican recruiter she calls "mother" and visits frequently, even taking care of Myrna when Myrna was recuperating from surgery. It might seem strange that Ileana would have great affection for African Americans. But in fact, Ileana describes herself and is described by Latina coworkers as one of the only Latinas who gets along well with Black coworkers. Part of this may be due to the peculiarities of her personality: she is goofy, boisterous, and unpretentious. Her gender presentation is nonthreatening, as she does not wear makeup to work or engage in flirtatious behaviors with men, as many women workers do. But a significant part of her positive relations with African American workers is undoubtedly attributable to the fact that she makes an effort to engage them despite her very limited English-speaking abilities, particularly through humor, playfulness, and camaraderie. She is cognizant of the fact that African American workers who know of the term tend to not like being referred to as *moyos,* and therefore avoids using the word, especially in their presence. Instead, she refers to African American workers by their names, contrasting herself to most Latinas/os, who she says usually refer to a Black worker as *el moyo* or *la moya.* Further, she appears to give some validation to Black workers who occasionally complain to her of other Latinas/os' attitude of looking down on them. Importantly, then, Ileana's self-conscious avoidance of *moyo* is both reflective of her more positive understanding of Black workers *and* constitutive of it. At the same time, Ileana understands workers like herself, besieged by the vulnerabilities of illegality, to be in the position of greatest disadvantage, a perception shared perhaps universally by Latino/a workers regardless of status, since the liabilities of illegality bleed onto *hispanos* as a group. The key distinction may be that Ileana sees her own tenuous position as inversely related to Black Americans' position of relative privilege and advantage as *Americans,* not as *Blacks,* an important point that will be discussed in the next chapter. Ileana once said:

You know, the *negros* treat you better. Because I see eye to eye with most of the *negritos*. There are *compañeros* that are like, "Ay no, Ileana. That Eileen [an older African American boning line worker] doesn't talk to anybody. But I see that with you . . . ! And if it's the other one, Bess, or Susie [African American boning line women]. These people with us . . . "But it's that you don't give them an opening!" I say to them. The *morenitos* even go around giving me chewing gum, they say hello to me. This Fred, this Tyrese—"Hey, Ileana, hey!" And they go around saying hello to me. "I don't know, Ileana, how do you get along with the *morenos*?" [She is recounting what other Latinas say to her]. "It's that they are *a todo dar* ["all good," in a slang sense]. You all are the ones who don't give them an in." Because I have asked them [Blacks], I've asked Bess. "Ay, [she makes a face]" that they [Latinas/os] have an ugly way about them. And I ask them [Blacks] about me, and they say "good" [she gives a thumbs up]. They say *hispanos* are very much like that, that they look at them like that [she makes a face]. Because Eileen told me the other day that *hispanos* looked at her like that. And she even said to me, "I am American from this country!" They [African Americans] tell me that when I leave for Honduras they're going to come to my house, they're going to come visit me there in Honduras.

Sandra says, "The only one who gets along well with the *moyos* is Ileana." But they don't get along with them. I don't know why. They're good people, at least the ones I've dealt with at the plant. Imagine, they even bring me gifts. "Bess brought you a gift?! That old lady doesn't give to anybody!" [Again recounting what Latinas tell her]. And the other one too, Susie, she also gives me a Christmas present. She wanted to come to my house. When I had surgery, she also called me, even though I didn't understand too well. "Is okay, Ileana?" "Yes." I get along well with them. It's what I'm telling you, I've asked them and they say that *hispanos* look down on them. I don't think so, I don't know. I've asked all of them, why don't they get along with the *morenitos*. They say they are racists. But then I ask them why, because even though I don't speak English I talk with them, sometimes I understand one word but nothing else. But I talk with them, even though I can't. But they feel, and I express to them, that I want to be their friend. And maybe the others don't. It's true, they give them mean nicknames. Sandra calls Bess La Huajolota [The Turkey]. And sometimes she understands because she's told me that she understands a little bit of Spanish. She says to me, "Sandra *widi-widi* about me"—that Sandra is talking about her, she'll say to me. And I go, "No," and she'll say, "Yeah, yeah! Me Spanish *poquito*!" she says to me.

So sometimes they [Latinas/os] will talk in front of them, and maybe they understand what they're saying. Because, don't be fooled, from everything they hear they have to learn something, just like us. From talking with them so much, I've picked up a word here and there. Since they work among us, they have to learn something. But what happens is they pretend they don't understand what you say about them. That's why we say they're racists, but sometimes we don't try, we don't try to get to know people first. I get along well with all of them. There isn't a single *moreno* in the plant that doesn't get along well with me! If you don't try to mix with people you will never get along with them. But one day Sandra told Melinda, "That Ileana is a kiss-up." This is a theme for us Hondurans. Like that because they're from this country, I try to get along with them, to get something out of it.

I was sitting in the living room of their trailer, their dog Benji on my lap. Ileana's husband Jorge explained how Blacks are typically referred to in Honduras, and how he came to learn about *moyos* and *bolillos*: "Over there [in Honduras] we called them *morenos*. That comes from Mexicans, saying *moyo* and *bolillo*. *Morenos* don't like being called *moyos*." Ileana then expanded on this explanation:

> They don't like to be called *moyos*. I first heard that word here at the plant. But I only call them by their names. "What's up, Fred?" "What's up, baby?" he says to me. Even if I can't pronounce it. To Tyrese I say, "What's up, Taris?" He'll come over to me on the line and give me a high five. He'll look around to see if Jorge [her husband] is around [laughing]. To Harvey, I say, "Hey Harvey." He's at the beginning of the line. He's worked there a long time. Elsa only refers to them like that [by *moyo*].

Jorge added, "They just refer to them as *moyos*. Or *bolillo* if they're American." Ileana concurred: "Horacio only talks about them like that—'That *moyo araganísimo!*' [super lazy *moyo*!]" Jorge explains, "Yes, because they don't like it when people tell them they're *moyos araganes* or lazy."

Ileana's sensitivity to the meanings of *moyo*, and how these are received by African Americans, can be contrasted to Claudia's aloofness to these issues. Like other Latinas/os, she first heard of *moyos* and *bolillos* upon arriving in North Carolina. When I asked her if these terms bothered those so designated, she was certain that they did not: "No. Because among themselves they call each other that. Sometimes a *negro* will say to another, 'That *moyo pendejo*.' Or the *bolillos* will say, 'That *bolillo pendejo*.' Among themselves! I don't think it bothers them. It's a way of distinguishing them. That's what I think." I inquired how she would respond if it did bother them. "I don't care," she replied. "It doesn't matter to me. I'm not *moya* or *bolilla*. Why would it matter to me?" Claudia is under the impression that, since they sometimes banter with one another using these terms, African Americans (and whites) are not offended by them. Rather, they are neutral categories by which to identify people. But Claudia makes clear that if these terms *were* considered offensive, it would not matter to her. The contrasting understandings about *moyo* that Ileana and Claudia's comments demonstrate suggest that the use of this designation for American Blacks is neither

FIGURE 5. View of the loin boning lines from atop the ribs-backbone saw machine tower.

merely neutrally referential nor only reflective of a pejorative view of African Americans. Rather, in using the term—or avoiding it, in Ileana's case—Latinas/os construct and embolden, or at times erode, the boundaries they symbolically articulate vis-à-vis African Americans.

LATINAS/OS AND NATIVE-BORN WORKERS NAVIGATING THE ROCKY TERRAIN OF ETHNORACIAL IDENTIFICATION

Despite the ubiquity, sometimes neutrally portrayed, with which *moyo* appeared in Latina/o workers' designations of African American workers, and even its occasional application in expressions of affection for a particular African American worker, the negative valence attached to *moyo* on balance is captured in a story Vincent told me when I interviewed him a few months after the encounter that opened this chapter, in which Vincent carefully explained the contexts that subtly determined the valence of *moyo*.[16] On this occasion, though, Vincent allowed little interpretive ambiguity when he heard Latina/o workers use the term. I asked him whether he had ever experienced discrimination at work.

> *Vincent:* I mean, at work, I don't really think it's too much because I don't socialize with a lot of people. I mean, I associate, speak or whatever. Me and Emilio call each other names. Bad names [laughs].
>
> *Vanesa:* Like what?
>
> *Vincent:* I mean, I call him *joto* [faggot] all the time.
>
> *Vanesa:* Oh yeah, that's right.
>
> *Vincent:* I mean, something stupid. I don't call him, like, a racist name. He has slipped up a couple times and talked about some *moyo*. You know *moyo*? He was talking about some *moyo* and shit like that. And I figured out what everything means. Cause, I mean, I work with a whole lot of Hispanic people and I'm always trying to learn something, so, if it's good or bad, I'm learning. So, I mean, I decided I wanted to know what it mean. I told him one day, "Quit that shit. Don't be playing that. I know what that means, motherfucker." So he cut that shit out though, 'cause, I mean, I don't know if he was just being funny or whatever.

African Americans not only attempt to make sense of or contest the ways in which Latinas/os identify them, as Vincent did, but also contribute to the repertoire Latinas/os draw from. Gerardo, a scrawny twenty-eight-year-old Honduran with shoulder-length curly hair, whose mother works on the Kill Floor and sister-in-law works in Belly Conversion, has the job of sorting ribs as they come down the line. He is a jovial and boisterous worker, howling like a wild animal for laughs and probably to keep himself awake, trading insults in jest with Alma, who weighs the ribs at a scale after Gerardo throws them up on another line. For a time, Jeremy, an African American man in his late thirties from Wadeville, North Carolina, whose dream was to work for himself as a bar owner, worked near him trimming ribs. The two men developed a buddy relationship, joking and teaching each other work vocabulary in English and Spanish. Gerardo says they got along well, and after a while Jeremy began teaching him a different sort of vocabulary: the word "nigger" and the proper contexts for its use. One day, Jeremy was standing in the way as Gerardo tried to reach a combo where he was piling ribs, so he shouted at him "*muévete de ahí nigger*" (move out of the way, nigger). Gerardo recounted that "the other *moyos*"—Thomas, Linda, and Vincent—standing in the vicinity all turned around at once and stared. For a moment, he was terrified that they were going to pounce on him, but Jeremy quickly defused the situation, saying, "It's cool, we joke like that." Gerardo has a nuanced understanding of the significance of this designation, and of others, including *moyo*:

It's a disparaging word [nigger], that they used in the old days when they were slaves. But if you are with friends, or people you joke around with . . . So I had already joked with him several times. It's pretty harsh, for them it's a pretty harsh word. If you are in a place where there are *gente de color* [people of color] and you say *negro,* they understand it. I imagine it [*moyo*] was a way of referring to them without them understanding that you are talking about them. Although now a majority of the *moyos* understand the word. Because there's a certain number of *gente hispana* who speak Spanish and start mixing with *personas de color,* and that's how they find out.

Recall from the encounter that opens this chapter that Vincent suspected that Latinas/os avoid referring to Blacks as *negros* because it might be misinterpreted by African Americans to mean "nigger." Gerardo gave some support to this explanation, adding that at least initially *moyo* may have allowed Latinas/os to talk about African Americans in their presence without them knowing it. The implicit admission that such casual references were imperatively racialized is in stark contrast to the rarity with which African Americans referred to Latina/o workers in ethnoracial terms.

In fact, perhaps ironically it was a *white* worker, one of the few who worked at Swine's, who articulated the point made at the beginning of this chapter about the much more muted ethnoracial identification of Latinas/os. Gerardo recounted a conversation with Kendra, incidentally a self-professed nymphomaniac, that made him consider this issue:

Kendra says, "You all call the *morenos moyos,* us *bolillos,* and what about you all? What do we call you?" At first I said to her, *hispano.* But she said no. She wanted a disparaging word, because they view *moyo* and *bolillo* as disparaging. So she said "wetback." Then I started to think about what she said, and I told her that phrase was not correct. Because that [a wetback] is someone who is here illegally.

Gerardo seemed to be trying to explain that, while a Black American is always a *moyo* and a white American is always a *bolillo*—ethnonyms—a Latino/a is not always a "wetback," which is a racialized term, to be sure, but one referring specifically to (il)legal status. This is a crucial distinction, and one that suggests the flimsier basis for the ethnoracial identification of Latinas/os, for whom there is no category to parallel that of *moyo* or *bolillo.* And yet, disparaging or not, the experiences that bring together Latin American migrants from diverse national contexts at Swine's as *hispanos*—as they most frequently refer to themselves—is an important part of this story.

CONCLUSION

If incorporation, as it is defined here, is a process of mutual adjustment by which groups both achieve and are ascribed social positions in a stratified system of belonging, then how groups negotiate identifications in relation to one another is in some measure a reflection of how they create and manage group boundaries that give meaningful symbolic expression to consequential social distinctions. The argument proposed in this book is that social relations between subordinate groups are usefully thought of as *prismatic engagement*. An important point at which to begin to understand incorporation, then, is to shed light on the categories, uses, and meanings through which a group identifies another with which it is articulated in some socially significant way—that is, in some way that has a bearing on, or is reflective of, these groups' relative positions in a stratified system of belonging. Such groups do not encounter one another in empty social space. Rather, Latino/a migrants and African Americans—the native-born workers with whom they most overlap in the workplace—encounter one another in a system of racialized structure and meaning that may involve several different points of reference across and within national boundaries, but which refracts their relationships through a single prism of white dominance.

Latin American ethnoracial panoramas considered briefly in this chapter prefigure some of the variation in the language of Latinos/migrants in the United States, and the degree to which Blacks are negatively racialized. Yet while these historical contexts precondition Latino/a migrants' characterization of Blacks in the United States, and support the notion of a global devaluation of blackness, it is their encounters with African Americans on the line, and their lessons in racialization schemes developed in the American context, that actually define the parameters of the social field in which group boundaries are shaped. It is in this sense that such boundaries demarcate a transnational field of ethnoracial signification—a sort of third space that is neither here nor there—in which "being Black," despite the universal devaluation of blackness and the scorn reserved for *moyos,* can come to be viewed by Latinas/os as a privileged status at the micro level of the American workplace.

Skeptical that relatively recent Latino/a migrants to the U.S. South have acquired their views about American Blacks directly from whites, researchers have proposed that migrants more or less bring such views with them from their origin countries. But not having studied in any depth the features of the most important social domain in which

Latinas/os and African Americans encounter one another in the American South—the workplace—these scholars neglect a critical sphere in which these intergroup relations are molded. Without a doubt, migrants from all over Latin America come to the United States with a lifetime's worth of schooling in the racial systems of their origin communities. And while there are important differences in the various Latin American schemas and the American racialization system, there is one feature they crucially hold in common. That feature, shared by all societies born of the devastations and developments wrought by European conquest and colonialism, is the universal devaluation of blackness and the concomitant valorization of whiteness (Frederickson 1981). Most of the Latina/o migrants at Swine's do not self-identify as Black (or white), are not typically identified as such by others in their origin communities, and are not identified as such by others here in the United States. Instead, their re-racialization in the United States refers to the (ethno)racialization of diverse migrants from Latin America as *hispanos*.[18]

Scholars have studied the formation of group consciousness by measuring either rates of self-identification with putative group labels (Roth 2012; Itzigsohn and Dore-Cabral 2000) or rates of reported feelings of commonality with other members of such putative groups (Sánchez 2008). For example, some scholars have studied Latino/a group consciousness by measuring rates of self-identification of individuals from diverse Latin American origins with various pan-ethnic group labels (e.g., Hispanic, Latino/a). Other scholars have studied Latino/a group consciousness by measuring feelings of commonality or closeness reported by individuals from diverse national origins with other Latin American–origin groups (e.g., [Hondurans] have a lot in common with [Mexicans]). Drawing on the political scientist Michael Dawson's (1994) seminal study of African American political attitudes, Sánchez and Masuoka (2010) argue for measuring Latino/a group consciousness according to how much putative group members feel that their individual fortunes, as well as the fortunes of their own national origin group, are contingent on the fortunes of Latinas/os more generally. In other words, according to these scholars, to be a meaningful category of analysis and action, "Latino/a group consciousness" should be a gauge of the degree to which putative group members feel their own fates are linked with the fate of "Latinas/os," and to some extent dependent on the fate of the group. I argue that the strong identification of *moyos* has its corollary in the indefinite ontological status inhabited by *hispanos*.

At Swine's, self-identification by putative group members as *his-panos*, I argue, was suggestive of all three group-consciousness processes. When Latina/o workers at Swine's talked about *hispanos,* this reflected the increasing adoption of this pan-ethnic label for purposes of self-identification and a progressive feeling of closeness or commonality with other putative group members given the imposition of conditions that tended to suppress national differences among Latinas/os, but also ripening the certainty that one's individual fortune was tied to the fate of the group. This will become clear in the chapters that follow, which delve into the social boundaries between Latino/a migrants and African American workers at Swine's. The next chapter offers an explanation for the bold symbolic boundaries that Latinas/os drew vis-à-vis their African American coworkers at Swine's—an account that carefully considers Latinas/os' perceptions about the position they occupy in the most crucial social domain of their lives in North Carolina: the workplace.

CHAPTER 4

"Painted Black"

Oppressive Exploitation and Racialized
Resentment

I was working with Cristina, carrying piles of rib racks from the pan to the table for her to trim, bagging the trimmed extra-meaty ribs, and throwing these back on the line to be sealed and packed in boxes, when she suddenly announced, "Tomorrow I'm going to come in painted black, so I don't have to work!" I chuckled nervously and busied myself stacking more ribs on the table. I noticed two African American workers, Jeremy and Adrienne, at the table talking to her and quickly gathered that she had repeated this comment directly to them. Jeremy gave her a sideways look from behind his round, wire-rimmed glasses, eyeballing her with displeasure and suspicion. He walked by and she smiled, nonchalantly calling him over. She said to me, "He's lazy [*haragán*]. And when he worked on the knife he was lazy." Jeremy walked past the table and said, "You're mean. I'm gonna take you to HR 'cause you're prejudiced. You have prejudices." Cristina asked me what that meant, and I translated. She smiled and kept working, all the while trying to get Jeremy's attention.

After a short pause, she turned to me and asked, "What's that? What you said before." "*Prejuicio?*" "Yeah, what's that?" "It's like . . . racist ideas," I explained in Spanish. "No!" she said, shaking her head, adding that she didn't think "they" were all like that. As if to further explain herself, she added that when she and Jeremy labored alongside one another at the ribs station, "I showed him how to work with the knife, and he would teach me words in English." A while later I noticed Adrienne telling Coreen, an African American woman in her thirties who normally worked bagging small hams at the end of the ham-end boning line, what Cristina said. Coreen proceeded to eyeball Cristina. Pretending I didn't know what was going on, I asked Coreen what was wrong. "Nothing, just what this woman said, that she was going to come to work painted black so she didn't have to work." I asked her what she had responded, and she said, "Nothing." Shortly after, I spotted a group of Black workers including Jeremy chatting, probably about Cristina's comments. Later that day, Cristina, apparently oblivious and still trying to get Jeremy's attention, told him excitedly that she wanted to show him videos of Blacks—Garifunas—in Honduras dancing *punta*. Feeling embarrassed, I translated this, and Jeremy just nodded.[1]

Perhaps the confluence of contempt, fondness, and obliviousness in this encounter between Cristina and African American workers represents a certain ambiguity resulting from the diverse sources Latinas/os draw from to articulate boundaries with African Americans, as shown in chapter 3. Yet the unmistakable impression that emerges from the thrust of Cristina's comments to Jeremy, and which was issued repeatedly by Latina/o workers, is that African Americans occupy a privileged position in the workplace. This perception is inextricable from Latina/o migrants' sense that they are the most oppressively exploited workers at the factory. They see African Americans as having advantages that are beyond their reach, and which relate to three dimensions of the labor process. First, African American workers are seen as being more likely to be assigned less-strenuous jobs. Second, they are felt to be domineering, delighting in the humiliation of Latina/o workers. Third, African American workers are thought to be subject to a less punitive labor discipline regime.[2]

The first section of this chapter outlines key issues in the literature on the economic incorporation of migrants and social relations between migrants and native-born workers in the labor market. It specifically discusses research that has developed around Herbert Blumer's "sense of group position" model, and highlights studies of Latino/a migrant incorporation in the American South that advance this framework. Following the review of the limitations of research to date, the second section delves into the substance of the argument. It exposes the character of social relations between workers, showing how the symbolic boundaries Latinas/os express are rooted in their perception that they are the most oppressively exploited workers and that African Americans occupy a privileged place within the social organization of labor. The third section demonstrates that within the context of oppressive exploitation at Swine's, the sharp symbolic boundaries that Latinas/os draw against their African American coworkers is linked to their conviction that African Americans occupy an advantaged position in the workplace. Because white workers are scarce but also because whiteness is valorized, and because blackness is universally devalued, this grievance is translated into a resentment that is racialized.[3]

LATINO/A MIGRANTS' INCORPORATION INTO A STRATIFIED SYSTEM OF BELONGING

U.S. immigration scholarship has focused extensively on assessing the labor market impacts of immigration, in particular the question of whether immigrants "hurt" native-born workers, especially Blacks, and whether economic competition results in conflict between the groups.[4] Some scholars who have studied African American attitudes toward Latinas/os have found these to be negative and hostile, and have argued that this is rooted in economic competition (Bobo and Hutchings 1996). But much of the concern could be deferred, it was thought, as long as Latino/a migrants and African Americans didn't tend to overlap in space (Smith and Edmonston 1997; but see Hamermesh and Bean 1999). But with the move to nontraditional destinations in the South, where African Americans are concentrated, scholars' preoccupation with intergroup relations has steadily gained traction (McClain et al. 2006).

In general, and depending on the emphasis given, the ethnic succession perspective has tended to view the situation of compositional shifts as involving replacement as opposed to displacement, but chapter 2 of this book has argued that both processes, along with growth in the case of many industries, are likely to co-occur. Intergroup processes are the critical means through which Latino/a migrants become incorporated in a stratified system of belonging; in a more proximate sense, intergroup relational dynamics are key to understanding how Latino/a migrants gain a sense of group position. In short, the ethnic succession model carries the assumption that when workforce composition is affected by replacement dynamics, intergroup conflict should be minimized, while intergroup conflict should be heightened by displacement dynamics. Although this is a plausible hypothesis, convincing tests of this proposition have not been undertaken.[5] More troubling, very little research has produced data based on direct observation of workplace intergroup dynamics. This chapter addresses that void.

Recently, a number of scholars have turned to Herbert Blumer's (1958) "sense of group position" concept to explain how the perception of threat from an out-group causes in-group members to react with prejudice. While scholars have usefully drawn on Blumer's concept to incorporate a diversity of threats—economic, political, and cultural—that bear on intergroup relations, and to emphasize that *perceptions* of threat may be as important as real ones, more must be done to contextualize these threats and to consider their possible bases. This book argues that our understanding of the mechanisms and conditions—the dynamic processes—that produce this sense of group position is underdeveloped, and that a "boundaries" approach inspired by Fredrik Barth's (1969) seminal work allows us to arrive at a richer understanding of the collective process that shapes a group's sense of its position within the American stratified system of belonging. To be useful, this approach must be situated within contexts that meaningfully condition patterns of intergroup relations—such as the workplace—and must be attentive to the relationship between symbolic boundaries and the real or perceived social distinctions that underlie them, and which are reinforced or challenged by them.

The Sense of Group Position: Origins and Development of a Concept

When Blumer (1958) proposed viewing "race prejudice as a sense of group position," he went against the prevailing view of prejudice as inhering in individuals' feelings of hostility, intolerance, and aggressiveness. Instead, he asserted, prejudice is the result of a collective process of group representation whereby members of a dominant group construct definitions of a subordinate group in ways that affirm the dominant group's superiority, the subordinate group's essential difference, the dominant group's rightful claim to privilege, and the dominant group's sensitivity to feelings of threat from the subordinate group. This view of prejudice, or perhaps conflict more broadly, has developed as a middle ground between the rational economic-conflict models of prejudice (Borjas 1998; Burns and Gimpel 2000) and the more social-psychological models (Allport 1954).

Numerous studies have attempted to bridge threat-based explanations for prejudice against, as well as among, ethnoracial and religious minorities and immigrants (Berg 2009; King and Weiner 2007; Dixon 2006; Alba, Rumbaut, and Marotz 2005; Oliver and Wong 2003; Taylor 1998; Wagner et al. 2006). Although Blumer's concept referred to the sociospatial (i.e., positional) relationship between dominant and subordinate groups, and the mechanism that produces dominant group prejudice toward subordinate groups (i.e., perceived threats to their position), scholars since have extended his group position approach to the study of intergroup relations and prejudice among subordinate groups (Hutchings and Wong 2014; Bobo and Hutchings 1996) and within class-stratified contexts (Waldinger and Lichter 2003). A critical contribution of Lawrence Bobo and V. L. Hutchings's work is the concept of "racial alienation" (1996, 956), which they developed as a measure of the degree to which group members feel enfranchised or aggrieved. They theorize that greater racial subordination results in greater racial alienation, which in turn is reflected in a heightened perception of competitive threats from other groups.

Roger Waldinger and M. I. Lichter (2003) extend the study of prejudice both across class lines and among subordinate groups. They show
how prejudice is context dependent, such that employers may dislike a
group but prefer them for certain jobs. For example, across low-wage
workplaces, (white) employers seeking workers who will make the best
subordinates see native-born whites as the ultimate in-group, Blacks as
an in-group to the extent that they share the same view of the proper
equation between effort and reward but an out-group as disliked racial
subordinates, and Latino/a migrants as an out-group in both senses—
and therefore Latino/a migrants are preferred on this basis. Waldinger
and Lichter incorporate Bobo and Hutchings's concept of "racial alienation" in their expanded, situational understanding of prejudice to
explain the contentious relationship between in-groups and out-groups
at work. According to these scholars, native-born groups, particularly
those who experience greater "racial alienation" (i.e., African Americans), are likely to feel that immigrants pose a competitive threat to
their sense of group position.

An unnecessary limitation to the explanatory power of the "racial
alienation" concept has been its narrow construction to the case of African Americans. Because it has been so directly tailored to fit the historical experience of African Americans as the quintessentially racially subordinated, and therefore most racially alienated, group in the United
States, it becomes difficult to imagine that another group could perceive
itself to be more deprived. And because economic competition has generally been viewed as the precipitating factor that leads a group to feel
its sense of group position threatened, other sources of grievance have
not been adequately explored. The importance of loosening the analytical constraints on the "racial alienation" concept, and redirecting attention to sources of grievance or deprivation other than direct economic
competition, will become evident as the data and findings on relations
between Latinas/os and African Americans at Swine's are explained.
The (ethno)racialization of Latinas/os in the contemporary South is a
recursive process of group formation, as *hispanos* develop an understanding of theirs as an aggrieved identity, deprived relative to what
they see as African Americans' privileged status at work.

In fact, the "sense of group position" perspective, unlike the predic-
tions of Waldinger's ethnic succession model, grants as much causal
force to the *perception* of threat as to the actual conditions of niche
overlap that would likely produce competition and conflict between
groups. In their study of low-wage jobs in Los Angeles, Waldinger and

Lichter found evidence of interethnic workplace conflict, particularly in workplaces where immigrants are at a numerical advantage, which they argue is suggestive of competition, but they conclude nevertheless that "the degree of tension falls below the level to be expected had blacks perceived themselves as being displaced."[6] Waldinger and Lichter seem reluctant to conclude that Blacks are in competition with Latino/a migrants for low-wage jobs or to consider that the conflict they observe may not be rooted in the attitudes and behaviors of African Americans. They also neglect the possibility that interethnic workplace conflict can have something other than competition as its source.[7] Of course, intergroup relations are a major concern of scholars who study Latino/a migrants' social and economic incorporation in new and maturing destinations.

New Destinations and Intergroup Relations

Latino/a migration to nontraditional destinations has produced a wealth of texts documenting the unprecedented transformation of the American heartland and Bible Belt regions (Anrig, Wang, and McClain 2006; Zúñiga and Hernández-León 2005; Arreola 2004; Sills 2010; Hill and Beaver 1998; Stull, Broadway, and Griffith 1995; Gozdziak and Martin 2005; Hamamoto and Torres 1997; Jones 2008; Johnson-Webb 2003; Odem and Lacy 2009; Mantero 2008; Massey 2008; Murphy, Blanchard, and Hill 2001; Peacock, Watson, and Matthews 2005; Smith and Furuseth 2006; Gill 2010; Schwartzman 2013). The vast majority of research on Latino/a migration to the U.S. South consists of case studies of particular localities, often painting a broad-strokes portrait of small-town demographic and economic restructuring that demonstrates the abundant contributions Latino/a migrants have made to the agro-industrial labor force. This growing literature has addressed the "challenges" that such changes pose for places with little to no collective memory of immigration, and reveals an undercurrent of concern over the destabilization of long-standing binary intergroup relations and the ongoing configuration of a new, more complex system of intergroup relations now featuring whites, African Americans, and Latinas/os.

Some scholars have focused their attention on intergroup relations at work as well as in the broader community, and the issue of conflict between Latino/a migrants and native-born non-Latinas/os, especially African Americans. Studying the rural Delmarva Peninsula on the East Coast, Timothy Dunn, Ana Maria Aragonés, and George Shivers (2005) document the growth of the Latino/a workforce in poultry between 1987 and the late 1990s, at which point about half of the workforce was immigrant, mostly Mexican and Guatemalan. Latinas/os played a big role in union revitalization in one plant in Selbyville, Delaware, where until they staged a wildcat strike as a result of an injury-related firing, they generally had no idea of the union presence, and the lone steward— an African American woman—apparently did not seek to engage them. The United Food and Commercial Workers decided to support the workers' strike, and as a result the union was revitalized in the plant. The number of stewards reached fifteen by 2001, fourteen of whom were Latinas/os, out of close to one thousand workers. According to the Latina woman by this time elected vice president of the union local, the incident brought African American and Latino/a workers together.

Discussing African American–Latino/a relations, these scholars find no apparent large-scale tensions, but some friction. They note that some workplace tensions are instigated by management, who let workers know they think Latinas/os are the better workers. In the community, Blacks begin to feel neglected by social services agencies. Timothy Dunn, Ana Maria Aragonés, and George Shivers also mention "public expressions of hostility" that drew public outcry, such as comments by the Bridgeville, Delaware, mayor at a mostly pro-immigrant conference, "Those people need to learn English!" and those of the Georgetown, Delaware, mayor that Guatemalan and Mexican immigrants were "lowering the region's standard of living" (180).[8] As to the future of race relations, the authors conclude, "On the one hand, if things play out as a zero-sum competition among subordinated groups, then there will likely be increased hostility, especially between African Americans and Latinos. . . . On the other hand, the increasing interest among local actors in cultural exchange with Mexican and Latino immigrants should help improve interethnic relations" (180). Immigrant activism will likely develop further as well, and they believe this will "contribute constructively to interethnic relations" (180).

William Kandel and Emilio Parrado (2004) share a similar guarded optimism about the prospects for Latino/a migrants' incorporation in the rural South, based on their case studies of poultry workers in Duplin County, North Carolina, and Accomack County, Virginia. These researchers recount that in September 2000, Latino/a workers at Carolina Turkeys, the largest turkey processing plant in the United States, held an "international festival," and later during the Semana de la Hispanidad in 2001, Latin American country flags were exhibited in the company hallways. According to Kandel and Parrado, "Following their lead, black employees decided to celebrate African-American Week in January 2002" (2004, 274). Unfortunately, aside from noting these rather superficial events, the authors do not examine what their significance was beyond the implicit assumption that both groups merely took the opportunity to express their ethnic pride: "None of the informants . . . suggested that the growth of the Hispanic population had caused concern among community residents" (274) but later they note that some mentioned hearing about job competition between Latino/a migrants and local Blacks, as well as concern over fake drivers' licenses and access-to-housing issues, while Latinas/os were concerned with being crime targets.

Rubén Hernández-León and Victor Zúñiga (2005) have examined the demographic transformation of Dalton, Georgia, nicknamed the carpet capital of the world. Earlier in the twentieth century, the exclusion of Blacks from mills led to their northward migration and local population decline. Industrial development created a stark two-class community united by race, in this case shared whiteness. Explaining the growth of the Latino/a population in Dalton, the authors note that initially, workers were recruited in south Texas for poultry processing, and by 1997, the local ConAgra poultry plant was 80 percent Latino/a. In the early 1990s, carpet manufacturers sent recruiters to south Texas, and later advertised in Spanish-language media and on town billboards. Many migrants in Dalton came from traditional urban destinations or from farmworker camps in Florida.

Among the community-level changes they note are the growing use of Spanish in public spaces and the growing Catholic presence. These authors gently critique past studies for attending almost exclusively to conflict, competition, and tension, an excessive focus they see as problematic. In addition, they critique the emphasis on dramatic events as opposed to examining less-sensational social interactions in everyday life, and what they see as a lack of attention to intragroup differences, particularly with respect to class (especially among whites) (see also Griffith 2005; Marrow 2011). They offer vague examples of positive interaction (e.g., Black and Latino/a coworkers "fraternizing" in carpet mills; more mixed marriages), but these are not well developed and do not appear especially salient. Their discussion of conflictive situations is more prominent: A long-term Mexican worker complained about how newcomers in the early 1990s were rate-busters, and this animosity was shared by white and Black workers. Whereas white workers used to switch jobs across plants routinely, these labor market strategies could not be sustained in the face of abundant inflows of Latino/a labor.[9] In addition to a pattern of separate coexistence in public spaces, Black lower-middle-class respondents were upset about the "takeover" of public and semipublic spaces. Although they lauded the entrepreneurialism and social capital of Latino/a migrants, they also conveyed a sense that whites were "catering" to Latinas/os in a way that no one had ever assisted Black Daltonians. At the same time, given the small local Black population, itself heterogeneous, some Black leaders have viewed coalition building with Latinas/os as a way to help Blacks gain some power.[10]

Another example is the case of Siler City, North Carolina, which experienced what appeared to some locals an "overnight" transformation of the community's demographic makeup. According to Steve Striffler (2005), the negative response of many whites to Latinas/os, whom they had thought were just "the Mexicans" passing through, was difficult to miss. Recruited by poultry processing plants in the area, the Latino/a population in Siler City swelled between 1990 and 2000 from less than two hundred to more than three thousand. Alarmed at these changes, Siler City formed a "Hispanic Task Force" that included no Latinas/os, and which produced a pamphlet warning Latinas/os that keeping chickens within the town limits and wife beating were against the law. Further, the Democratic county commissioner submitted a letter to the INS in August 1999 requesting federal intervention to assist the town in dealing with "the problem."[11] The letter set off fear among migrants, who sensed that a backlash was to follow, and perhaps even a round of INS raids. What did follow was a rally sponsored by a local self-identified "Aryan" at which David Duke, the former Klan leader, was the headline speaker. Though the rally was well attended (estimates were about three hundred supporters and another one hundred onlookers), the obvious associations with publicly identified white supremacists gave pause to many white residents about the heightened animosity directed at Latino/a migrants. At the same time, the county commissioner responsible for the letter to the INS went on a trip to Mexico sponsored by UNC's Center for International Understanding and returned promising to set aside his incessant focus on questions of migrant illegality and focus instead on integration issues (Striffler 2005; Cuadros 2007). African American churches made efforts to reach out to Latinas/os, the Duke rally not sitting well with Blacks, no matter what the intergroup tensions in the community were (Silver 2011).

Helen Marrow's work (2011; 2007) is the most comprehensive analysis to date of Latino/a migrant incorporation in the South and the status of intergroup relations in the region. Based primarily on interviews with native-born and foreign-born Latinas/os, native-born white and African American workers and managers across several industries, and public institutional actors, Marrow (2007) evaluates several competing theories that seek to explain African American–Latino/a relations. Distinguishing between what she refers to as personal (see Borjas 1998) and group (see Burns and Gimpel 2000) economic interest models and the group position model derived from Blumer (see Bobo and Hutchings 1996; Bobo and Johnson 2000; Morawska 2001), she explores several hypotheses about the relationships between whites, African Americans, and Latinas/os, while taking account of the relative sizes of the groups at the county level.[12]

According to Marrow, Latino/a migrants experience greater discrimination from Blacks than whites, and she explains this using a group position model, since Blacks are mostly at the bottom of the social class structure, while whites are generally split between working and middle class. African Americans, facing threats to their sense of group position, react in an exclusionary fashion toward Latino/a migrants. Marrow (2007; 2011) builds on Claire Jean Kim's (1999) racial triangulation theory, which posits that Asian Americans occupy dual places within a "field of racial positions" that is overdetermined by white hegemony—as valorized insiders relative to Blacks but as civic outsiders perpetually estranged as foreigners. She argues that "Hispanic newcomers experience discrimination and exclusion not just along one vertical skin color axis along which white natives can mark them as racially inferior, but also along a separate horizontal (non)citizenship axis along which both white and Black natives can mark and ostracize them as undeserving civic and cultural 'outsiders'" (2007, 30). She says this latter axis is experienced most strongly, and that Blacks are seen as its "worst perpetrators."[13] Furthermore, this intergroup dynamic is even more pronounced in areas with higher African American population levels—majority-Black "Bedford" county has more tense intergroup relations than majority-white "Wilcox," even though Latinas/os constitute a much larger minority in the latter.[14] Given her findings, she argues tentatively alongside other scholars for an emerging Black/non-Black ethnoracial divide in the United States, at least one in which the boundary between whites and Latinas/os is less rigid that that between Latinas/os and Blacks (Yancey 2003; Padín 2005; Lee and Bean 2007; Feliciano, Lee, and Robnett 2011). At the same time, scholars also find evidence that suggests a more enduring ethnoracialization of at least a segment of Latinas/os currently thus categorized through their research on dating preferences (Feliciano, Lee, and Robnett 2011), census self-identification (Haney López 2005), and political solidarities (Jones 2012).

Despite the interest scholars have shown in the potential for large-scale Latino/a migration to the U.S. South to multiply the complexity of race relations in the region and beyond, there have so far been few studies that examine the racialization process as a historically conditioned, context-dependent phenomenon. Studies of migrant incorporation in nontraditional destinations that engage with "race" seem especially concerned with a set of narrowly defined questions. One such question is whether Latino/a migrants and native-born groups (typically whites and Blacks, but usually the latter) experience conditions of competition and perhaps conflict. In particular, studies ask whether Latino/a migrants experience exclusion or racial discrimination, and from who. These questions correspond roughly to a broader agenda to study how migrants are socially and economically incorporated in nontraditional receiving communities in the South and the Midwest. These are important questions, but studies that address these questions have been conducted in a way that limits our scope of understanding.

A critical limitation across much of the literature on migrant incorporation and intergroup relations in the U.S. South—even the literature that extends Blumer's group position model—is its inability to adequately account for relations among subordinated groups. With respect to relations between African Americans and Latino/a migrants, scholars have tended to focus on one dimension of the relationship—African Americans' attitudes and behavior toward Latino/a migrants. But from an incorporation perspective as defined here, Latino/a migrants' understandings about African Americans take on equal significance. There is little agency for Latinas/os in models that focus primarily on African Americans' attitudes and behavior toward them. Worse, in attributing attitudes and behaviors to African Americans when these are reported by Latinas/os, African Americans' agency is also circumscribed and misrepresented.

Several factors account for the limitations of the research to date. First, most of the data gathered pertains to interviews with Latino/a respondents embedded in a variety of arenas. This methodology yields rich data for gauging the perceptions of Latinas/os across a broad range of social situations and spaces, but it is important to distinguish between *a claim about Latinas/os' perceptions*, whatever the objective conditions that produce these perceptions, and *a claim about the fact of*

African Americans' role in essentially pushing Latinas/os to embrace a position closer to whites by displaying exclusionary attitudes and behaviors toward Latinas/os because they feel threatened. A related problem is that scholars seem to underestimate the built-in incentives Latinas/os have—and were likely well aware of before arriving—to distance themselves from Blacks or other highly stigmatized groups and identify with whites, or at least view them more favorably. Chapter 3 showed that Latinas/os are predisposed to view blackness as a subordinate status given the ethnoracial meaning systems in their origin communities. More importantly, as this chapter will show, by situating the analysis of intergroup relations in the crucial domain of the workplace, it becomes clear that Latinas/os have strong reasons for representing Blacks in a negative light.[15]

A second critical limitation across much of the literature concerns the fact that intergroup relations are considered in mostly binary or dyadic, as opposed to multiplex, fashion. In other words, this involves insufficient attention to how Latina/o–African American relations may be mediated by whiteness, or may implicate whiteness, despite the fact that whites themselves may have a minimal, if important, presence in contexts where African Americans and Latinas/os interact. This limitation is related to the tendency among scholars to assume that the most salient aspect of the potential reconstitution of systems of race relations has to do with the relationship between Latinos/migrants and African Americans.[16] This focus is understandable and in some ways warranted, since until relatively recently Latino/a migrants and African Americans generally did not live in the same places and therefore were less likely to experience niche overlap leading perhaps to competition and conflict (Smith and Edmonston 1997, 223; but see Hamermesh and Bean 1998 and Bean and Bell-Rose 1999, who dispute the NAS interpretation).

But this is problematic, for two reasons especially.[17] On the one hand, the sharp emphasis given to conflict between African Americans and Latinas/os is rarely situated in concrete contexts of structured interactions such as particular workplaces or neighborhoods, and is instead usually surmised from interviews with a cross-section of individuals over a range of actual institutional contexts. Further, narrowing the scope of interest in Latino/a–African American relations to "conflict" unnecessarily restricts the range in modes of intergroup interaction that might be observed, and precludes a richer, more complex representation of boundary processes and intergroup relations. By almost exclusively considering conflict to stem from competition, scholars fail to consider alternative grievances that might underpin conflict, particularly that which is projected most by Latinas/os.

On the other hand, a near-exclusive focus on the potential for "tense" relations between Latinas/os and African Americans fails to adequately account for these groups' relationships with or position vis-à-vis whites, and obscures the continued white dominance most apparent at the highest institutional levels of communities, counties, and the state. Indeed, we learn remarkably little about the contexts that nurtured the wave of anti-immigrant legislation currently sweeping the U.S. South, with Georgia, South Carolina, and Alabama passing Arizona-inspired bills that target unauthorized migrants in increasingly punitive ways (Golash-Boza 2012; Gill 2010; Odem and Lacy 2009; Weissman et al. 2009). But even a cursory glance at these cases tells us one thing: that these measures were sponsored not by the working-class African Americans that migrants are supposed to threaten the most, but by conservative white political activists (Brown 2013; Chavez and Provine 2009). Recent work by Jennifer Anne Meri Jones (2013) moves in this direction. Drawing on research in Winston-Salem, North Carolina, Jones proposes that Latinas/os (whom she identifies as mostly mestizo and Afro-Mexicans) and African Americans develop a common identification as minorities through their shared experience of discrimination, which they attribute to whites and white-dominated organizations. These understandings lead some to expressions of solidarity between the groups. This theme will arise again in chapter 7.

Rubén Hernández-León and Victor Zúñiga (2005, 252) see new destinations for Latino/a migration as a "unique opportunity to study the destabilization of existing patterns of interethnic relations—largely based in terms of black and white polarity—as well as the formation of yet to be defined positions and structures of inter- and intra-group interaction." They correctly point out that "this transitional stage requires a great deal of attention to processes of interaction and group position formation rather than a commitment to a particular theory of interethnic relations" (252). However, their assertion that a "sense of group position" does not yet exist at the point of "initial intergroup contact" should be qualified. It may not exist in a fully settled form, but contours of an emergent sense of group position are perhaps discernible. And from the perspective of posterity, understanding how and why Latinas/os became incorporated as they eventually did will depend crucially on piecing together clues from the early phase of incorporation. At the same time, Latino/a migration to "new destinations" has been unfolding rapidly for at least twenty years, so their settlement and incorporation experience is maturing already.

The next section draws the reader into the most crucial domain of Latino/a migrants' incorporation into American racial and class stratification systems. It is, fundamentally, through their experiences in the workplace that Latino/a migrants develop a sense of their group position as *hispanos*. It is these workplace experiences too that condition Latinas/os' relations with native-born groups, particularly African Americans, given their perceptions about the positions of both groups in the workplace.

PERCEPTIONS OF PRIVILEGE AND THE EXPERIENCE OF SUBORDINATION

The encounter between Cristina and Jeremy retold in the opening scene is striking because it conveys in no uncertain terms the sense Latina/o workers have about African Americans' position within the social organization of labor, and, by implication, their own group's position. Cristina's comment to me, which she reiterated to Jeremy and Adrienne, has a very clear interpretation: if she were Black, she wouldn't have to work, but as long as she is not Black, she has to work. Her subsequent comments fill in the sharp boundary that her initial remark draws between African American workers and Latina/o workers: Jeremy is lazy, now that he has an easy job, but he was also lazy back when he had a hard job. In attributing laziness to African American workers who are seen as occupying a position of privilege within the social organization of labor, Latina/o workers strive to even out their statuses, at least symbolically, by adding to the expressive boundary drawn relentlessly through ethnoracial identification of African Americans as *moyos*, *negros*, and *morenos*.[18]

The encounter that opens this chapter is remarkable also for the rather restrained response on the part of Jeremy, Adrienne, and Coreen to Cristina's sharp barb. Although he called her out on her initial offending remark, Jeremy let slide what followed, which would be clearly recognizable within the context of American racial sensibilities as a faux pas. After all, what would an African American meatpacker from Wadeville, North Carolina, care about a Honduran Garifuna dancing *punta* in a faraway coastal village? Jeremy's muted reaction to these kinds of comments from Latina/o coworkers was evident on other occasions as well. Leticia, a thirty-six-year-old Honduran woman from the north Atlantic department of Colón, moved to North Carolina from Houston, following her sister Carina. Because she had become pregnant, Leticia was taken off the loin bagging line where she normally worked and performed a variety of lighter tasks as instructed by Itty or Michael, usually bagging tenderloins, putting labels on bagged meat after it had gone through the *tortuga*, or pushing a cart stacked with bagged bellies to and from the line. One day she was bagging tenderloins while Jeremy stood in front of her to chat, assisting her by placing two tenderloins on the spoon for her to bag—something he did when not doing his paperwork, throwing bagged meats onto the line from combos, or procuring materials from the supply rooms. After a year working a knife job trimming ribs, Jeremy had been given an assistant-type job: checking the status of orders, ordering and retrieving product and box labels, throwing bagged meats from combos onto the line to be vacuum sealed, and doing assorted light tasks.

Leticia was being playful, having me translate to Jeremy that he was "very handsome," teasing him. "What do women do when you go to the mall, do they want to kidnap you?" or, "All the women think you are handsome," then taking it back, saying that only she thought so. In the midst of this playful banter, Leticia told me she knew Jeremy when he started here at the ribs station. "There," she says, "*él era muy traba-jador*" (he was a hard worker), which I translated to him. "*Pero ahora es muy haragán, muy* lazy," she said, which he could obviously understand without a translation. She mocked his "assistance," asking in an exasperated tone, "What is this?" She rubbed the tenderloins on her white butcher coat, smearing it with meat juice. "He does this so it looks like he worked!" Jeremy protested this claim mildly: "I work hard!" Henry, the white product reconditioner (the person who picks up meat from the floor, washes it, and brings it back to the line) and self-described ex-hippie from upstate New York with a serious heart condition and a probable drinking problem, stopped to chat with us. Referring again to Jeremy, Leticia said, "*Él parece un gorilón.*" Henry, who was always friendly with everyone and tried to pick up Spanish words, guessed correctly, "a gorilla?" Jeremy turned to Leticia: "I look like a gorilla?" "A big gorilla!" she responded in English. Henry seemed slightly uncomfortable but Leticia was unperturbed. Jeremy sort of chuckled, and I ignored this, looking down and feeling mortified when she wanted me to confirm, "Doesn't he?" All of a sudden it occurred to her to blurt out, "King Kong!" "I look like King Kong?" Jeremy asked calmly.[19]

Even Ileana, Cristina's relative, who was proud to say she got along well with Black workers, sometimes teased them about being lazy. She described a routine interaction she had with Bobby, an African American Quality Assurance worker, when a loin reached the end of the line and had not been properly deboned. "'Like Bobby, he says—throwing me the bone—'Ileana!' I tell him, 'Hey Bobby, what happened? Easy! You—knife!' I tell him to grab a knife from Horacio so he can remove the bone. 'No, you!' he tells me. So I say to him, 'You—lazy!' [laughing] And he says, 'Oh Ileana' [sighing]. I say, 'Bobby' and high-five him. And he high-fives me. Now when I go to the line and a bone is coming down he'll grab a knife and remove it. I say to him 'Good!' because he's helping me. Nah, I get along well with all of them [African Americans]."

Latina/o workers' frequent characterization of African Americans as lazy corresponded to their perception that Black workers occupied a privileged position in the workplace. Such perceptions revolved around three crucial distinctions, namely, that African Americans had easier jobs than they did, that they were domineering, and that they were subject to a less harsh labor discipline regime.

"Los moyos no la hacen"

Working at the ribs station, in the packing area set off from the end of the loin boning lines, gave workers ample opportunity to interact. Trimming, bagging, and packing ribs around tables and deep pans meant that they were in close proximity to one another, and being somewhat off the main lines meant there was a little less pressure to keep up, since ribs would inevitably have to be piled up in a giant pan or in combos for later processing. In April, two young Black women were hired and almost immediately assigned to work at the ribs station bagging ribs. Aisha was twenty and had been living for a while in Florida, but moved back to Perry to try to save money for school. Her parents were both longtime Swine's employees; her mother worked in Hamboning and her father had worked in Water Treatment and the Cut Floor box room. Aisha made clear from the beginning that working at Swine's was only temporary for her, and that factory work was not her thing. She was only here to save enough money to buy a car; then she planned to go back to school. Adrienne was twenty-one, funny, and seemed more mature and less naive than Aisha. She had a two-year-old son and was separated from the child's father. As it turned out, Adrienne was close with Michael, the floor supervisor. Her father and Michael were best friends, and "Uncle Michael," as she called him, frequently called her house to speak with him.

Aisha was the object of both derision and entertainment for the Latina/o workers at the ribs station: Cristina, Daniel, Gerardo, Hernán, Rosa, Alma, Andrew, and even people who came by this area to throw bagged meat on the line for sealing at the *tortuga*. Carina, Leticia's sister, was doing this one day when she remarked on Aisha's demeanor to me: "She seems tired, like she doesn't feel like working." Her permanently glued and heavily mascaraed eyelash extensions, which a Quality Assurance employee informed her were prohibited, drew laughs and commentary. "She won't look pretty anymore when she takes them off!" Cristina predicted, which I did not translate despite the fact that Aisha asked me to. Even more humorous to the other workers was the day Aisha showed up with voluminous hair extensions that she had trouble keeping covered under her hairnet and hard hat. Aisha was a goofy, mostly friendly woman with a flirtatious streak but very little interest in breaking a sweat. She took off for the bathroom numerous times throughout the day, made frequent trips to the supervisors' office for supplies, and visited the nurse regularly. When she was working, she kept a steady pace, but never seemed hurried or even concerned about giving supervisors the impression that she was working quickly. Because she was easygoing and nonconfrontational, she wasn't despised in the way that some of the older Black women workers were, for instance Constance, who was ironically named because she was, along with the Hondurans Doris and Tania, among the crankiest and most impatient women I have ever met in my life. But Aisha could be exasperating to work with. As irritated as I got, having myself internalized some of the logic of super-exploitation, I tried to avoid complaining about her because usually my coworkers responded in racialized terms.

At times, though, the banter and jostling at the ribs station seemed relentless and infused with hostility. One Tuesday in April, Daniel,[20] Claudia's Mexican boyfriend who had switched his pallet jack driver job for a job trimming ribs, was flirting with Aisha. I found myself bewildered at their flirtation, as it was mixed in with him being a jerk to her and her being spacey and slow, as was typical for new workers. Daniel had told me, "This *moya*, this *moyita*, I tell her she's pretty." A while later, Claudia yelled from the *tortuga* that the ribs we were bagging weren't reaching the bottom of the bag, and therefore the bag wasn't sealing properly, which Daniel conveyed to me, adding, "It must be the *moya*." The following day this treatment escalated. At first Aisha would ask me, "What'd he say?" when Daniel made remarks about her. Aisha told me to ask Cristina, "What does English sound like to her?"

When Cristina responded, "Exactly what Spanish sounds like to her: blah blah," Daniel interjected, "What does this *moya* know? She doesn't even speak English. Who knows what she speaks, maybe Jewish!"

When I'd first gotten to the table in the morning, there was already a mound of ribs waiting to be bagged, and Cristina had proclaimed loudly, "*Los moyos no la hacen!*" (*Moyos* don't get things done! or, *Moyos* can't hack it!). Daniel repeatedly complained about Cliff, an older African American man with a limp, who had been moved from the ribs saw machine and was now being "trained" to trim ribs: "This *moyo* doesn't work." He also complained about Thomas, in his presence. When others were complaining that Thomas wasn't working the knife, that "he's a knife worker but he doesn't want to," Thomas was packing ribs and doing assorted light tasks (*pelándosela*—slang for jerking off). Daniel exclaimed, "This *moyo pendejo,* if it were up to me I'd send him home because he doesn't work!" Interactions between Daniel and Aisha escalated when, in the context of him rushing her, egging her on—"*Apúrate! Trabaja!*" (Hurry up! Work!)—and urging her to quit—"Quit! Quit!"—he called her a "*pinche cabrona!*" Cristina opened her eyes wide. I told Aisha this basically means "fucking bitch." "Don't you call me a bitch," she told him, and he repeated, "*cabrona.*"

It is not that Latina/o workers do not identify *any* Latinas/os who are able to escape the most oppressive elements of exploitation, and who may therefore be resented or disparaged as lazy. Indeed, I was quite astounded at the degree to which workers had so internalized exploitation and labor discipline that they would constantly scrutinize and criticize the performance of others and compel them to work faster and harder, shooting them dagger eyes or badmouthing them. Rosa and Rafael were singled out by Latina/o and African American workers for slacking and shirking, but such assessments weren't racialized in any way. Sometimes, Black workers would accuse Latina/o workers of laziness, too. The back and forth slandering could reach comical levels.

One Wednesday in May, I was bagging ribs with Cliff, a middle-aged African American man who had worked in boning for a year but was constantly being reassigned to different jobs, partly because of health problems. After working as a mechanic for many years, he had been laid off and taken a job at Fresh Birds Co. in Linden for three weeks before getting called back for a job he had applied for at Swine's, an opportunity he snapped up because the pay was much better. Alma, a short and round Honduran woman in her thirties, and Alexis, a Mexican man in his forties, weighed and sorted the ribs at two scales along

FIGURE 6. Workers in the Loin Boning and Packing Department bagging ribs in pairs.

FIGURE 7. Workers in the Loin Boning and Packing Department trimming ribs in the foreground, weighing and sorting ribs in the background.

the line before they reached the trimmers and baggers. Alma kept yawning and climbing down from the platform where she stood behind the scale all day, making unhappy faces, stretching her sore body. Cliff looked at me and in his thick country drawl said, "She's kind of lazy, ain't she?" I thought at first he meant me, but he said, "No, from what I can tell, you work." The irony was that two days earlier I had been bagging loin chunks near the boning line, and Cliff had been sorting different loins at the end of the line. Cristina had popped around at some point, bantering with him indecipherably, calling out "Cliff!" and holding out her cupped hand with her fingers outstretched. Cliff exclaimed, "No, no!" protesting her gesture and laughing heartily. Even though I knew what it meant, I asked her about the gesture and she told me it meant *"que es huevón, que los huevos le pesan"* (that he's lazy, that his balls are heavy), and laughed.

Banter, teasing, and other taunts were a common communicative practice among the workers, despite the English-Spanish language barrier, in ways that sometimes blurred playfulness and hostility, as the example of Daniel and Aisha suggests. Not infrequently, these jokes revolved around someone's work effort. Sex was another common theme. In the first week of my transfer to Loin Boning, a Salvadoran ribs trimmer named Rosa came to help Vincent, Linda, and me finish bagging ribs at the end of the shift. Vincent ripped into Rosa, and I couldn't tell if the banter was playful or not. "You so lazy, Rosa. Finally you're doing some work today! What you been doing all day anyway?" She frowned, seeming to understand some of what he said. She called him *"pendejo"* and "lazy, *haragán"* to me. He caught the *pendejo* part and commented on this. He asked her how her kid was doing, and when she said he was fine, he continued, "Did you just make up that excuse to be out of work?" She explained to me that her kid had been in the hospital for three weeks and that she had been given leave. He protested that he was asking her for real about her kid, and was truly interested in hearing details. She said to me, "He doesn't work, that's why they put him over here at this table." He continued ragging on her, now about her young boyfriend, who is in his twenties and works on the boning line. "Ask her!" he said to me. Rosa said he was twenty-six, and boasted that there was a lot of *chaca-chaca* (hanky panky). Vincent continued, "That's just because she was his first that he likes it. Hey Rosa, do you take out your teeth for your man?" I noticed that her front teeth appeared to be missing, or perhaps her gums had receded. He told me to translate, and I refused, feeling embarrassed for her. Linda was now listening in and said, "Vincent is terrible!" howling in her throaty smoker's voice.[21]

What was important was that Latinas/os' vilification of the African American workers' labor effort more often than not was leveled at the entire group—*los moyos, los morenos,* or *los negros*—while African Americans' vilification of the Latina/o workers' labor effort was directed solely at individuals.[22] Further, when Black workers tried to pass judgment on the work effort of Latinas/os, the response was indignation. In my second week in Loin Boning, Michael assigned me to work with Doris, a Honduran woman in her forties, bagging *japoneses* (loins cut and bagged according to different specifications for export to Japan), some of the toughest loins to work with. I was tasked with pulling loins off the line, laying them on a stand, and placing absorbent paper on the surface. Doris would then wrap the opening of a bag over the top of the loin and push the entire thing into the tight bag, finally throwing it back on a line. It was hard work. Doris was surly, her chubby face always bright red, and most workers tried to avoid getting on her bad side. She seemed to be exasperated by my pace. Even though it was fast, it was not frenzied. For a moment, though, she loosened up and told me she had worked here for nine years but was thinking about quitting because the long hours and heavy work were wearing her down. Later in the day, two middle-aged African American women, Eileen and Eve, came to bag loins on the line. Doris got upset when, apparently, Eileen commented that we were "just talking" when there was a brief lull in the loin line. This got Doris riled up, and a while later, again, Doris snapped at Eileen to "take it easy!" Later, seeing the two women standing about during a lull, she said to me, her voice tinged with bitter anger, "They can stand around without doing anything and no one says anything to them." "Who?" I asked. "The *negras.* If only they worked like they complain!"

The brazenness with which Latinas/os charged Black workers with laziness is perhaps startling given how politically incorrect it is in the context of contemporary American sensibilities around race. But even if it is startling, it is probably not *surprising* to most people, it being a racist trope as old as slavery itself. This characterization has also been documented by scholars studying poultry workers in other parts of the American South and Southwest (Stuesse 2009; Gleeson 2010). In the context of as demanding a workplace as this, however, accusations of being lazy—*haragán* or *huevón* being the most common slurs, followed by "lazy," and frequently accompanied by a palms-up cupping of the

FIGURE 8. Workers in the Loin Boning and packing Department bagging loins in pairs.

hand that connotes heavy testicles—have a patently relative meaning, and would certainly ring hollow to anyone who has ever set foot in a meatpacking plant. Few people would consider even a person standing idly all day in a frigid, unpleasant environment from before sunrise to after nightfall to be lazy. And of course, at Swine's nobody stands idly for long.

On the other hand, it would probably surprise most people to imagine that Black workers would occupy a position of privilege and advantage in a workplace. But because privilege and advantage are assessed in a relative sense in a context where group ascriptions signal distinct vulnerabilities, it should not really come as a surprise that Latinas/os perceive American Blacks as enjoying advantages they do not and resent them for this. A crucial point, however, is how these advantages, which we might expect native-born workers to have for a variety of reasons, including citizenship and nativity, English fluency, social capital, and seniority, are seen to accrue to them as Blacks rather than as Americans more generally. The thrust of intergroup conflict, if it is to be thought of as such, is not competition over jobs and resources, in which case the motivation would be African Americans' sense of competitive economic threat. Rather, it is about the perception of group-based advantages and disadvantages relative to oppressive exploitation, and this draws our attention to the configuration of group relations in the workplace.

"The negros always want to humiliate you, just because you are hispano"

Some Latinas/os perceived African Americans coworkers to be domineering, unfairly insisting that work be done on their terms. This was described by some as a bitter and humiliating experience. Leslie, an older Honduran worker, explained that she resisted such efforts at humiliating Latina/o workers:

> That *morena* doesn't do anything, that Janice. No, that *negra*! And that's the problem there. There's too little personnel, and they want the work to get done. And more so now that there are lots of work orders. It's a killer for me. You feel desperate, leaving work at eight or nine at night. No, the *negros* always want to humiliate you, just because you are *hispano*. The *bolillo* is more . . . but the *negro*! The *negro* always wants to see you as lesser, he humiliates you. Let's say me, on the ham line you have the *morena* Eileen. She's always like that. She wants you to do what she says. But I don't go along with it. I talk back to them, the little [English] that I know I talk back. And so they don't say anything to me. But they always want to look at you as being lesser. There's always racism. Because you're not from this country. For everything. You're an immigrant here. They always see you as being lesser.

A similar depiction was given by Reina, whose perceptions of how whites and Blacks treat her echoed those of Helen Marrow's (2007) respondents in important ways. Furthermore, Reina conveyed the same kind of indignation that some of Marrow's respondents expressed upon having their expectations of "moral hierarchy" upset by the perception of worse treatment from Blacks than from whites. We were discussing her perception that supervisors treated Black and Latina/o workers differently, a topic chapter 6 addresses in greater depth, when she explained her perception of differential treatment from white and African American workers more generally:

> I think *negros* are more racist. I imagine maybe it's because the *negros*—since the *moyos* used to be treated badly. But yes, sometimes you look at *moyos* and *blancos*—*blancos* are also racist toward us. But as I see it, it's more

Blacks than whites. And since there hardly are any *blancos*, you know. There are more *negros* than *blancos* [at work]. I once had problems with a *morena*, that Shameela. I had problems with her. I feel like sometimes they think that since we don't speak English or we're from another country, we don't understand. But sometimes. The good things don't stick, but the bad things do. So I talked back to her in English what came to mind. She didn't like it and went upstairs to say that I had pushed her. She told Itty's grandson, and they agreed to say that I had pushed her. Supposedly, I'd already been fired. But then Renata Chatuye [the Honduran Garifuna Human Resources assistant manager] took a look at our records, and I had never had any problem. And she had, people had complained. I got suspended for three days, but thanks to Renata, she's the one that helped me. Because according to Larry [Human Resources manager] I was already fired, because she gets along well with him. The other day Patricia was throwing the carts around and now I know I'm not going to fight with them because they end up winning and we end up losing. So what you have to do instead is go upstairs to complain.

Reina feels that supervisors will defer to African American workers' versions of events and therefore finds herself subordinated not just to management, but also to Black workers who will always end up winning. When I asked her how she thought *hispanos* were treated in the broader American society beyond the workplace, Reina made it clear that her experience of American society was defined almost entirely within the workplace. She expanded on her view that whites are less racist than African Americans despite her earlier comment that there are hardly any whites at Swine's, the context that defines her experience in the United States:

I haven't really had much of a life here. I've never been one to hang out in the *discotecas* or anything like that. I only know about work. But I think the *blancos* aren't so racist. I see that sometimes they treat you a little bit more . . . with less of that racism, that uneasiness, whereas the *moyos*, if you graze them they go like this [jerks away]. And the Americans, the Americans I have dealt with—there must be, because there's always all sorts—but I think it's more the *negros*. I think there must be whites but maybe they don't show it more than the *negros*. It probably has to be, I imagine, that since whites are really more from here than even *negros*. . . . Because the *negros* got here like us, actually worse than us, because the *negros* got here as slaves. Exactly, slaves that didn't earn anything, whereas we get paid for our work but not them. They got here in a worse position. Actually, they shouldn't be this way because they have been through what we are going through. Their situation was even worse than ours. They actually shouldn't be this way. I wonder why they are this way.

Reina was perplexed at the treatment she perceived from African Americans, who she reasoned should be more understanding of her plight given their own history of oppression rooted in slavery. As she saw it—her perspective informed almost entirely by her experiences in the workplace—African Americans are "more racist" toward Latinas/os than whites, who she nevertheless notes are almost entirely absent from the workplace.

"Things have to be parejas"

Latina/o workers were convinced that Black workers "don't have to work"—perhaps because they are given easier or more desirable jobs—and that they are therefore lazy. But they also perceived that African Americans—who they felt should be more sympathetic to migrants given their own history of oppression—preferred instead to humiliate and dominate them, as Leslie and Reina's stories illustrate. Latinas/os also felt that African American workers were able to escape some of the more oppressive elements of the labor discipline regime because supervisors were more likely to defer to their wishes and subject them to less-intense surveillance and discipline. Latina/o workers were sure that supervisors were more likely to choose pleasing an African American worker over pleasing a Latina/o worker.

Early in May I was at the ribs station when Natalia asked me to come upstairs to tell our superintendent George about what she considered an unfair incident. She had been bagging Japanese loins when a recently hired African American worker named Trina, arriving late to the floor for whatever reason, insisted that Natalia move from the spot where she was working, and Natalia refused. The floor supervisor, Michael, had then told Natalia to move. She was incensed. "I don't understand this discrimination since all of us here, white, Black, and *hispano,* are supposed to be equal." I conveyed to George her complaint about discrimination. His response was, "Did she ask Michael why he moved her? Michael maybe had a reason for moving her. I'll have to ask Michael and get back to her." Of course, he never did.

Latina/o workers were also certain that supervisors applied different disciplinary standards to African Americans. One afternoon in May, we were coming back from break, which we had taken a little early. I had smoked a cigarette and had a shot of coffee really quickly outside, and I noticed when I came back into the cafeteria that people were already rushing to get back on the floor. It was clear that they were going back to work early, or at least earlier than usual, and I was annoyed. I got my butcher coat, apron, sleeves, and gloves back on quickly, and as I returned to my station, I noticed that Aisha and Adrienne were not yet back, and I knew Linda couldn't possibly be back because she had been going out to smoke as I was coming back in. I accused Cristina, Adriana, and José of coming back from break early, which they denied. I was standing there for about a minute when I noticed that George, the African American superintendent, was at the stairs peering out at us. Thomas had just gotten back, was putting on his gear, and was talking to someone. Adrienne had just returned, and Aisha came shortly after, standing under the stairs with the belly cart out of George's view. I saw George signal for several people to go upstairs to the supervisors' office. Janice, an African American rib trimmer, met him halfway up the stairs and they chatted briefly before she returned to her station. Then Alma and Rosa were told to come upstairs, and I was summoned to translate. As we climbed the stairs, Hernán grinned and shouted, "They're going to make you sign the paper [a write-up]!" I asked them jokingly what they had done now, and they started ranting.

"This racist old man, how come the *morenos* can get here late but they don't get called up here, and only *hispanos* get called up here but they don't say anything to the *morenos*." Rosa released a flurry of curses in rapid succession: "*viejo serote! viejo culero!*" (old turd! old faggot!). Alma echoed her rant with a look of righteous outrage. George sat in his office chair and said sternly, "I've talked to y'all a couple of times already about coming back from break late. Apparently it doesn't work when I try to be a nice guy about it, so now I'm going to do it the other way. The next time that y'all are late it's going to be a written warning, and the next time it's going to be a three-day suspension." Rosa kept saying things to me in Spanish, such as, "And why only us?" but George kept interrupting, saying, "Listen to me, this is the last time, I have warned y'all several times, and it's not going to be a supervisor who brings you upstairs next time, it's going to be me [the superintendent]." As if to add insult to injury, he said, "If I can work without you for ten minutes I can work without you for three days. Thank you." Rosa kept trying to say things, and he just repeated, "Thank you." As we were about to walk out, I asked, "Do you all want me to say something to him or what?" Rosa said, "What for? Racist old man." When we got back, Adriana commented, "Why only the two of them if there were other people, the *morenos,* who hadn't gotten here? He only calls out the *hispanos,* you see?" I said I thought he had talked to Janice too, and she said, "But there were others who hadn't gotten here and who weren't working yet." Echoing a statement I heard many Latinas/os make, Adriana concluded, "Things have to be *parejas* [equal]."

CONCLUSION

Scholars interested in Latino/a migrant incorporation have not adequately addressed the collective processes through which this group attains a sense of its position within the stratified system of belonging in the United States. While researchers have drawn on Blumer's model to account for the character of intergroup relations in the transforming American South, and have considered the implications for how working-class Latinas/os are becoming incorporated in a now more complex racialized stratification system, there are important limitations to their approaches. A critical flaw has been a nearly exclusive focus on how African Americans react to Latinas/os, and how the perception of exclusionary behavior resulting from competition is pushing the latter toward a particular route of incorporation. This has resulted in a failure to attend to how Latinas/os construct understandings and representations of African Americans, and what this tells us about how they view their own position in the system. Most researchers seem to assume that only African Americans, and not Latinas/os, have a sense of group position, and therefore the capacity to feel threatened. Yet the overwhelming sense of grievance that Latinas/os express as embittered subordinates has its counterpoint in their perception that African Americans occupy a privileged position within the social organization of labor, a perception that breeds a strong resentment toward Blacks and is articulated through the elaboration of a variety of symbolic boundaries. It is this feeling of relative deprivation, not competitive threat per se, that fuels resentment *toward* rather than *from* African Americans. Latina/o workers at Swine's are indignant about what they see as their disadvantaged position within the social organization of labor, a position in which they are the most oppressively exploited. Comments from several workers suggest that a part of this indignation stems from the upending of a moral hierarchy: they did not anticipate that Blacks would occupy a position higher than their own, as Marrow's findings also suggest, and this is in line with the more or less universal devaluation of blackness. When Latina/o workers find that, at least as they perceive it, African

Americans occupy a relatively more advantaged position at work, a gnawing resentment builds.

Given how this resentment is racialized as advantages that accrue to American Blacks as opposed to Americans in general, and recognizing that the vulnerabilities that migrants confront, exacerbated by the disciplining functions of illegality, are racialized as attaching to *hispanos* as a group, several issues must be considered. Scholars have drawn on Bobo and Hutchings's (1996) concept of racial alienation as being particularly helpful for explaining the character of relations among subordinate groups. But this leads to several plausible accounts about relations between Latinas/os and African Americans. The first, which is the conventional take and the conclusion put forth recently by Marrow (2011) for Latino/a–African American relations in the American South, is that African Americans—the quintessential racially alienated group—react negatively toward Latinas/os, whom they identify as a socioeconomic competition–based threat to their sense of group position. The second, which is the more pronounced tendency in my data, is that although both are subordinated groups and therefore prone to experiencing racial alienation to some degree, Latinas/os *perceive* themselves as occupying a disadvantaged position relative to African Americans within the social organization of labor of a meatpacking plant in the U.S. South. Whether or not African Americans concur with this perception, they apparently do not feel sufficiently aggrieved to contest it in group terms.[23]

There are a number of limitations inherent to interview data—the inability to evaluate distinct modes of action (what people say versus what they do) or talk (what people say when prompted by an interviewer's questions versus what people say in spontaneous, unprompted exchanges). These have been amplified by a reliance on reports from Latinas/os as to their perceptions and attributions of discriminatory treatment and exclusionary behavior to draw conclusions about the actual behavior of African Americans toward this group. Studying the meaningful boundary-making processes through which Latina/o workers distinguish their experience within the social organization of labor from that of African Americans sheds a bright light on an important dimension of Latino/a migrant incorporation in the American South and beyond. But now that I have shed this light on Latinas/os, understandings and representations of African Americans, what about the other dimension: African Americans' understandings and representations of Latinas/os? This question arises again in chapter 7, after a discussion of how the composition of the authority structure mediates Latinas/os' perceptions of African American privilege in the workplace, the topic of chapter 6. But first, chapter 5 will delve more deeply into the perceptions and experience of vulnerability that convince Latinas/os that there is a cost to being *hispano* and a value to being Black at Swine's.

CHAPTER 5

The Value of Being *Negro*, The Cost of Being *Hispano*

Disposability and The Challenges for Cross-Racial Solidarity in The Workplace

Late one evening in March 2010, soon after my transfer to the Loin Boning and Packing Department, Leticia, who was in the third trimester of her pregnancy, complained to me about not being sent home after working eight hours, as some pregnant workers got permission to do. After we were finished bagging all the combos of loins that had accumulated over the course of the day and were feeling relieved at the prospect of being done, Michael directed us to another three combos of loins and ribs to pack. "Maybe they think we are idiots," she said, as an explanation for why we in this department get "wrung out and exploited," the words I responded with when Michael brought out more work for us, thirteen hours into our shift. Leticia asked me why I had transferred to Loin Boning and Packing from Marination, and I told her it was a long story that I would relate another time. She asked me if I had worked with Constance yet. Constance was an older African American worker who was persistently cranky, even mean. What had I thought of her, how had she treated me? I shrugged with an expression that could be read as "not good." Leticia replied that even though "among us" there's a lot of gossiping, "we" still stick together, unlike Constance. Leticia said someone had told her that Constance said she "didn't like *hispanos*."

Not long after this, Leticia was telling me about how she was initially assigned to a knife job when she first started working at Swine's almost a year ago, but that gradually she had been reassigned to packing. Because knife jobs paid better than packing jobs, I asked if she had kept the higher pay rate even though she wasn't doing knife work. "Ha! No, I would have to be of *that* color for them to do that." "Which color?" I asked, feigning naïveté. "*Morena*," she responded, matter-of-factly. She added that if she stands around and Itty sees her not working he gets mad, then pointed over to Aisha and Adrienne, who were pretty much not doing anything because it was slow at the ribs station. "If it's them," she said, "he doesn't get mad." We were killing ourselves to finish bagging combos of loins that had piled up, and just then Itty's grandson Dwayne came by the packing area after finishing his work skinning tenderloins on the line. He stood watching us. Leticia signaled for me to look at him. "It's worth it to be *negro* here. He's Itty's grandson and look how he's standing around."

In the context of oppressive exploitation at Swine's, the perception of one group's advantages is inextricably tied to another group's position of disadvantage. It is in such a context that being Black comes to be viewed by some Latinas/os as a valuable resource, despite the fact that blackness retains a universally disparaged status, even (or especially) in the migrants' countries of origin. Like Leticia's comments, Cristina's declaration (described in the previous chapter) that she would come to work painted black so she wouldn't have to work illustrates this subtle insight rather powerfully. Given the backdrop of white supremacy in the United States and the well-documented continuity of racial inequalities across life domains, from education to health to labor markets, it is difficult to imagine that being Black could be a valuable resource, as some Latinas/os suggest. Within the world of work, there is an abundance of research that demonstrates employers' negative assessments of Black workers, particularly when compared to the virtues of hard work and subservience that they perceive among other types of workers, namely immigrants (Harrison and Lloyd 2013; Karjanen 2008; Zamudio and Lichter 2008; Donato and Bankston 2008; Waldinger and Lichter 2003; Moss and Tilly 2001; Holzer 1996; Kirschenman and Neckerman 1991). The "soft skills" immigrants bring to the workplace, which employers refer to as having the right attitude toward work that offers limited extrinsic and intrinsic rewards, have been interpreted differently by scholars. These scholars have identified "soft skills" as shorthand for immigrants' "tractability" relative to other kinds of workers in the face of employer demands for compliance and subordination (Zamudio and Lichter 2008; Donato and Bankston 2008; Waldinger and Lichter 2003).

Indeed, it is this distinction-making that informs employers' documented preference for hiring immigrants over native-born workers across a variety of industries. Employers may prefer to hire immigrants over native-born workers because they are viewed as the ideal subordinates. But for the same reason, it could be hypothesized that *once hired, native-born workers are situated relatively more favorably than immigrants within the social organization of labor,* an important extension of the ethnic succession theories proposed in chapter 2. Remarkably little is known about how workers perceive distinctions among themselves, and what conditions shape these perceptions, as discussed in chapters 3 and 4. This analysis is important, because if we understand employers' preferences not as objective evaluations of individual workers' abilities to perform some job, but as different types of workers' relative capacity and suitability for oppressive exploitation, then we must imagine that this feature is likely to be reflected somehow in the social organization of labor, and therefore in social relations among workers. Herein lies one key to resolving the paradox of the "value" of being Black at Swine's when all indications point to the lack of value attached to being Black in American society more generally.

This chapter examines the rather surprising claim that it is "worth it" to be Black at Swine's, focusing attention on the vulnerabilities of migrant illegality that, on the shop floor, have the tendency to bleed onto Latinas/os as a group, and results in the perception of a cost to being *hispano*. Perhaps because *hispanos* come together as a group through their subordinated status in the workplace, it is a group identity that is fraught with internal tensions, much as Leticia's comments in the opening encounter suggest. Leticia let me know that even though "we" (*hispanos*) gossip about each other and put one another down, "we" stick together, apart from and unlike African American workers.[1] The first section of this chapter proposes that a crucial corollary to the vulnerability through deportability that illegality produces for the migrant is the vulnerability through disposability that illegality produces for the migrant *worker*, especially in the context of intensified immigration enforcement policies in the United States, particularly in the South. It shows how such vulnerabilities came together in Cristina's harrowing experience at Swine's. The second section demonstrates the challenge that group-based vulnerabilities such as those produced by illegality, which radiate onto the entire group of *hispanos*, poses for solidarity among workers in the struggle for dignity and justice on the shop floor. The third section argues that Latinas/os' perceptions of the different positions that they and African Americans occupy within the social organization of labor may well be rooted in reality—a possibility that should not be surprising given the bases for employer preferences in hiring.

THE VULNERABILITIES OF "ILLEGALITY"

If Latina/o workers were sure that African Americans were a privileged minority at the factory, they were equally certain that *hispanos* were a disadvantaged group, as numerous quotes throughout this book demonstrate. Although different immigration authorization statuses are tied to different *objective* risks and susceptibilities, a common perception of subordination was shared by Latina/o migrants regardless of their particular status. Indeed, Swine's Latina/o workforce spanned the spectrum of immigration authorization statuses, even as the increasingly stringent employment authorization verification requirements resulted in the slow purge of workers lacking authorization. On the factory floor, the vulnerabilities of "illegality" are likely to mean (as Billy, a Coharie crew leader identified by workers as a *bolillo,* told Honduran boning line worker Elsa) that "you're a wetback, so you'll do what I say." Some Latina/o migrant workers also contend with what Cecilia Menjívar (2006) has termed the "liminal legality" produced by certain forms of immigration authorization status, such as Temporary Protected Status, which grants temporary work authorization to vulnerable groups. For Latina/o workers with TPS, including Hondurans and Salvadorans who left their countries under dire circumstances, partial and ostensibly temporary legal status in the present tense coexists with uncertainty and impermanence in the long run. For Latinas/os with TPS, their future legal status is defined at best as the perpetual renewal of temporary and incomplete legality, since no avenue for legal permanent residency is built into Temporary Protected Status.[2]

Of course, there are Latina/o migrants who have obtained legal permanent residency and others who have become naturalized citizens. But in the social context of a workplace characterized by workers of mixed legal statuses, Latina/o migrants share a distinct vulnerability in that they have limited English-speaking skills and are not "from here," traits easily identified by supervisors on the shop floor. The fusing effect of these shared characteristics, which brings heterogeneous individuals together as a group, is magnified by supervisors' attaching to this group the special vulnerabilities of "illegality" that objectively only pertain to some (migrants lacking work authorization) on the basis of ethnoracial attributes held in common by all (socially coded phenotypic features, language, and cultures).

Scholars have drawn attention to the legal and political processes of "illegalization" through which the category of the "illegal immigrant" has been rendered an object of state intervention and public concern (Calavita 1998; Ngai 2003; De Genova 2005; Chavez 2008; Cacho 2012). The relevant historical timeline for the production of this state of subjection usually begins in 1924, when Congress enacted the first broad immigration control legislation, which initiated numerical restrictions and national origins quotas, and created the Border Patrol. The recent surge in legal and political efforts to control unauthorized migration and unauthorized migrants goes far beyond the border enforcement initiatives that began much earlier, and is typified by state legislation such as Arizona's SB 1070 and copycats in Alabama, South

Carolina, and Georgia. These measures were preceded by provisions included in the 1996 Illegal Immigration Reform and Immigrant Responsibility Act that allowed local officials to partner with federal authorities and become vested with immigration law enforcement powers. In the everyday life of an unauthorized immigrant worker, the vulnerabilities of "illegality" are both immediate and transcendent.[3]

Cristina, an unauthorized migrant worker from Honduras, followed developments surrounding the Arizona law closely, and for weeks we had been discussing it across the worktable, sharing the latest updates and debates we had picked up on Univision, the Spanish-language TV network. Perhaps because of my level of education and the fact that I studied migration, Cristina seemed to think that I had some special knowledge or intuition about where U.S. immigration law was headed. Did I think Obama was going to give papers? Did I think the Dream Act was going to be approved? Did I think the Arizona law was going to pass? What would happen if they passed a law like that here in North Carolina? When not at work, Cristina had to worry about *retenes*, police checkpoints set up routinely around the area to nab drivers without licenses. A favorite barricade for police was right around the corner from Cristina's trailer park, just down the street from Walmart, where practically the entire county could be found shopping on weekends. People dispatched scouts to detect police checkpoints and called one another to warn of *retenes*, but even so, most people got snagged at one point or another, and the widespread and frequent fines amounted to a substantial tax on the undocumented. The intensification of immigration enforcement policies in North Carolina, as elsewhere in the United States (Hagan, Rodríguez, and Castro 2011), was felt acutely by Latina/o migrants, even in Clark County, which did not participate in some of the voluntary programs that other counties did.

The disciplinary functions of migrant "illegality" work through the fear-inducing feature of "deportability" (De Genova 2005) but also more proximately for the unauthorized *worker* through the mechanism of "disposability." Only weeks before Cristina was apprehended by police with the collaboration of Human Resources personnel, Adriana faced a similar, if less precarious, situation. Cristina herself had told me about it when I returned to the worktable from fetching a box of bags: "Adriana got called to the office. Her papers came back bad." I rushed to the locker room and found Adriana, who was pregnant at the time, emptying out her locker, collecting her knives and gear, sobbing quietly. All workers at Swine's were disposable—in fact, we were made to sign a statement during new-employee orientation that said as much in fancy legalese; a major point was made out of the fact that our employment at the company was "at will." And as Michael made clear one night in mid-April when, fourteen hours into our shift, he castigated workers for daring to go to the bathroom, all of us were entirely replaceable.

But unauthorized workers have a distinct target on their heads, a special disposability that serves a labor disciplining function for management just as their unique deportability gives management a basis on which to make important distinctions among potential sources of labor. Ironically, deportability "favors" migrants when they receive preferential treatment in the hiring process, but once hired, disposability places them in a position of singular disadvantage relative to other groups within the social organization of labor. Although much has been made of migrants' dual frame of reference for evaluating conditions of existence "here" relative to conditions "there" (Waldinger and Lichter 2003), my fieldwork taught me that Latina/o migrants—unauthorized or authorized—are not always the happy, willing subordinates they are imagined to be. And, in fact, their deep grievances are of critical importance for understanding their relations with African Americans, and perhaps for grasping their emergent sense of group position within the American system of racial and class stratification.

The vulnerabilities of "illegality" do not just apply to unauthorized workers, though they do so more severely and more consequentially. This is especially true in the current sociopolitical environment, when U.S. immigration enforcement policies have intensified both at the border and in the interior, inaugurating a third era of mass deportations and workplace raids (Hagan, Rodríguez, and Castro 2011). In the hustle and bustle of a factory, supervisors can and do treat ethnoracial group ascriptions, such as being Latina/o, as shorthand for the kinds of people that approximate those associated with some trait, namely illegality. This was plainly evident one day when Claudia asked me to accompany her to the supervisors' office so I could translate her message to our superintendent, George. I informed George that Claudia had gotten special permission from Human Resources for a monthlong leave of absence. She was not required to inform George personally, and George noted this, telling her how much he appreciated that she bothered to let him know. But then he asked, "Where is she going?" She said to tell him she was going to her country, El Salvador. A sly smile appeared on his face, and he asked, "Is she going to be able to get back into the United States?" Understanding full well his insinuation that she lacked authorization to enter the country legally, I translated for Claudia, and she answered simply, "Yes." Perhaps unconvinced, George added with a laugh, "Because if she can't get back in, tell her I know someone who will marry her." As we walked out, she told me George had a nephew who worked in the Shipping Department who had always liked her. Claudia had Temporary Protected Status, which means she can get permission from the immigration authorities to travel to and from El Salvador, and she had work authorization. She had worked in the same department for nine years, yet her head supervisor could not shake the idea that she was unauthorized.

The vulnerabilities of "illegality" were quite literally embodied in Cristina's pain and injuries: the inflamed tendons in her wrists, the chronic back pain, the stiffness in her neck. Cristina had never sought medical attention in two years of work, despite paying for the company's insurance, or even visited the company nurse, for fear of finding herself on the shortlist for firing. Indeed, Myrna, the Human Resources recruiter, warned unauthorized workers that given the increasingly stringent enforcement of employment verification requirements, it was better for them to "take care of their jobs" and avoid seeing the nurse or making complaints to Human Resources. "For what?" Myrna admonished Cristina's relative Ileana about visiting the company nurse. "To rub people the wrong way? It's better to take it [the pain]." Because she knew she was especially disposable, anticipating that any moment her papers would turn out bad, Cristina never missed work or used the days off she accumulated, figuring she better earn a check working as many hours as possible while she still had a job. Within a few weeks of working with Cristina at the rib-trimming table, I told her about my research. She was, I believe, unsure at first whether I was some kind of undercover police agent, but I gained her trust precisely by entrusting her with this information about me (though I did not and could not request that she keep it a secret) and by becoming a sounding board for her doubts and questions.

Because I had been having problems with my fingers due to repetitive motion injury and overexertion, I visited the nurse, and later several doctors. Over this period of time, we talked extensively at our worktable about this process, and about things like workers' compensation and the workplace rights of undocumented workers. Cristina would stretch out her arm and grimace from the pain in her tendons, wrist, and back. Sometimes she would have me grab hold of her wrists and pull as though I were yanking her hands off their worn hinges. Sometimes I would rub her shoulders, neck, and back through the thick layers of sweaters, giving momentary relief from the immiserating pain. She began to visit the company nurse, and began to contemplate making a doctor's appointment, but was still afraid. Daniel and Hernán, who frequently worked at a table with us, mocked our conversations, dismissing my explanations of undocumented workers' rights as "pure lies." "You see! It's because of these guys that I haven't been to the nurse this whole time!" she snapped. I was struck by the dissuasive influence they had on her in terms of quelling her interest in learning about her rights as an undocumented worker and discouraging her from pursuing those rights. But Cristina finally made an appointment with a doctor, and her voice quivered with fright as she gave "her" social security number and details to the receptionist over the phone. She told me that she hated lying. She did go to a doctor, but that would be the only time, since her worst fear, which she nonetheless never really anticipated, would become a reality.

On a Friday at the end of July, my morning started off badly. I woke up late for the first time since I'd started working at the factory. I had to be at work at six thirty in the morning and was fifteen minutes tardy making it onto the floor. Every morning as we arrived at our workstations, Cristina and I would exchange greetings. "*Buenos días!*" she would exclaim, loudly and cheerfully, and I'd respond, "*Buenos días, alera* [Honduran slang for friend], how are you?" "Good, did you sleep well?" This morning, Cristina was surprised that I was late. "What happened? I was worried, I told Gerardo to go get my phone and call you to see if something happened, because you live by yourself. He joked that no, you live with your cat." During an unofficial morning bathroom break, we talked again about my being late and how worried she had been. When we went on our official morning break at nine thirty, she waited for me to catch up to her as we streamed out toward the cafeteria, a cold and hungry army of workers, and held my hand as we walked together, wanting me to feel her icy hands.

Back on the production floor after breakfast, I was dumping a heavy tub of meat trimmings into a tank when I noticed that Cristina was under the stairwell to the supervisors' office, and George was telling her something. I didn't think anything of it; I figured he was giving her instructions, or telling her to go work on a different line. A little while later, Rosa mentioned that George had told Cristina she was wanted up in Human Resources. Immediately we were worried, as unauthorized workers assumed that this meant that they were going to be fired or worse. La Madrina, an elderly Salvadoran worker everyone called the

Godmother, assured us that Cristina was having her hearing checked. After a while of feeling at ease with this, it occurred to me that she had had her hearing checked in April, the week of "Cristina's" birthday, which is when the company nurse gives workers their annual hearing test.

A sinking dread, a horrible sensation of alarm, came back. I worked at different points in the morning with Claudia, who kept coming to help me bag ribs because work at the *tortuga* was slow. I was getting extremely worried because Cristina had left at around eleven, lunchtime was approaching, and she was not yet back. Claudia was calm. "Aaahhh, I'm not worried, don't worry, what's there to be worried about? You worry when someone's sick, or something happens, when your kids are sick." She told me about her son's recent bicycle accident. "I don't have kids, so let me worry about other people," I snapped. "Why don't you worry about *my* kids, then," she suggested dryly. We went on lunch break and Cristina was nowhere to be seen. I kept asking Rosa and La Madrina if they had seen her, but they had not. We went back on the floor, close to one o'clock, and still Cristina was not back. Claudia was bagging ribs with me, and little by little information began leaking through the rumor mill that police had been at the factory. And then it was confirmed. Cristina had been hauled away by police in handcuffs.

My heart dropped. My mind raced with flashbacks to all the conversations we had had about everything going on in Arizona, as recently as the day before. I recalled her right-below-the-surface-but-always-there feeling that she was being persecuted, her sense of fear and dread and anxiety and confusion, her incessant questions. I squatted down to hide among the steel and boxes, and called Cristina's house on my cell phone. Her twelve-year-old daughter picked up. "Where's your mom?" "She's in jail," the girl said flatly. I kept working with Claudia. I wondered if the workers were going to do or say anything, or what was going to happen.

I was feeding Claudia ribs, and my eyes welled up with tears. Adrienne, a young African American worker, looked over from where she was bagging Safeway. She asked, "What's wrong?" and I broke down crying. I put my head down for a second, resting my arm on the pile of ribs in the pan. Claudia hit me on the hard hat with a rack of ribs, telling me to stop crying and get it together. "If you're going to be like this, you should leave," she said. At two thirty I saw George and told him I had an emergency and needed to go. He looked at me with his cockeyed smile and said, "I'm not going to give you a point, let me just see what time it is." I was sure he knew why I was leaving. Cristina and I had run into him and his wife at Walmart one day, so he knew we were friends. I left, spending the rest of the day with Cristina's husband, Ernesto, trying to find a lawyer and collect money and property titles for bond, all the while unsure whether my friend was going to be released or transferred to the custody of ICE. When her husband and I posted bond and she was released from jail at midnight, her eyes calm, tired, but wide awake, I could not help but be amused as she recounted how when the police officer told her she was under arrest for identity theft, she told him it couldn't be true because she had bought the papers, not stolen them. The disciplining features of illegality, which at work are transmitted through the mechanism of disposability, are communicated with great force in the community beyond the workplace through the mechanism of deportability.

Latina/o migrants struggle to survive in "the prison" that is work at Swine's and in the "cage of gold" that is life outside the factory gates. As Ana, an unauthorized Honduran worker told me, police harass them constantly, putting up license checkpoints in places Latinas/os are likely to travel through, making her fearful to leave her home. And yet it could be worse, since Clark County is one of the few in this region that has not enlisted in the 287(g) program, which deputizes local law enforcement to exercise authority on immigration matters (Gill 2010; Weissman et al. 2009). Ana's sense of defeat is echoed by Cristina's in-law Ileana, who told me, "Before people emigrated from there to here, but now we have to emigrate from here to there." She feared losing her job at Swine's because she had heard that not even the hog farms would hire workers without papers any more. Adriana was fortunate enough not to have been arrested. But this seemed to be of little consolation to her when, only weeks before Cristina's ordeal, I saw her crying as she emptied her locker: Human Resources had decided that her papers were no good. Cristina herself, now confined to taking care of working parents' children for what amounts to pennies per hour, views her entire migration experience with regret. Her son she left in Honduras, she says, has probably lost his love for her and for what? she says. She would not have starved to death if she had stayed there. Workers like Cristina, Adriana, and Ana are the most disposable workers because they were never really (supposed to be) here in the first place.[4] As the anthropologist Susan Bibler Coutin (2005, 195) explains, "Because their presence is prohibited, unauthorized migrants do not fully arrive even when they reach their destination." In the workplace, this incomplete state of being transforms them into "ghost workers" (García 2012). The next section discusses how the costs of being *hispano* radiate beyond the group, constraining cross-racial solidarity in resisting oppressive exploitation.

"*MORENOS* HAVE TO WORK LIKE WE DO": COLLECTIVE ACTION AS A RACE TO THE BOTTOM

Because supervisors apply to the broader group expectations for labor subordination designed with reference to a uniquely vulnerable kind of worker, the disciplinary functions of "illegality" shape the working conditions of all Latina/o migrants at Swine's. The liabilities entailed by other ethnoracial attributes that characterize the group—namely, not being "from here" and having limited English-speaking skills—also play a role in their subjection. For Latina/o migrants unhappy with these working conditions, the disciplinary functions of "illegality" and the silencing effect of not being English-fluent in turn circumscribe their ability to openly challenge labor subordination. Latina/o workers are often ready and willing to talk back to supervisors, but find themselves quite literally bereft of words, their rebellious urge smoldering inside. On several occasions, Latina/o workers discussed the possibility of presenting their complaints about working conditions, including supervisor mistreatment, to Human Resources personnel. As these workers knew, it was important to present these complaints collectively as a group, rather than as individuals who could then be singled out for retaliation. These enthusiastic surges of courage were usually short-lived, succumbing within moments to the discouraging sense of certainty that others wouldn't dare to join in the protest because they didn't have papers and would be too afraid, or stifled by the dissuasive influence of those who thought resistance was folly. Most Latina/o workers, including Cristina, Reina, Leticia, Ana, and even Claudia, expressed their support for a union at Swine's, regardless of their authorization status. But most of them felt there was too much at stake for them to take action, especially since the increasingly stringent employment verification requirements and the slow purge of unauthorized workers meant they were only biding their time until it was their turn.[5]

Given the objective and perceptual conditions I have laid out, perhaps it was inevitable that of the few instances of collective action in which Latina/o workers sought redress for their oppressive working conditions, the target shifted from improving the conditions of work to demanding that African Americans be subjected to the same labor discipline regime as they were. In the dog-eat-dog world of Swine's, challenging the structure of power on the shop floor that dictated the conditions under which workers labor was a daunting task, perhaps more distant-seeming than the immediate injustice that was protested when Latinas/os perceived African American workers to be advantaged.

One afternoon in May, two months into my job in Loin Boning, I got called up to the superintendent's office. George, the African American superintendent of Loin Boning, wanted me to translate for several groups of workers, most of whom were Spanish speakers. He delivered a speech to each consecutive group with declining enthusiasm, explaining that production levels were not going to decrease (as most people expected for the summer) and that work hours were going to stay the same: brutally long. "This is a profit-making company, and we're the only plant making money right now, so this is where production is going to be. You all have three options: transfer to another department that isn't even making forty hours, stay put, or leave." To drive home the point, he repeated, "It's all about the bottom line." Lupe, a Mexican woman who worked on the loin-bagging line, complained that more people were needed on the line to keep work from getting backed up. Workers were annoyed that Itty, a Black man in his sixties who had worked there for forty years and had supervisory functions even though he was a regular worker, took workers off the line to do other tasks, which caused things to get backed up. "Why don't you tell Itty to bag them, then?" George replied flippantly. When Lupe brought up the need to rotate loin packers and ribs packers, because bagging loins for an entire shift was extremely grueling, he feigned ignorance about the idea of job rotation. George finished by telling the group to put their concerns and suggestions in writing, which would "force him to respond." Lupe and several others asked me to draft a letter on behalf of the packing workers. They knew I was well educated, could read and write English, did not have kids or a spouse to care for, and was more "from here" than they were, given that I was a citizen, factors that they felt made me suited to the task.

On a break in the bathroom, I approached Lupe with a draft of my letter, which I read to her as others gathered around. She kept voicing agreement, and Doris joined her enthusiastically: "Absolutely!" Lupe, Doris, Natalia, and other Latinas became quite animated, saying they wanted me to include that "*Hispanos* aren't treated the same as *morenos*. *Morenos* can work the way they want, but if *hispanos* are standing around they get yelled at but *morenos* don't get yelled at." These workers agreed that "*Morenos* should have to work like we do.

The supervisors don't say anything to them, they give them easy jobs and let them leave early." Immediately I felt some dread. Someone said, "If supervisors looked at who did all the different jobs, they'd see that the Blacks have all the easiest jobs and *hispanos* have the hardest." Later, I was helping Ximena (Guatemalan) and Elsie (Honduran) pack bellies and Ximena told me, after bringing up the letter to George, "If you just look around, you see so many *morenos* just standing around, but if you or I did that we'd quickly get yelled at." To make her point clear, she pointed to several Black workers who were standing nearby talking.[6]

Latina/o workers were quick to protest what they saw as the privileged treatment African American workers received, and even mobilized as a group to demand that African Americans be subjected to the same level of oppressive exploitation that they were. But sometimes Latina/o workers recognized that their own internalization of the logic of exploitation at Swine's, or at the very least their powerlessness to contest their disposability, made them complicit in their oppression. Reina felt that, moreover, African American workers had the advantage of solidarity. Latina/o workers, on the other hand, united in the experience of shared subordination, were beset by the pressures to conform to oppressive exploitation that in-group members placed on their fellow workers. I asked Reina how she thought *negros, hispanos,* and *blancos* got along at work:

> Well, among the *moyos*, they shelter one another. And *hispanos*, as I told you before, there's always that *egoísmo* [selfishness]. Instead of getting along, they're trying to backstab, to point the finger at someone. Yes, instead of helping you, of being united, the *hispano* is actually selfish. Instead of helping you, the *hispano* tries to drag you down. He isn't *unido* [united, solidaristic]. The *hispano* that is *unido* is rare. It's rare. Always selfish. You see it in Packing. If you're standing around, one of the women will say, "Look at so and so doing nothing, she's standing there doing nothing!" It bothers her that you're standing around. "*Qué haragana! Qué huevona!*" [What a lazy ass!]. But then you notice that the *morenas*—if a *moya* sees another *moya* standing there, she won't say anything to her. They're more *unidas*. That's why I say that it's our own fault.

Cristina gave an explanation for how *negros* and *hispanos* got along at work that clearly demonstrated an awareness of Latina/o and African American workers' differing views on what Roger Waldinger and M.I. Lichter (2003) have termed "the proper equation between effort and reward," which caused frictions:

Because they don't like to work alongside you. The truth is that they—I don't know if it's that they don't work, or if it's that they can't or don't want to. But they say they're not going to kill themselves working for so little. They say they don't earn enough to kill themselves. And that when it's overtime, they don't work the same as during the day. When it's overtime, they don't like to work the way they work during normal hours. It's slower. They say that they don't need to be rushed, because it's past the eight-hour workday.

And yet, asked how she personally got along with African American workers, Cristina articulated a nuanced response that profoundly illustrates the ways in which her own racialized resentment of African American workers was tied to her own internalization of the logic of capitalist exploitation, which caused her to submit to her subordinate position in the workplace:

> I didn't dislike them. Sometimes I told them they were *haraganes* [lazy], that they didn't work. But it was never that I didn't like them. I've never disliked them. Racist, no. Well, yeah, they follow their own rules. They do what they want. The truth is that if they don't work, and we work, it's our fault. That's what I think. It's our own fault, working more than they do. Sometimes, they do demand more of us. But it's up to our bodies what we can take. What happens is that sometimes we strain our bodies beyond the strength we have for working, when we like to work. So of course, if we're tired and the other person isn't doing anything, that's when we don't like it. But the truth is, they say, "You work if you want to work. Leave me alone. What are you looking at me for?" And sometimes they're right because nobody has a knife to our back to make us work faster. Sometimes I would tell myself to work slower, because that way I leave work well rested. But after a little while I would forget. Until a while later I would remember again. But sometimes one's body just can't be without working.

Latinas/os at Swine's develop a group identity that is mired in the struggle for dignity and status, a struggle most immediately mounted vis-à-vis the group they most overlap with in the social class, a group whose position within the social organization of labor at Swine's appears to upend the racialized hierarchy that the migrants expect. Latinas/os' position as embittered subordinates unites them across national lines, muting such distinctions in favor of a pan-ethnoracial identification as *hispanos*.[7] Yet we must not read such reactive solidarity in overly rosy tones. Some workers, like Leticia, Reina, and Cristina, may not even refer to such a shared sense of group identity as solidarity at all, making cross-racial solidarities perhaps even harder to attain. The next section accounts for the ethnoracial composition of the Loin Boning and Packing Department in order to put into perspective Latinas/os' perceptions that groups occupy different positions within the social organization of labor at Swine's.

THE SOCIAL ORGANIZATION OF LABOR: PERCEPTIONS ARE REALITY?

Let's lay out the ethnoracial composition within the social organization of labor. While I worked in Loin Boning and Packing, the total number of workers was approximately two hundred. Usually this was broken down as three loin, shoulder, and belly deboning lines consisting of about twenty to twenty-five workers each, two ham-end deboning lines consisting of about twenty-five workers, two butt deboning lines consisting of about fifteen workers, several loin and tenderloin bagging lines consisting of about fifteen workers, ribs trimming and bagging lines consisting of about ten workers, several box packing lines consisting of about fifteen workers, four *tortuga* operators, two to five saw operators, and three to five jack drivers. The remainder were assigned to work at various positions on different days. Around 25 percent of these workers were African American. Of this 25 percent, 69 percent had worked at the plant for at least a year. This suggests that there is a stable core of African Americans working at Swine's and a smaller number of positions that turn over multiple times.[8]

Of great significance, as will become clearer in chapter 6, the authority structure in this department was identified as predominantly Black. Itty and TJ, both longtime African American employees, held positions as "worker-supervisors," a term used here to refer to workers who, despite not being classified officially as supervisors, are given a mostly supervisory role in the delegation and coordination of work. It is perhaps also the case that among regular workers, Blacks were more likely than Latinas/os to be assigned to more coveted and less onerous jobs. Shameela, Patricia, and Jeremy had all been given assistant-type jobs after some period of doing straight or whizard knife work. On the ham line where twenty Latinas used straight knives to debone ham ends, Coreen had the job of bagging the hams at the end of the line. Bess, Eileen, and Susie worked the whizard knife trimming fat off loins at the end of the line. Ten of the thirty-six Black (28 percent) workers had been assigned primarily to the ribs station, considered by most workers to be somewhat lighter work compared to loins, shoulders, and bellies, even though ribs station jobs accounted for only about 10 percent of all the jobs in the department. Close to half of the ribs station workers at any given time were African Americans. The concentration of African Americans in certain jobs and not others in the Loin Boning and Packing Department suggests that Latinas/os' perceptions about their advantage have some basis in objective conditions. Yet it is important to remember that these "advantages" are only construed as such in relation to the position that Latina/o workers tend to occupy as a group. These are "advantages" that might seem minor, even negligible, to an outside observer, but that take on extraordinary significance to workers who face on a daily basis some of the harshest working conditions imaginable.

CONCLUSION

Although it is not necessary for subjective experience to faithfully reflect objective conditions, in this case, it is likely that African Americans *as a group* occupy a *relatively* more favorable position in the Swine's workplace than do Latinas/os. Many Latina/o workers, especially in the super-exploitative Loin Boning Department, feel they are treated differently than Black workers, that supervisors set higher bars for them in terms of work performance, that labor discipline is more stringent upon them, that they are more surveilled by supervisors and their agents, that they are given harder jobs, and that they are at a disadvantage when it comes to a supervisor deciding between pleasing a Black worker and pleasing a Latina/o worker. The fact that these supervisors were African American only solidified the Latina/o workers' perception that Black workers were given preferential treatment, a topic that comes up again in the next chapter. Given their perceptions, which in fact correspond with the expectations of these groups' relative positions in the literature on ethnic succession and employer preferences,[9] Latina/o workers ascribe to Black workers the qualities of receiving unearned privileges and being lazy in an effort to even out their statuses—at least symbolically, filling in the initial boundary drawn boldly against American Blacks via an elaborate array of symbolic resources that relentlessly designate them using ethnoracial forms of identification, and which frequently acquire pejorative significance. The compliant, subordinate hard worker does not exist in itself. Supervisors continually hone that compliance to their demands, and Latina/o workers are extremely resentful of their subordination, but the immediate objects of their resentment are Black *workers*, not supervisors. Latina/o workers understand their subordinate status to be tied to their own vulnerability as non-English-speaking immigrant workers, some of whom are particularly handicapped by their lack of work authorization. But in the frenzy of fifteen-hour workdays at Swine's, this understanding recedes into the background next to what they see as the more favorable treatment Black workers receive. Perhaps unable to imagine that Swine's could ever operate as anything more than a prison—that working conditions might be improved for everyone, and especially for them—Latina/o workers insist that African Americans be subject to the same unrelenting labor discipline regime.

CHAPTER 6

Black, White, and Latino/a Bosses

*How the Composition of the Authority
Structure Mediates Perceptions of Privilege
and the Experience of Subordination*

One afternoon, my work was slow at the ribs, so I intermittently went to second-seat my Salvadoran friend Claudia at the *tortuga*. We were chatting, passing the time, when she told me: "When I leave this job, before I go I'm going to say to Michael, 'bye stupid nigger.'" I responded in shock. "What?!" "That's what I'm going to say. Goodbye stupid nigger! You are a stupid nigger!" After repeating this over and over, she said to me: "They don't like it when you say that, right?" "No," I responded. She went on, railing against Michael. Conversations like this with Claudia and others could be tough for me, and on this day, I grew impatient. "I'll never understand why *hispanos* here see the mistakes Blacks make so clearly, but when whites make mistakes, they're totally blind to it. And whites are the ones who have power, they're the ones wanting to deport them and pass laws against them. They're the ones who really want to oppress *hispanos* and migrants!" In a moment of seriousness—this whole conversation was all the more frustrating because Claudia seemed to think it was hilarious—she said, "But, the thing is that from my point of view it's *them* here at work."[1]

Although she did not recognize the ugly history within which the "nigger" slur is embedded, Claudia knew that it was a pejorative designation for African Americans. Availing herself of an opportunity to malign Michael, our African American supervisor whom she detested, Claudia's comments suggest that while she must inhabit a subordinate status while she is employed at Swine's, if she were to leave the job she would exact her revenge, bidding farewell to Michael with this most insulting epithet. Her explanation in a moment of seriousness conveys clearly that from her most proximate and immediate perspective, African Americans—not whites—are the real oppressors at Swine's.

This chapter examines how the composition of the authority structure mediates the intergroup dynamics described in previous chapters. At

Swine's, African Americans have made small inroads into positions of authority at the level of the shop floor, mostly as crew leaders but also as department supervisors, and less so as division superintendents. Latinas/os have made fewer inroads, and whites still dominate most supervisory positions as well as higher levels of management. Given the dynamics discussed in the preceding chapters, it is important to consider how the ethnoracial composition of the authority structure conditions intergroup relations on the shop floor (Reskin, McBrier, and Kmec 1999). In particular, an African American–dominated authority structure exacerbates Latina/o workers' perceptions of African American workers' privilege, and this resentment is expressed in racialized terms. While I worked in the Loin Boning and Packing Department, the authority structure shifted from African American–dominated to white-dominated. Therefore, I had the opportunity to study how this shift affected Latinas/os' perceptions about how the composition of the authority structure magnifies or undermines the privileged position that African American workers are presumed to enjoy. In addition, as discussed later in the chapter, I also worked for almost half of my time in the Marination Department, where the composition of the authority structure was different.

Most Latinas/os in Loin Boning perceived that the new white superintendent was fair, treating all workers equally (*parejo*), unlike his predecessor. Some workers celebrated a white superintendent because to them this meant that finally "*morenos* would have to work like we do." The implicit association between whiteness and fairness—meaning that all workers would be treated the same—ran strong among Latina/o workers. Ultimately, however, because the white superintendent intensified labor discipline and redoubled the oppressive exploitation of *all* workers, a few Latina/o workers showed signs of redirecting their grievances from racialized resentment of African American workers' privileged position to the deterioration of working conditions for all. Very little research has considered the role of the composition of the authority structure in shaping intergroup relations, even though this is a key dimension of the social organization of labor.[2]

The first section of this chapter discusses Latina/o workers' perception that the privileged status of African American workers was augmented when African Americans also occupied positions of authority, especially when they were at the helm of the authority structure in the Loin Boning and Packing Department. The second section discusses how their perceptions were affected when the African American superintendent of Loin Boning, George, was replaced by a white superintend-

FIGURE 9. View of the packing area of the Loin Boning and Packing Department, showing the staircase to the supervisors' office.

ent, Don. The third section shows that rather than viewing *hispanos* who occupy positions of authority more favorably than either whites or African Americans, some Latina/o workers singled them out as the most oppressive supervisors of all.[3]

LATINA/O WORKERS' PERSPECTIVES ON
AN AFRICAN AMERICAN–DOMINATED AUTHORITY
STRUCTURE: THEY FAVOR *MORENOS* "BECAUSE
THEY ARE THE SAME RACE"

As her comments in the encounter that opens this chapter would suggest, Claudia was certain that Michael, the African American floor supervisor, and George, the African American superintendent, gave preferential treatment to Black workers:

> Michael shows favoritism toward *morenos*. The jobs for the *morenos* are less difficult. And he will never turn down a *moreno*'s request for permission to leave work. I think Michael is racist. Same as George. He can see a *moreno* being lazy and he won't say anything to them. Michael fired Don Anselmo [an older Latino worker] a few weeks ago when he refused to stay

late, which he would not have done to a *moreno*. Poor Don Anselmo threatened to have his "good friend" Arnold Schwarzenegger intervene on his behalf!

Cristina too was certain that Black supervisors treat Black workers more favorably than they treat Latinas/os. In her explanation, this favoritism is based on their supposed understanding that Black workers will do the work according to their own prerogatives, not those of any supervisor, as will *hispano* workers:

> If a *negro* is a supervisor and has workers on the line that are the same race, they treat them differently. Because they know how they are, and they know that if they say something to them they're not going to change. Whereas we will.

Clara, among the minority of Mexican workers at Swine's, was unequivocal in her belief that supervisors gave African American workers privileged treatment. Moreover, she tied this differential treatment to her belief that supervisors—and African Americans in general—assumed that all *hispanos* lacked authorization, and were therefore more inclined to accept poor working conditions:

> They don't stick the *morenos* from here [the United States] on the line.[4] Because they can't take it. There are very few *morenos* on the line. But there's always that racism [from African Americans], because they know we are not from here. And because for them every *hispano* doesn't have papers.

Ana, a Honduran worker in her forties, turned quickly to her perception that African American workers receive privileged treatment from supervisors, especially from African American supervisors, when I asked her how Latina/o and Black workers get along ("not very well"). And like Clara, she also felt that African Americans view Latinas/os as outsiders who do not belong:

> Most *morenos* look at us *hispanos* like we're strange insects. Like you have to be from here [the United States] to be viewed favorably. There are plenty of *moreno* people who have a good heart, but there are people who have a bad heart. I've seen it and experienced it. We have some *morenas* that work with us. If they don't want to do something . . . When I first started working here I had problems with some *morenas* because they lost a cell phone.

After accusing Ana of stealing their phone, a misunderstanding exacerbated by their language barrier, Ana was taken to the supervisor's office to speak to George, the African American superintendent of Loin Boning and Packing:

> George became angry because they had wanted to beat me up. George got angry because he knew deep down that I wasn't capable of stealing a cell phone, nor did I speak English well enough to tell them that I did not have it [as they claimed I had]. George had a talk with both of the women because they said they were going to wait for me in the parking lot to beat me up. I was going to fuck them both up! When I was leaving work, I took my *chaira* [sharpening steel] with me. Actually, George accompanied me to my car. But I was still ready with my *chaira*. He told me to put it away, but I didn't believe him, since they're the same race. So, yes, you encounter a lot of problems with *morena* people.

Even though George took her side in the matter, refusing to believe the Black workers' accusations, Ana had nevertheless suspected he would take their side, since they were "the same race." Her comments also resonated with the strong feelings of exclusion from American Americans that Latinas/os have reported in other studies (Marrow 2011). Like some of the Latinas/os interviewed by Helen Marrow in North Carolina, who prefaced their views about how African Americans treat them with a balanced assessment of the group as a whole, Ana vacillated between saying that some African Americans have a "good heart" and some have a "bad heart." But the thrust of her comments suggests, much like Marrow found among her Latina/o respondents, that she feels African Americans treat Latinas/os as foreigners who do not belong—"strange insects" who are not "from here."

In eleven years of employment at Swine's, Leslie, a Honduran worker, had never gotten a point for missing work, a feat that is beyond spectacular. She was happy to report that supervisors did not give her a particularly hard time. Although she noted that supervisors harangue workers for going to the bathroom, she blamed workers who take overly long bathroom breaks for bringing this discipline on themselves. Nevertheless, Leslie had no doubt that supervisors treat *negros* preferentially and that *hispanos* always get the most tongue lashings. She felt this was the case especially when the department was run by an African American, George, even though George never treated her poorly:

> I've never been treated badly. They [supervisors] know who they're going to chew out. But sometimes there are people, workers, who take advantage. Let's say, now, they're controlling who goes to the bathroom and when. I only go for like five or seven minutes, but others will be in the bathroom for twenty minutes. Like I said, supervisors fulfill their obligations. Sometimes they go

overboard. They treat people badly. But they are also being pressured. Some-times I think that there is preference. There are people who don't do anything, just pass the time walking around. It used to be that there was favoritism toward the *negros*. With George. But I would be lying if I said he ever scolded me. No supervisor has ever scolded me. The Americans—those *moyos*—had the easiest jobs and they got paid more, supposedly. And for us *hispanos* it has always been more . . . You can see the racism toward us *hispanos*. They always scold *hispanos*, but never Americans, because of racism."

Leslie was certain that supervisors—especially African American supervisors—treated Black workers preferentially on the shop floor, giving them easier and better-paid jobs and scolding them less. She asserted this despite the fact that she herself had never personally experienced a scolding from a supervisor, African American or not. Regardless of whether Leslie developed this view by observing a pattern of treatment of which she was an exception, or whether she merely internalized this view from the claims of other workers, it was a perception that informed her assessment of the status of African Americans in the workplace.

LATINO/A WORKERS' PERSPECTIVES ON A WHITE-DOMINATED AUTHORITY STRUCTURE: "THINGS ARE GOING TO BE EQUAL NOW"

The particularly racialized character of Latina/o workers' resentment became clear when a white superintendent took over as head of the authority structure in Loin Boning and Packing. If Latina/o workers felt that Black workers occupied a privileged position at Swine's because they shared, with all native-born workers, the advantages of being "from here" and especially of being American, then one would not expect their perceptions to change when a white superintendent took over. But this was not the case. The universal perception among Latinas/os was that a white superintendent, not sharing any racial affinity with Blacks, would negate some of the privileges that the Black workers had previously enjoyed when laboring under a Black authority structure. Clara laid out this general perception succinctly:

> Donny is *parejo* [equal] with everyone. He doesn't care what you are, whereas George was more patient with the *morenos* and maybe demanded more of others. But not Donny. He is *parejo*. He punishes everyone the same. George wasn't *parejo* and Don is.

Natalia, a Honduran worker in her forties, framed the issue within the broader context of the dog-eat-dog world of surviving at Swine's:

There is a lot of selfishness. Because there [at Swine's] people don't care if they make you look bad or get you in trouble. There people are just out to save their own skin. They [supervisors] want *hispanos* to be working. If a *negro* doesn't want to work, they let him be. But now that Donny is there, he's *parejo*.[5]

Leslie, who believed that African American and Latina/o workers were treated differently by George, the African American superintendent, even though she had never felt personally targeted, agreed that the climate had changed with Don:

It has changed because this American, this *bolillo*, now he is *parejo* with everyone. He scolds *negros, blancos,* and *hispanos* alike. I haven't heard people say anything about him, and he's never said anything to me. But I see that he comes down from his office to keep an eye on the work.

Interestingly, Cristina did not think that white supervisors would display the same biases as African American supervisors, if only because there were so few white workers at Swine's. In her explanation, then, whiteness is associated with fairness, but perhaps only because white supervisors lack a corresponding white workforce to whom they can show racial favoritism. Her comments imply that the affinity is racial, not about shared status as Americans. She explained this when I asked her whether the same affinity she thought existed between Black supervisors and workers would exist if the supervisors were white:

If the supervisors are white? If they're American? I don't think they would have a preference, because there aren't many Americans there, same as them, who are white. For example, how many are there in Packing?

For Claudia, who was blunt in her view that African American supervisors treated workers differently, and that they were especially oppressive in their treatment of Latinas/os, the shift to a white-dominated authority structure was reason to rejoice. Like most other Latinas/os at Swine's, Claudia believed that Don was *parejo* with everyone. But whereas this new equality between workers—equality in being treated like animals[6]—caused some workers to redirect their attention away from the supposedly privileged position of African American workers and toward the deterioration of working conditions more generally, for Claudia things were different indeed: "Things have changed with Don." Seeing my distress during our conversation in the encounter that opens this chapter, Claudia later tried to console me, saying she only hated two *negros,* presumably Michael and her coworker at the *tortuga*, Lauren, whom she also loathed. In fact, Claudia's many racial commentaries were altogether contradictory. One day she would distance herself from the claim to hate all Blacks except for two, then on other occasions make blanket condemnations of African Americans. The weekend before our conversation at the *tortuga*, we were at her house cooking *pollo en crema* when she told me of her great delight at her perception that Don was making African Americans work like everybody else:

> I have it up to my eyebrows with the *moyos*. They don't work! And everyone has to work *parejo*. I like how Don is doing. I like how he is making everyone work. You see that Janice doesn't spend the whole "test" [a special order run] sitting down like she used to. George didn't care. He wouldn't say anything to her. Now she has to do something. That *moya* doesn't work. And the one at the machine [her African American coworker at the *tortuga*, Lauren] doesn't work. Now we'll see what she does.

I tried to argue with her but she was quite charged, though she did offer her view of the exceptions to her general statements about African Americans: "It's not all of them. I'm not going to say it is. I think Thomas works hard. That *moyo* works hard. And Vincent, despite what anyone might say about him, he works. He's not a perfectionist but he gets the work out." I tried to counter that there are not any lazy people at Swine's—that everybody works hard. I admitted there were some people who practically killed themselves, but maintained that that should not be necessary. Illustrating precisely the internalization of the logic of exploitation—she was a veteran of Swine's, having worked there for ten years—Claudia made it clear to me that the only option is for African Americans to work like "everybody" else. She defended Don's speed-up of the production process, telling me it was both good and necessary, and endorsed Don's firing of workers who "don't want to work": "No! Everyone has to work the same. How are we ever going to leave work? We have to finish. And all of us have to work *parejo* for that to happen."

Whereas the transformation of the authority structure made Claudia delighted at the prospect of African American workers having to work like "everybody" else, Reina responded to the changes brought about by the new white superintendent somewhat differently. Reina was, like many others, sure that under Don, all workers were treated equally. But she did not feel especially heartened, since the working conditions at Swine's had become even more unbearable. Indeed, she intuited in the new superintendent's actions his intentions to squeeze workers even more, and in doing so make himself look good to the higher-ups:

Right now, the new supervisor wants to be the hero. He wants to get people out earlier, not like George. Now he wants to get everyone out at six thirty at the latest. But he's wanting to speed people up a lot. Now they don't want to let anyone go to the bathroom, especially the line workers. I don't think that's right. We haven't signed any paper that says we don't have the right to go to the bathroom. That is everyone's right. He doesn't want anybody to go to the bathroom because he wants to get the production out earlier. In other words, he wants to be the hero, not like George. This Don is a great friend of Larry's [the Human Resources manager]. He didn't like George. They clashed. So I heard he pushed George out so that Don would take over. George would ask for more workers, but they would never give him more. But they do with Don, since he and Larry are friends. Do you think George *wanted* to leave work at nine at night?

She seemed to feel sympathetic to George, but still believed that "at the end he had become racist." Nevertheless, she viewed Don as merely self-interested, using workers to meet his ever-expanding goals for faster production:

George used to be different, but at the end he had become racist. He only protected the *negros*. He turned sort of racist. I imagine it's because since he is *negro*. Up to now, this guy Don is *parejo*. He's *parejo* with *moyos* and with *hispanos*. Because Don wants to look good. What he cares about is getting the production out earlier. At the end, I guess George didn't care since he could never come out looking good. This guy tries to look good. What he is concerned with is getting the production out. With me, this guy wanted me to keep packing bellies, but I refused because I'm pregnant. So while he is using people [he is nice to them]. But now that I'm in the condition I'm in [pregnant] . . .

Most Latina/o workers who perceived a general deterioration of working conditions under Don did not articulate their resentment in racialized terms, whereas the articulation of racialized resentment of an African American–dominated authority structure was common, no doubt in part because Blacks being in charge was thought to magnify the privileged position of Black workers.[7]

LATINO/A WORKERS' PERSPECTIVES ON
LATINAS/OS IN POSITIONS OF AUTHORITY:
"THE *HISPANO* IS THE ONE WHO MAKES AMERICANS
BEHAVE THAT WAY WITH US"

Latinas/os did not necessarily have a more sanguine view of Latino/a supervisors. In fact, some Latina/o crew leaders and supervisors were widely despised by Latinas/os, who expressed even greater dissatisfaction with their treatment of workers given that they were Latinas/os themselves. Interestingly, the only Latina/o worker who said she did not perceive differential treatment between *hispanos* and *negros* was Rita, a recent hire who had worked under white supervisors at hog farms in North Carolina for much of her time in the United States. On the other hand, she was certain that *hispano* supervisors were the worst: "They want to humiliate the *hispano*. Among *hispanos*, we should get along, not treat each other like animals."

Reina, who was discussed in chapter 5, thought that Latina/o workers lacked solidarity and felt similarly betrayed by Latinas/os in positions of authority. Interestingly, her discussion of this followed on the heels of saying she wished Swine's had a union that would protect workers, especially *hispanos*:

> The way they treat us and the way they treat Americans [is different]. Because they know that we put up with it. They try to humiliate you. There's another Pig Corporation where they have an organization that protects people, the union. My sister-in-law works there. I would like for one of those organizations to come here so that we would be protected, especially *hispanos*. Because there's a lot of discrimination here. They humiliate you. There is racism. The union protects people. The company is the one that doesn't protect you. The company people are the ones who are the corrupt exploiters. And let me tell you, sometimes it isn't so much the Americans, the owners of the company. Rather, sometimes it's other *hispanos* who are selfish. You know Héctor. He's *hispano*, just like us. And he doesn't have papers either. He's Mexican and he works with Honduran papers. The *hispano* is the one that makes Americans behave that way with us the most. It is *hispanos* who stick the knife in you. The *hispano* isn't solidaristic [*unido*]. We should support each other, since we're all the same. Good for those who were able to fix their papers, but they might have family members who are in our same situation. But sometimes it goes to their head.

Clara also found *hispano* supervisors to be particularly "brutish," even a Mexican floor supervisor who had worked with and befriended Don at Berkshire Chicken and had been hired at Swine's at the same time:

> The new floor supervisor, Javier, walks around giving orders brutishly. Sometimes I think they demand more out of us. Too much! Even to go to the bathroom. It feels like we're in prison. You have to get permission to walk off the line. They scream at us and they don't even know the work. There are days when your knife is sharp, and it's good. But there are other days that, no matter how hard you try, you can't get your knife to sharpen.

Even Leslie protested that some Latina/o supervisors were especially abusive toward Latina/o workers. She mentioned this in regard to Héctor, the Mexican crew leader disliked by most workers, Latina/o and African American:

> Héctor used to be bad, but he has changed because the Dominicans [several Dominican boning line workers] went to complain upstairs. It wasn't right, how he treated us, even with foul language. "*Pinches huevonas!*" [Fucking lazy asses!] he would say to them. And he would scream at you, but not anymore. He knows he has to take care of his job. If they fire the bigwigs, they'll fire a rat too!

"WE CAN'T ALL BE INDIANS": AUTHORITY AND RESISTANCE IN A MAJORITY–AFRICAN AMERICAN DEPARTMENT

Joe, a supervisor, was angry with us one day about a month into my job in Marination. Like a disappointed father, he huddled us together for a stern speech, which he began by declaring: "We can't all be Indians." He explained that certain people were supposed to do certain jobs and others shouldn't try to get in their way. For example, Davis and Tanesha were operating the machine that runs the meat, and only they should be changing the roll of plastic film. "So we can't all be chiefs," he concluded. "I thought you said we can't all be Indians?" I countered, with malicious delight.

Compared to my time in the Loin Boning and Packing Department, a somewhat muddier picture emerged during my earlier seven months in Marination. Over that period of time, the department was headed by a white supervisor, Joe, and overseen by an African American crew leader, Clyde. The majority of the twenty-some workers—all newly hired to staff the department's night shift, as the department had recently reopened—were young African Americans. The sharp compositional contrast with core production departments such as the Cut Floor and Loin Boning was likely due to several factors. For one, the majority of new hires at this particular time were African Americans, native-born Latinas/os, or older Latina/o migrants with legal status, and some whites or Indians (as these persons self-identified). Second, Human Resources personnel had a tendency to steer African Americans, young and old, into the further processing departments, which had shorter or inconsistent working hours, and into the later shifts. Of the handful of Latina/o migrants employed in this department, almost all were in their fifties—much older than the average in the core production departments, where Latinas/os were the majority.

Whereas Clyde was a longtime employee who had cut his teeth boning hams on the line, Joe was a career management type who had previously been a supervisor at the nearby Big Bird plant. Because Clyde and many African American workers shared common backgrounds, being local to the area, they occasionally demonstrated rapport with one another that Clyde clearly lacked with the Latina/o workers in the department, whom he referred to uniformly as Mexicans despite the fact that they were mostly Honduran, Salvadoran, and South American. Yet Clyde, often frantic and distressed by the pressures of running production, was the butt of jokes and the target of African American workers' vitriol and protestations, not their affections, and his frequent sexual harassment of women workers led to resentment among that contingent. African American workers in Marination were not shy to denounce working conditions or supervisor treatment they deemed harsh or unfair, and these accusations were aimed squarely at the perpetrators.

A few weeks into my job in Marination, work orders were mounting, and we had been told we would be working several weekends in a row. At the start of the shift, workers were huddled around a prep table where we wrapped "chunked and formed" tenderloin tips with bacon and seasoned them with various herbs, stacking these in tubs that we then ran through the line to seal in packages to be boxed for shipment. I mentioned that word was we'd have to work the upcoming weekend (again), and Jay muttered, "Slave drivers!" Our crew leader Clyde offered a tepid apology to the group about his behavior the night before, when he had become furious that the product count was twice wrong. Macy was unforgiving, probably because Clyde had blamed her for the miscount and angrily told her to "go home." By the time I had gotten to the locker room that night, Macy was denouncing Clyde, asserting that she was going to school and wasn't going to work at Swine's forever and he couldn't talk to her that way. Later in the shift, Clyde and Jay got into a shouting match because, as Jay later explained to me, he was ignoring her questions. Over the next few months, Jay and Clyde would butt heads over his rude manner of addressing her and her refusals to abide by his demands.

Some days after the "Slave drivers!" comment, I was at the bacon wrap table with Macy, Carmen, Jay, and others when Clyde walked over and hovered at the table. Macy commented to his face that he was "like our slave master watching over us." He just gave her a deadpan look. Macy's blowups with Clyde continued in the subsequent days, and even months: "This is just a hobby for me. I just work here for pocket change! I go to school." This time Clyde had grabbed Macy by the arm and angrily pulled her to a labeling station to work. She insisted she was going to ask Joe for a transfer the next day because she "didn't want to work for Clyde any more." Months later, Macy was still working in Marination, now pregnant and still at odds with Clyde, who she repeatedly claimed was on crack. Joe gave her a disciplinary write-up for acting "ignorant and belligerent" toward Clyde. When I gave Macy a ride home after work some nights, she complained that, while she liked everyone we worked with, she hated Clyde and Joe.

Jay and Macy weren't the only ones to call out our supervisor, and especially our crew leader, for perceived transgressions and abuses. One afternoon, we were prepping a new order of meal kits consisting of precooked noodles with sauce and meat packs in plastic containers, labeled and couponed and ready for supermarket shelves. Valerie was at times working—it even seemed to me—at quite a leisurely pace. Clyde noticed and instructed her to "tighten up" and work faster. Valerie was unfazed, barking back, "This ain't slavery. Don't try to work me like no damn slave." She and Kim repeated this with gleeful purpose. "You're daydreaming over there!" he fired back. "I'm allowed to daydream!" And once, in the smoke break room, I overheard Deandra and Davis talking about Clyde, making fun of his role vis-à-vis Joe—Clyde sometimes referred to Joe in warnings to us as "the man"—by calling him an "Uncle Tom." Over the course of my seven months working in Marination, Deandra became progressively intolerant of Clyde because he sexually harassed her, and she felt that he sometimes treated her poorly because she rejected his advances. Deandra did not feel entirely defenseless, though: "He done messed with the wrong bitch. My brother kills people just for fun."

Clyde was also in the crosshairs of Ms. Angie, an older African American worker. One evening, Clyde huddled us to explain the "game plan." When I said I couldn't hear him, Clyde lowered his head in immediate frustration. He explained that he wanted the same people on the same jobs as the Saturday before. Thinking we were going to be reassigned to work in the Pork Chop Department, Ms. Angie asked, "Can I go to the nurse?" because it was too cold for her in Pork Chop. Clyde, in typical fashion, dropped dramatically to the ground in exaggerated frustration, leaving Ms. Angie furious. In the smoke break room after this, she angrily declared she wanted to see "that motherfucker" somewhere so she or her "old man" could knock his ass down, leaving me and three Black workers in stitches.

Joe lacked rapport with anyone despite his corny attempts early on. The mostly young, mostly African American women in the Pork Chop Department, which he also supervised, ridiculed his awkward paternalism, referring to him as their "daddy," while in the Marination Department Lydia would often tell one of us coworkers that "*tu papá*" said this or "*tu papá*" said that. One evening some Marination workers were sent to work in Pork Chop, sorting chops by weight for a standing order with the diner giant Pancake Express. After a USDA inspector walked through and saw a worker placing product on a non–product surface, Joe gathered everyone for a warning: If he got a second "NR" (noncompliance) this week for the same issue, he was not going to be happy. Nicky, a young African American lesbian who is kin to Maya, cracked us up as she translated for the group that "Joe said he was going to be a bitch tomorrow." A short while later, coming back from break, Felicia told some of the other workers what "your dad" said. I laughed, telling her that some workers in my department also called him this. Apparently, his paternalistic camp-counselor style was known across departments.

In short, Black workers in the Marination Department at times took aim at their supervisors but did not seem to think that, as African Americans specifically, they were treated any better or worse than the Latinas/os. My Black coworkers had no great love for Joe, and they seemed to view Clyde with particular disdain, perhaps in a similar fashion to my Latina/o coworkers in Loin Boning who expressed a strong dislike for Héctor, their Latino crew leader. Being both Black—or both Latina/o in the case of Héctor and workers in the Loin Boning and Packing department—made the sour taste of subordination that much more acrid, but maybe also that much easier to verbally spit out.[8]

In contrast, Latina/o workers' resistance to authority was sometimes expressed in strongly racialized form, either by the particular language chosen to chastise Clyde (but not Joe) or by ethnoracially framing their grievances vis-à-vis Black workers. Because product orders for this department were inconsistent, the hours varied wildly from day to day. There would be weeks when workers would not make forty hours, and get dismissed after a few hours of work. Then there would be weeks when the later shift didn't end until two in the morning. Other weeks we would be sent to work in other departments, like Hamboning, Pork Chop, Dry Salt, or Bacon Slice. This rollercoaster of instability irritated workers, but also necessarily generated ambivalence in work motivation. Workers needed hours in order to make a decent paycheck, but it could also be a quiet relief to be done early. Carmen and Lydia frequently complained that Joe or Clyde let "the *negras*" go home early and kept them working—or kept "the *negras*" on working and sent them home early—depending on their particular aggravation at the time.

From the very moment our cohort was hired to work in Marination, Carmen apprised me of her loathing for Joe. It turned out that Joe had been her supervisor at Big Bird Turkey, where she said he made a habit of "firing everyone—*americanos, blancos, morenos,* and *hispanos*—with particular gusto." Joe appeared to similarly dislike Carmen, constantly picking on her work performance, and even asking me on various occasions to confirm his observation that she worked too sluggishly or carelessly (I did not). Carmen told the story of a Black man named Jason who was fired after working at Big Bird for many years. She said everyone except Joe liked Jason, who was very funny, and she spoke affectionately of him, saying if she knew where he had gone, she would get him to come work here. She said Jason would talk back to Joe. When Joe would ask him where he had been if he went missing, he would say "in Evisceration, looking at women." She said everyone was happy when Joe got fired from Big Bird Turkey, where workers called him *el ruso* ("the Russian," a play on his real name). Lydia confirmed his reputation, having worked at Big Bird too, and though she knew him only from a distance, she said he was "racist against *hispanos*," treating Hispanics poorly. In contrast, she believed that here, "*como los negros predominan*" (since Blacks are predominant), he had calmed down. "Why?" I asked. "*Porque el sabe que las negras lo hacen trapo*" (because he knows that the *negras* will tear him to shreds) and "they can charge him with racism and he would lose his job." I said I doubted he had any greater appreciation for Blacks than *hispanos*, which she agreed with, but said perhaps he still "didn't dare."

At the end of shift one night, I found Carmen chatting with Edgar's wife in the locker room, complaining that "*pinche negro*" Clyde had let her go early. When we walked out together, she repeated that the "*pinche moreno*" had told her to go home. Earlier, after dinner break, Carmen had come back a few minutes late and made a funny face to him in humor, but he had not cracked a smile. As I walked with Carmen to her car, she lamented having had to leave Big Bird Turkey, where she was so settled and work was close to her house. She could do every job there, she told me, though she didn't like to do evisceration because it was so hot. *Pinche ruso* messed up her job there, she said, but she was going to wait the six months she was told it would take to clear her record (of the two write-ups, because at the third write-up you get fired and cannot ever come back) and then probably reapply.

Just a few weeks into my job, I was walking into the locker room to get ready for work and Capreese informed me that we had to work on Saturday *and* Sunday. I expressed frustration because I had made plans for the weekend, and Valerie was not happy either. Capreese remarked that it's double pay on Sunday, as Tanesha and many others did throughout the day, with some excitement. I was told to mention the weekend work schedule to Edgar and Carmen, since I frequently translated for them, and Edgar was aghast: "Slaves! Slaves! That's how they treat us! I've never worked a Sunday in my whole life! Sunday is sacred. Didn't you finish high school?" "Yes," I responded. "Well, don't you know about workers' rights? Workers have a right to a day off!" Later, he was still fuming at the meat grinder, threatening that if this "*negrito*" (Clyde) said one more thing, he was going to throw off his gloves and leave. I tried to redirect his anger, pointing out that it was Joe, the supervisor, who really had power and authority over us. He said, "Yes, Joe, that guy is who I'm talking about." But Joe is not a *negrito,* and I don't think he had intended any irony. Edgar, whose own work performance was derided by Carmen (she joked that Edgar "worked with such patience you would think the meat he was handling was eggs"), seemed to think that African American workers didn't work as hard as others. One night Edgar was bringing tubs of tips to the bacon-wrap table and said to me and Carmen, "You all work more than the *moyos*!" And when I went to get more meat from him, I asked him to help me take a bin, and he replied, "No, let the *moyo* do it." I looked around and only saw David coming, which was interesting because Edgar knew he was (at least part) Honduran Garifuna.

If an African American worker got into an argument with a supervisor, my Latina/o coworkers might respond with a generalization about African Americans' temperament. One particular shift started out at the bacon-wrap table with Carmen, Jaycene, Ms. Angie, and Lydia. We were seasoning and wrapping with bacon very stinky globs of meat chunks referred to as tenderloin tips that had been ground by a machine and pumped into cylinder-shaped plastic bags, frozen overnight, and sliced into "filets." When the line started to run, Jay went to work her scale, where she weighed and labeled packaged product. Not long after, I heard Macy shouting something. I looked over and Jay signaled to me to go work the "spec" ("product inspection," as the machine spits out sealed product). I walked over, but by then Clyde was there, telling Ms. Williams to work the spec, to which she said no, she was working the scales. It devolved into a sort of face-off, and Clyde ran off to get Joe, but not before telling me to go back to my station, that "she has no right to tell you to do anything." I was silent, head down, and walked back. Then I walked back to Jay, and she said, "It's okay." Joe appeared on the floor and took Jay away, probably for a reaming or a write-up, and she was sent home. It turned out that Capreese had gone to the bathroom and left the "spec" unattended without telling anyone, which caused a mess and people had been hollering for someone to cover. When Clyde told Jay to do it, she apparently declined, telling me later, "that's not my job description." Lydia turned to me and said, "Some *morenas* are not easy."

In mid-February 2010, Lydia, Carmen, and I picked up Macy—I had been giving her rides for months—and on the way to work we stopped at a Chinese restaurant to get food. Lydia and Carmen had spent the night at my apartment due to a snowstorm, and we had stayed up late drinking and talking about work, especially about sexism at work, which Carmen referred to as *"racismo."* In regard to Clyde's constant frantic berating of workers, Carmen said (and Lydia agreed) that it was "as if we were slaves; he's just missing the whip." Macy complained about her incident with Clyde and Joe the night before, and how Joe said she acted "ignorant and belligerent" toward Clyde. "Oh yeah, Clyde is an angel," I said sarcastically. Carmen laughed, saying, *"Un angel negro"*—meaning an angel of darkness but also a Black angel. Macy said she'd heard something about "Black" so I explained the irony, and she said she understood. I told Macy that Carmen calls Joe *"Satanás"* (Satan) and how I had joked that Clyde was *"Satanasito"* (Little Satan), which she got a kick out of. Carmen scolded me in Spanish, saying I should not tell her these things because *"ellas son todas traicioneras"* (they are all traitorous) and may snitch. I turned to Macy: "Don't snitch," to which she replied, "Do I look like a snitch?"

On days when mistakes or mishaps occurred while running product orders, workers could become frustrated, especially if they perceived that it was not their fault and if it meant redoing the work. On one such occasion we encountered numerous snags while running an order, including that Clyde had the wrong "use by" date label (the date was four days short), so we (mostly I) had to redo about seventy-five boxes after they had been iced and sent down the line for shipping. To this, Lydia remarked by my workstation, "This Black son of a bitch doesn't know what he's doing!" On another similar occasion, as discussed in chapter 3, Lydia remarked, *"Por eso es que no quiero tener un negro parado al lado mio porque llegando o saliendo la joden*" (That's why I don't want a Black standing next to me, because coming or going they are going to fuck up).

In short, although the pattern was more muted in Marination than in Loin Boning and Packing, Latina/o workers perceived certain advantages to being Black, and their efforts to resist subordination were also racialized in particular ways. Specifically, while Clyde's blackness was frequently mentioned in condemnations of his actions as an authority figure, Joe's whiteness went largely unmentioned despite the contempt held for him. In contrast, African American workers directed their antagonism squarely at supervisors, never articulating grievances against Latina/o coworkers in ethnoracial terms but demonstrating an awareness of racial subordination in their protestations of supervisors' treatment.

CONCLUSION

The demographic past and present of Swine's collide. While the highest levels of management have remained closed to African Americans, Blacks have made small inroads into supervisory positions on the shop floor (though long after the early 1990s, when they were the vast majority of the regular workforce). It would be a mistake to overstate the access to positions in the authority structure that African Americans have achieved at Swine's. Most superintendents and supervisors there are white. To my knowledge, Swine's had only one African American superintendent (George) for any of its five or six divisions (department groupings). At the level of department supervisor, of which there are about fifteen positions, three to five were filled by African Americans. There was a somewhat greater proportion of Blacks in crew leader positions—the lowest rung in the authority structure above regular production worker. Their modest advances into management have come at a time when the workforce has shifted and is now predominantly Latina/o.

Conventional sociological and economic analyses of the economic effects of immigrants on native-born workers posit the idea of "complementarity" as a beneficial feature that neutralizes possible negative effects (Smith and Edmonston 1997), a view also consistent with a version of ethnic succession through replacement dynamics. In other words, given differences in human capital, for example, a majority of native-born workers are poised to be "pushed up" by labor migrants whose low levels of human capital make them most suitable for bottom-rung positions.

Yet, aside from the troubling presumption that such a "complementarity" will be viewed as beneficial by everyone involved, it also obscures the possibility that grievances inherent in this arrangement will motivate the relationships among those so engaged. Indeed, this is precisely the social dynamic I observed, and one that other scholars have documented as well. A hotel manager interviewed by Roger Waldinger (1997, 382) noted that when "the old black attendants" (presumably those having long tenures) moved into floor supervisor positions as the regular workforce became predominantly Latina/o, this became "a source of tension."

If scholars are right to propose that African Americans—indeed, any group—are likely to do better on average when some of its members occupy positions of authority, then we could expect this to hold true at Swine's (Cohen and Huffman 2007; Elliott and Smith 2004; Zatzick, Elvira, and Cohen 2003). For example, Philip Cohen and Matthew Huffman (2007) show that having women in higher-level positions of authority in a workplace improves the status of women employed there and reduces gender inequalities in outcomes such as earnings.[9] Organization scholars have also shown that having members of one's own minority group in positions of authority reduces turnover (Zatzick, Elvira, and Cohen 2003). But even before we might expect this dynamic to work for African Americans as Blacks, we would expect it to work for them as Americans. Scholars who study low-wage employers' attitudes toward different groups of workers have found that such employers view African Americans as having the same sense of entitlement to a certain effort-reward standard that they perceive from white workers, making native-born workers least suitable to work that involves the greatest subordination (Waldinger and Lichter 2003). Whether this "privileged" treatment of Black workers resulting in part from an African American–dominated authority structure reflects a real dynamic or whether it is merely Latinas/os' perception scarcely matters at Swine's. What is important is that Latina/o workers there are certain that American Blacks occupy a privileged position in the workplace, and that their positions of authority augment their status while contributing to disparities in treatment between Latina/o and African American workers. In this way, we confront a dilemma that appears to pit Latinas/os against African Americans, at least from the perspective of Latinas/os' interests, as they perceive them, not from the perspective of African Americans.

Some readers may wonder whether this analysis substantiates "split labor market theory," an alternative to the Marxist-derived perspective that the divide-and-conquer strategies pursued by capitalists are more or less intentional devices to discipline and isolate workers. Split labor market theory in particular highlights the role and interests of "privileged" workers in fueling group-based conflict in order to maintain their group's higher status (Bonacich 1972; Bonacich 1975; Bonacich 1976). My findings suggest that managers need not be particularly active or intentional in the production of distinctions on the shop floor in order for these to be manifest and consequential. Of course, it may be happening here and elsewhere as well, especially at the hiring phase when workers are initially assigned to specific departments. But nor do "privileged" workers, in this case African Americans, need to be the primary drivers of conflict. This presumption again is founded on the narrow focus of researchers on competition-based threat, rather than other sources of conflict such as those highlighted in this and the preceding two chapters.

CHAPTER 7

Exclusion or Ambivalence?

Explaining African Americans' Boundary-Work

It was the end of July 2010, and Arizona's SB 1070 was making waves in the news and across Latino/a communities in the United States. Cristina grew more anxious by the day, wondering aloud how these kinds of laws might make her life more difficult, and the ominous mood perhaps foreshadowed her imminent arrest. But work was work, and like any other day, workers crowded around their raw material, chitchatting now and then to break up the disquieting monotony of ceaseless labor. Late in the afternoon, Cristina and Rosa were trimming extra-meaty baby back ribs at the table, and Linda, an older African American worker, was bagging their work, throwing it on the line to be sealed at Claudia's machine. I was nearby, bagging ribs from the pan by myself, and Linda kept calling me over to translate because their choppy pantomimed English wasn't quite working. Cristina had just joked with Rosa that she needed to marry her so she could get residency, since Rosa was a legal permanent resident. Linda called me over and said, "Tell Cristina she needs to get married to *me* so that she can be able to stay here." I told Cristina, and she made a funny, perplexed face.

Linda said, "Wait, what about her husband? Her husband also needs to marry someone so he can stay here, too!" I went along with their plot, but cautioned, "Actually, it's not going to work because even if she married you in one of the states that allowed same-sex marriage, she still couldn't get her papers that way." Linda didn't understand: "But you can in some states get married. I know because my niece got married to a woman. Where was it?" I offered, "Massachusetts has it, Hawaii." Linda wondered, "Maybe Philadelphia?" We all cracked up and Cristina laughed too, scandalized at the suggestion of same-sex marriage. Linda continued, "We got to get someone to marry her husband." Cristina exclaimed "*Un hombre!*" Linda gasped and returned to her marriage proposal, saying "No, we got to get him a woman and we got to get Cristina a man to marry. Tell her I was kidding about that whole thing, about her marrying me or whatever." Linda must have thought Cristina had been offended, but when I translated this to Cristina she protested, "Oh no, tell her she already asked me, she already promised!" Linda laughed heartily at this. Thomas joined us at the table, and Cristina told me to tell him, "I'm going to marry him so I can get papers." Thomas chuckled, "*Mucho dinero!*" I said, "Thomas, did you say it's going to cost her a lot?" He said "Yeah, a lot!" Cristina eyed him askance, smirking.

The playful exchange between Linda and Cristina at the rib-trimming table was comic and a bit surreal, but not altogether unusual. Although many of the chapters in this book have spotlighted the negative content of symbolic and social boundaries that Latina/o workers draw vis-à-vis their African American counterparts, the modal tendency in their daily interactions with one another was simply to get along and not infrequently to make one another laugh. Moreover, the intense resentments that punctuated Latinas/os' discursive repertoire about African Americans were largely absent from that of African Americans toward Latinas/os. Indeed, in this opening encounter, Linda and Cristina do not just have a friendly and funny interaction. Rather, Linda's suggestion that Cristina should marry *her* in order that she "can stay here" conveys poignantly her sympathy for Cristina's situation as an unauthorized migrant and even a desire, however lightheartedly expressed, to assist Cristina in regularizing her status. On numerous occasions throughout my time working in Loin Boning and Packing, Linda would affirm that "I don't think it's right for them to get rid of them just 'cause their papers ain't right." And recall from the encounter that opens the introduction to this book Linda's conviction that Cristina *should* be able to get her authorization issues worked out. Referring to Cristina by her real name, Elvia, Linda had said, "Elvia here needs to start being real. Elvia needs to start being Elvia. So how much would it cost for her to get her papers?" Linda and other African American workers expressed views about Latinas/os that were rarely unambiguously exclusionary, as the scholarship built around competition theories would predict, and more typically ranged between ambivalent and sympathetic.

If competition is the linchpin of theories that explain intergroup relations in the social and economic realms (Waldinger 2000; Hamermesh and Bean 1998), a key concept used to explain intergroup relations in the political realm, especially within and between subordinate groups, is "linked fate" (Telles, Sawyer, and Rivera-Salgado 2011; Sánchez 2008; Kaufmann 2003). Scholars interested in the question of minority political coalitions understand that there are opposing perspectives on the likelihood of such political unions, which in the long run are contingent upon the nature of mass attitudes and behaviors (Kaufmann 2003). On the one hand, competition perspectives emphasize that minority groups may come into conflict if they compete for economic resources. On the other hand, differing perspectives focus on the overlapping objective group interests among subordinate minorities with respect to policy preferences. The concept of linked fate refers to the extent to which members of a group feel their individual fortunes to be tied to the plight of the group as a whole. Scholars posit that a high level of linked fate among members of a subordinate group is likely to produce solidarity with members of other subordinate groups (Sánchez 2008). In turn, linked fate is derived from the assumption of homogeneity among members of a group, making felt commonality among group members a prerequisite to a sense of linked fate (Sánchez 2008; Dawson 1994). Critically, this concept was developed with reference to African Americans in order to explain their high levels of solidarity on policy issues, despite growing differentiation by class (Dawson 1994).

This chapter demonstrates the significance of this concept, which, coupled with the expanded idea of racial alienation delineated in chapter 4, helps to explain African American workers' views of Latinos/migrants. Although Lawrence Bobo and V. L. Hutchings's (1996) original formulation unnecessarily limits the analytic utility of racial alienation by presuming that African Americans are the most racially subordinated group, here that assumption is relaxed in order to instead consider how particular contexts such as the workplace condition the sense of racial alienation. This allows for an understanding that within the context of Swine's, Latinas/os—not African Americans—are the group whose members feel most aggrieved and therefore most racially alienated. The concepts of linked fate and racial alienation together serve as useful heuristics to explain the softer and less negative boundary-making actions of African American workers toward Latinas/os.

The objectives of this chapter are threefold. The first section gives the reader a more robust impression of the boundaries that African Americans articulate vis-à-vis Latinas/os working at Swine's, since much of the focus thus far has been on the reverse. The second section anticipates potential challenges to the findings about African American boundary making vis-à-vis Latinas/os, considering evidence that gives some support but largely neutralizes such challenges. Several interactions with African American workers are discussed. These at first glance appear to support an argument for their exclusionary treatment of Latina/o migrants, but upon further analysis—and in the context of the full range of boundaries that African Americans do or do not articulate vis-à-vis Latinas/os—bolster my findings. The third section seeks to explain why, despite the expectations of competition theories and in contrast to my findings regarding the symbolic and social boundaries drawn by Latinas/os, African American workers at Swine's do not draw very strong nor very negative boundaries vis-à-vis their Latina/o counterparts. I consider whether the relatively weaker and less negative boundary-drawing action on the part of African Americans vis-à-vis Latina/o workers might be indicative of something more than African Americans' generosity of spirit. Alongside other explanations, it might suggest that Latinas/os' perceptions about the place Blacks occupy relative to them in the workplace are at least tacitly experienced as such by African Americans themselves. This condition would imply that within the context of Swine's, Latinas/os experience the highest degree of racial alienation, and therefore the greatest susceptibility to feelings of competition or, as already argued, other sources of deprivation that are likely to motivate conflict. In combination with the highly developed sense of linked fate among African American workers, which scholars would hypothesize to extend to other subordinate groups, these factors explain my findings regarding intergroup relations.

"ME, PERSONALLY, I DON'T GIVE A SHIT. THEY COME HERE TO WORK": CHALLENGING THE PRESUMPTION OF COMPETITIVE THREAT

On a Monday in mid-September, I was doing "Louisiana" with Vincent at a table at the ribs station. Vincent trimmed the ribs, which were weighed, sorted, and dumped into a giant pan by Alma and Alexis. I packed eighteen ribs to a box, then lifted each fifty-pound box and moved it to the line, where it would be stacked by workers for shipping to its destination. These ribs were a long-standing order with Louisiana Barbecue, a restaurant chain specializing in ribs, and most days several workers were assigned to trim and pack "Louisiana." Vincent, an African American in his late twenties, was a talker. He could talk indefinitely on a wide range of topics, from personal experience ("My girlfriend is getting on my nerves!") to sociopolitical issues ("What is the difference between Dominicans and Puerto Ricans?"), though he just as often was engaging in inappropriate sexual banter ("What you wearing under there, boy shorts?").

On this day, our conversation as we worked began with a personal turn, as he recounted his drug bust and the two years he spent in jail, and I ended up telling him about my alcoholic father. At some point, we discussed Cristina. Ever since Cristina was arrested by police at the factory about a month before, Vincent had asked me about her from time to time. The Thursday before, he'd asked me for the second or third time whether Cristina was "going to get exported." No, I said. ("*Como manzana!*" [Like an apple!] Cristina exclaimed with a chuckle when I told

FIGURE 10. Worker on the pallet jack hauling vats of carcass remnants.

her later what Vincent had asked, confusing "exported" with "deported.")
And he brought her up again on Monday, asking, "You talk to Cristina?
How's she doing? Is she all right? Is she working?" I was unsure of his
motives, and leery about creating more troubles for her, so I answered
evasively, "She's doing a little cooking, a little caring for kids. Why?"
"Just wondering how she's doing. What about her husband?" I said I
didn't think her husband had much work these days. In fact, her husband seemed to be going through a long spell of unemployment or
underemployment, unable to secure work as easily without papers as
before, perhaps feeling disillusioned, and drinking heavily. "Can she
come back to work if her papers get straight?" Vincent asked. "I guess,
yeah, probably," I answered, not sure how her having been arrested at
work for identity theft—and fired summarily—would affect her eligibility to regularize her status, if a legalization program finally came to pass.
I remembered Cristina telling me how many workers at Swine's had been
working under assumed identities when Hondurans were granted Temporary Protected Status in 1998, and again in 2001, and had the names
on their hard hats change from one day to the next. "What did she get
arrested for?" Vincent asked. "Identity theft," I said plainly, not wanting

to talk about her business but realizing that most people at the plant knew this much, so it wasn't a secret. "So her papers ain't straight?" "Yes, that's the issue," I said, wondering why Vincent was acting like this was news to him, or whether he actually hadn't known for sure.

"Me, personally, I don't give a shit. I mean, they [immigrants] come here to work and whatever. What bothers me is when they come here and they work but then they send all their money home." I found it strange that his concern was not with economic or political competition, but migrant remittances. That got us talking about why "they" do that. "In a way it's because a lot of people don't feel like they really belong here," I offered, trying to explain migrants' dual orientations and their attachments to family in origin countries. "I don't agree with that," he snapped. I tried not to be preachy, but inevitably I was. "But they have good reason to. A, you have all these hate groups and even regular people telling them 'we don't want you, go home.' B, they don't have citizenship, and don't have the same rights and status as citizens do. And they have little hope of gaining that. C, all their family is over there." "Well, I can understand that. But I don't agree that they should feel like outsiders," Vincent maintained. Then he made a poignant comparison to his own situation—a situation shared by a growing proportion of working-class and poor Black men, whose citizenship is increasingly proscribed. "Just because I got picked up on a drug charge and got busted for selling dope once, I don't have the right to vote." I said, "I disagree with that, too. I think felon disenfranchisement is another way of screwing Black people."

Vincent expressed the kind of ambivalent sympathy toward Latina/o migrants that other African American workers articulated, even when directly asked about their views regarding crackdowns on undocumented migrants. Sitting in my kitchen one evening for a formal interview after I left my job at Swine's, I asked Vincent what he thought about immigration enforcement policies such as the 287(g) program, which many North Carolina counties participate in, which make the apprehension and deportation of unauthorized migrants far easier than ever because police officers can inquire about immigration status when a person is stopped on suspicion of any sort of lawbreaking. Again he drew parallels to his own encounters on the wrong side of the law, displaying a confused ambivalence about illegality as an embodied status produced by law:

> So you mean, deporting is legal or illegal? That's like me defending selling dope. You know what I'm saying? If it's illegal, what can you do about it? If

you're doing something illegal and you get caught, you get caught. So, I mean, that's similar to me. If I'm doing something illegal and I get caught, I get caught. I can't complain about you trying to increase something to catch something that's not right. That's how I see it. If it's not right, it's not right. But just 'cause they said it's not right, don't mean it's right. But if they [authorities] are doing it to enforce the law instead of trying to make it stricter on the law, I mean, they do that every day. It's not just immigration or illegals. They do that on everything every day. So, I mean, that'd be hard for me to try to explain. I wouldn't understand that. I wouldn't understand how to explain something like that because if it's illegal, it's illegal.

Vincent's ambivalence with regard to the illegality of immigrants vacillated between adherence and resistance to the constructive force of law as both coercion and ideology (Haney López 2006 [1996]). His repeated comparisons to his own proscribed citizenship as a felon suggested an empathic basis for his wavering. I prodded him to elaborate, wanting to better understand his views on unauthorized migrants:

I mean, I can understand. Now, how they say about Honduras. Honduras is poor. Obviously. I mean, very poor. I can understand if that would be a draw. I imagine that'd make a person feel real good to be able to work, take care of themselves, and their family, their whole family. I mean, it makes me feel good every day to be able to take care of my family. That's my immediate family in my house, and my other two kids that's outside my home. I mean, it makes me feel very good to do that. But for you to be able to . . . that's the little difference I make because my money doesn't go as far, but it covers enough. But for a person to come here and work and support a whole family back there, that's got to make them feel good. I understand that, but I don't understand. You know what I'm saying? I mean, if you're legalized, you're legalized. If you're not, you're not.

Ultimately, Vincent conceded to an inherent human drive to survive, and therefore to migrate in spite of any obstacles in order to support one's family:

A person got to eat no matter what. I mean, you're gonna survive. That's human nature. Just wanting to survive. I mean, like you said, of course I would try to go to Canada [if the economic situation in the United States were dire] 'cause I don't want my family living like this, and I mean, you do whatever you have to. I mean, you'll try to do it the right way, but if it don't work the right way, you'll do it whatever way you can do it.

Vincent's qualms with "Hispanics" were a far cry from the "immigrants take jobs that belong to us" line that competition perspectives would expect. Aside from a fixation on the idea that the problem with immigrants is that they remit all their earnings, Vincent's other gripes were superficial, even comical. "Why do they throw their dirty toilet paper on the floor?" he asked me with disgusted wonder. Or, "Why do Hispanic guys touch each other's asses all the time?" I asked him what he thought Americans' views of Latinas/os were in general, especially of immigrants:

> I mean, to me, everything's alright. I've always been a person—I'll be friends with anybody. I can speak with anybody. I can do whatever with anybody. I can hang out with anybody. That's how I've always been, but you can get bad vibes off any race or any person. I can't say it's really a race thing or whatever. I mean, you know, it's some stuff that you see at work that shouldn't happen. Like in the bathrooms. That's ridiculous to me. The tissue in the bathroom! That's just fucking ridiculous, man. I don't understand. I try to understand that shit, but I don't really understand it. It's like, I asked one of my homeboys. He's actually married to a Mexican chick. I was like, "Man, why in the hell they do this shit?" [throw dirty toilet paper on the floor]. He was like, "Man, I think the plumbing's just bad in Mexico so they don't really do that, actually." That's the way he put it. I mean, why the hell they don't put trash cans in the bathroom, so you can put it in the trash can? Or let 'em know there's . . . they can . . . it will flush. But then, I don't know. I see a lot of them as hard workers, but then, like everybody else, you got lazy asses in every bunch. You got ones that's gonna be good in every bunch, and you have some that's bad in every bunch. A lot of the Hispanic males, most of them are alcoholics. That's a stereotype. They have DWIs and all that shit. I mean, you do get that, but every race has stereotypes. So, you can't take it as a bad. That shit happens in every race.[1]

Quite unlike Latina/o workers' views of African Americans, Vincent generalizes that Latinas/os are for the most part "hard workers," but this does not seem to suggest that other groups are not. After all, he says, "you got lazy asses in every bunch." And his use of the term "stereotype" in qualifying his other views of Latinas/os—that many of the men are alcoholics—and his concession that "every race has stereotypes" suggests a much subtler mode of boundary making than what prevailed among Latinas/os.

Thomas, an older African American worker, had a distinctly pragmatic perspective on African American–Latina/o relations. At work, he tended toward a quiet laboriousness. He could be conversational, if someone else started it. Thomas was generally easygoing and solicitous, rarely engaging in the sort of cranky skirmishes or playful banter that most workers succumbed to in order to pass the time or when work took its toll on their spirits. His views perhaps reflected these more general dispositions. Over beers one weekend afternoon at Wing World,

I asked him about how African Americans and Latinas/os got along at work:

> There are more Hispanics in my department than there are Blacks. But, as I said, once people are trained, everybody knows their job, what they're supposed to do, what it's gonna take for us to get the job done. Everybody wants to go home. We work together, pull together for the common cause, and go home. On the boning lines, on the loin lines, you got Blacks and Hispanics working side by side. You have to trust the man next to you because their knife is [right there]. You got to have a certain amount of trust and camaraderie to get the job done without injury.

Thomas's comments indicate a sense of solidarity and shared purpose among workers, whether Latina/o or African American. Working together cooperatively "to get the job done" and get it "done without injury" demands trust and camaraderie, a view that is consistent with having a sense of linked fate among workers of different ethnoracial groups.

But African American workers were not entirely ambivalent about their perceptions of Latinas/os as coworkers. In fact, those working in the predominantly Latina/o Loin Boning and Packing Department experienced a number of difficulties trying to get along in the workplace. Some African Americans felt that Latina/o workers shunned them, teased them, or otherwise sabotaged their work effort, an issue other scholars have documented in the retail, hotel, restaurant, and light manufacturing industries (Waldinger 1997). Vincent discussed his experience working among mostly Latinas/os on the boning line when he was first hired, describing a pattern of marginalization and noncooperation:

> When I first started, I started straight on the knife. Actually, I was on the line, cutting the little bone out. I didn't really understand it, and then you know, it's mostly Hispanics in front of that line. I mean, busting on the line period, it's Hispanics, and a lot of the guys, they don't really want to help you. If you're not Hispanic, they don't want to help you. I mean, I feel that way. That's what a couple of other people said. They'd rather send a Hispanic guy over there than send somebody else over there. When I first got there, I met a couple people there, see they alright, but when I first got there, they wouldn't help me at all. I'm talking about at all, and then they'd run to the bathroom, stick me on line. First thing! Stuck me on line with the knife, trying to cut this mess. He gone to the bathroom, one of the other ones gone to the bathroom, I'm stuck there. I don't know how to do this mess. Know what I'm saying? Billy [crew leader] kept standing back and watching, but they kept leaving. So, I'm trying to help out, but I got frustrated with it. And then so I think I told Billy, I was like, "Man, I can't do that mess, man." I

was like, "Right now, I can't do it. They're not trying to teach me for anything." Actually, I ended up cussing one of the dudes out. I asked him, "How you do this? How you do that?" He would never speak to me. He'd say something in Spanish, that was it. I don't remember his name, but he's right there. So, I think he didn't speak English, so I messed around, he would never help me. I asked him, he'd act like I ain't saying shit. So I ended up getting frustrated 'cause he kept looking at me, shoving the meat back to me, and I'm like, "Man, fuck that. It's your shit. You won't help me? What I'm supposed to do? Either you're gonna show me, or stop getting a . . . " I mean, I'm not saying it and keep getting madder and trying to do something that I can't do, but you know how to do it, but you're not trying to show me how to do it. So I told Billy, "Man, I can't do this, man." 'Cause I ended up meeting the dude. I mean, I cussed the dude out! And he acted like he didn't understand. Like, "Whatever." So, I didn't think he understood either. They started to put me on the other line, on the ham line. I did that for a while. I actually got something I could do. It started making me feel better about myself, more confident about myself, 'cause the other job, I couldn't get it. But now, I could go up there. I think I can do it now 'cause I know how to sharpen my knife and all that, so it's no problem now. But before, I struggled, and then with no help, that was too frustrating.

Even after working at Swine's for a year, Vincent dealt with taunts from Latina/o coworkers.[2] One day, I was bagging ribs by myself when Vincent asked me to come help him open up rework in the back. Rework consists of product that has to be re-bagged and re-run through the *tortuga* because it hasn't been properly sealed. "That bitch is slow!" he said about Bo, the rotund African American worker who opened up "leakers" behind the *tortuga*. "I mean, there's a lot of work back there, but he's slow." I was helping him open up rework when Eros, a Honduran packer, began to rush us and joke about our work effort. Eros kept twirling his finger, as in, "go go go," and telling us to hurry up. Vincent said to me, "You know I ain't racist, right?" "Why do you say that?" I asked. "This guy really gets on my nerves." "Okay, and?" I prodded. "Well, I think some really racist shit." I kind of laughed, asking, "Like what?" "I don't know," Vincent responded, trailing off, never telling me what "racist shit" he conjured up when Eros pressured him. Right then, Eros did the *huevón* (lazy ass) gesture with his hand about Vincent. "He knows I'm mad, and then he goes and says shit." Eros was just laughing, enjoying this provocation. Crucially, Vincent was fully aware of the racialized nature of the resentment that Eros's taunts caused him to feel, but in the end he did not articulate it to me or to Eros.

Susie, an older African American worker who had recently transferred into Loin Boning and Packing from Hamboning, had a similar experience working on the butt-boning line. Susie was bagging loins with me one evening after her work on the butt-boning line was finished, and recounted a pattern of harassment from her Latina/o coworkers. Every time she went to the bathroom and left her plastic arm guard behind until she returned, one or more of her Latina/o coworkers would fill it with scraps of meat and fat. Worse, Susie was hurt that Eugenio would tell her, "Black women no good. Hispanic women good." He would tell her to watch Latinas work so she would learn how to do the work properly. This sort of marginalization of Blacks and their targeting for pranks has also been documented in Latina/o-dominated workplaces in the furniture manufacturing, restaurant, and hotel industries in Los Angeles (Waldinger 1997). In the hotel industry studied by Roger Waldinger (1997), such pranks were common and employers referred to them as a way of explaining why Black workers would not make it in these jobs. One hotel manager reported: "Housekeeping is all Hispanic: you try to put a black in there, they won't last. They intimidate. We have had situations where we have different cultures that get put together and we lose the person. The Hispanic houseman will play pranks and not deliver linens to the black housekeeper and then they don't get the beds made" (382).

AFRICAN AMERICAN WORKERS' "REAL" VIEWS ABOUT LATINAS/OS: WAS I MISSING SOMETHING?

But perhaps Black workers were simply very good at hiding their true feelings from me, since I was not African American. Maybe African Americans did indeed draw boundaries vis-à-vis their Latina/o coworkers that were just as salient and as negative as those drawn in the other direction, but I was just somehow not privy to it. This possibility occurred to me throughout my fieldwork, but especially in the wake of Cristina's arrest for identity theft.

Several days after that event, I coordinated a collection box to help defray Cristina's impending court costs. As workers streamed back into work after lunch, I stood by the doorway leading from the cafeteria to the production floor with the box. Workers passing by chipped in a dollar or two, sometimes asking what the collection was for. Patricia, an African American worker in her thirties, stopped and asked, and I explained that it was to help Cristina with her bond and court costs following her arrest. "I can't believe y'all!" she exclaimed. "After all the time she worked here!" Her remarks were ambiguous, but clear in insinuating that collecting money for Cristina was not a legitimate cause. Perhaps Patricia thought that Cristina should have enough money herself and that we shouldn't be collecting for her, or maybe she felt that Cristina didn't deserve the collection considering that she had "made out" with a lot of money while working at Swine's under an assumed identity. Patricia did not donate to the collection box for Cristina, but other Black workers did, including Bess and Thomas.

Other African American workers also expressed a certain ambivalence around the legitimacy of Cristina's arrest. One afternoon, I was bagging loin ends when Bess, an older African American worker, called me over to the boning line where she worked on the whizard knife. She asked me about Cristina. I explained what had happened and Bess was responding sympathetically when all of a sudden she said, "How could she do that? She knew that was going to catch up with her!" But after this moment of judgment, Bess reiterated her sympathies: "She got kids though, right? She got a family." I told Bess it was especially unfortunate for Cristina because upon being arrested and summarily fired by Swine's she lost all her earned time off, which could have been cashed out, as well as her attendance bonus. "Oh they [the company] don't care, they don't care. They don't care about anybody," she said. Critically, Bess expressed some sympathy for Cristina's situation, despite the fact that in general Bess felt that Latina/o workers looked down on Blacks and talked about them in negative terms, as she had confided to Ileana in the encounter retold in chapter 3. Her remark that management "don't care about anybody" conveys a sense of shared experience among *all* workers, much as Thomas's comments about the necessity for cooperation and trust among Latina/o and African American workers suggests.

Sometimes the vulnerabilities of migrant illegality were a source of humor among African American workers. Soon after Cristina's arrest for identity theft, Vincent and Adrienne made light of her circumstances, and that of other unauthorized workers who inhabit the surreal world of assumed identities. I was bagging ribs with Adrienne, a young African American worker, when Vincent expressed a desire to look me up on Facebook. I said, "You're not going to find me on Facebook because this isn't my name" [referring to the "Janet" on my hard hat]. Realizing my remark was confusing, I clarified: "No, it's my name, it's just not what people call me." Vincent and Adrienne proceeded to whisper to each other. "What are y'all saying? What's so funny?" I asked. "When the immigration bust happens, everybody's going to know your real name." They chuckled over this, but at the same time exclaimed, "That's so wrong, that's really messed up, it's not funny." Adrienne added, "That's why she had left that day with Cristina" [when I left work after Cristina was arrested to bail her out]. They chuckled again, but reiterated, "That's not funny." Although they were making light of Cristina's arrest, Cristina herself had frequently made light of the "artistic" name on her hard hat, as workers who labored under assumed identities referred to these, often to the amusement of Black coworkers. And crucially, their whispers and self-reproaches suggest a much softer, more self-conscious boundary making on the part of African Americans vis-à-vis their Latina/o counterparts.

Indeed, the muted tone of African American workers' suggestive comments contrasts sharply with the brazenly racialized denunciations of Latina/o workers. The latter were expressed on a regular basis by many Latina/o workers, and sometimes were expressed directly to African Americans, as in Cristina's remark to Michael about coming to work painted black so she wouldn't have to work. I asked Thomas and Vincent directly whether I had missed something, because African Americans did not identify me as Black, but rather as white or Latina. Perhaps this had inhibited their commentary to me or within earshot of me. As usual, Thomas responded matter-of-factly, understanding that my question was about whether he might have felt inhibited "because you're one of *them*":[3]

> I don't pretend to speak for everyone, but I don't have any problem working with Hispanics or any other ethnic group. I've always been about: You do your job, I'm gonna do my job, we'll get along fine. It's all about getting the job done. The sooner I can get out of there, the better. I really don't have any problem with Hispanics or other groups working, as long as they do their job. Now, you've got Hispanics, Blacks, and Haitians who are out there just for the paycheck. You gotta work together.

Once again, Thomas emphasized the need for African Americans and Latinas/os to "work together." I asked him to offer a counterexample to getting along with Latinas/os. Understandably, he pinpointed the language barrier as a potential obstacle to cooperative relations between native-born and foreign-born workers. "The Hispanics speak Spanish. Most native people, people born in this part of the country, don't speak Spanish. It's increasing now, but most Black people don't speak Spanish. Most Caucasian people don't speak Spanish. And Hispanic people don't speak English. So there is a communication gap. Being able to relay something to a coworker who might happen to be Hispanic or Haitian."

I asked Felicia, a young African American Pork Chop worker who had recently become crew leader, whether she had ever heard African Americans complain about Latinas/os at work or worry that they were "taking their jobs." She said that, while she has heard comments like that before, she does not hear it at Swine's. Here, she said, it's not about "your color or ethnicity." Actually, she said with a giggle, some of the African American workers in her department say they'd rather work with Latinas/os because "they'll get it [the work] done!"[4]

Vincent was even more blunt in his response, boosting my confidence that the patterns I documented were not the result of a concerted, coordinated, sustained effort on the part of African American workers to censor themselves around people who might understand what they were saying, such as me.[5] Ultimately, he returned to his main hang-up with Latinas/os: "the tissue issue."

> *Vanesa:* What about at work? I always try to keep my ears open and try to listen for any kinds of commentary, but I don't know if because I'm not Black, other Black people wouldn't necessarily share their thoughts. And because eventually most people knew that I was Puerto Rican, even though I look white.
>
> *Vincent:* Shit, I tell you!
>
> *Vanesa:* Yeah, well, maybe people wouldn't feel comfortable talking shit about Latinos to me, but maybe they do. And so I'm asking you, what do people say? 'Cause I'm not exactly clear.
>
> *Vincent:* It's basically the tissue issue. And then, I mean, I get a one-week vacation. If I was Hispanic from somewhere else and I decided I wanted to go home or say I was going home, I can get a month off, unpaid. Me, personally, I can't get a month off and say I'm going home. So, I mean, it's certain things I see as not fair, but then it just could be something that they are taking advantage of and I just don't know how to take advantage of it yet. Something that I might've overlooked, not being able to take advantage of it.

When African American workers lashed out at Latina/o workers in ways that could be interpreted as taking on ethnoracial dimensions, this tended to be in the context of having perceived a personal slight, not systematic deprivation in the configuration of workplace relations. And even Vincent's response to Eros's taunts demonstrates a substantial level of restraint, much as Jeremy showed in his response to Cristina's proclamation about coming to work painted black so that she wouldn't have to work. For example, after a tornado destroyed his home, Vincent accused Latinas/os specifically of not contributing to the collection box taken up for him. And Linda lashed out at Salvadoran worker Sara after the two got into a quarrel when bagging ribs together one day. Sara had been bagging ribs that Linda handed to her, some of which were meant to be packed in black bags and others in clear bags. Sara was not paying much attention to the distinction between ribs that had to be packed in one kind of bag or another, much to Linda's chagrin. When Sara held open the wrong bag, Linda passed her the right bag, annoyed that Sara was being indifferent. Sara snatched the bag from Linda and threw it back at her. It was at that point that Linda told Sara that it was good that "Obama wasn't going to give them papers," holding her fist up menacingly.

Such denunciations, however, were rare, and the ethnoracial identification of "Hispanics" in everyday complaints and grievances was remarkable for its absence. The African Americans' grievances within the workplace rarely took the form of contention organized and expressed in ethnoracial terms. When it did, it tended to manifest in defensive outbursts resulting from personal affronts. Remarks by Leticia—"*no todos son malos*" (not all of them are bad)—and Vincent and Thomas—"there's bad apples in every bunch"—illustrate the different tendencies in their orientations to one another. In this sense, the conclusion that Black workers' attitudes and behavior toward Latinas/os is sharply exclusionary would seem to draw on weak evidence, particularly in light of the fact that Latinas/os—not African Americans—engage in the boldest and most frequent boundary-drawing efforts. On the other hand, it is plausible that Latinas/os would single out African Americans as the most exclusionary toward them for several reasons: First, it could be a reflection of Latinas/os' own negative views of African Americans as Blacks, a status also devalued in their communities of origin, as argued in chapter 3. Second, given the relative scarcity of whites at the workplace, African Americans are for the most part the only other group Latinas/os interact with. And given the perception that African Americans occupy a position of privilege in the workplace relative to their own, conditions are ripe for Latinas/os to demarcate stronger boundaries against African Americans than the boundaries drawn by African Americans toward them.[6]

But still. Maybe if I had worked in a majority–African American department, I would have seen the inverse of the patterned dynamics I observed in Loin Boning. Maybe I would have observed African Americans drawing sharply negative symbolic boundaries vis-à-vis their Latina/o coworkers. This could have been the case if, by simply being the majority, African Americans found themselves in the position of being the most oppressively exploited—if only because as a majority they would be depended on to carry the bulk of the production process. Or, if the whole business of boundary drawing was just a question of volume, if the composition were reversed, the volume on Latinas/os' boundary making would be muted while that of African Americans would be amplified and reach my eyes and ears. Fortunately, I am able to consider the size of groups as a factor that may affect intergroup relations, as other researchers have argued (Olzak 1992; Marrow 2011).[7] Recall that in the first seven months of my sixteen-month-long employment at Swine's, I worked in Marination, a small (approximately twenty-five-person), majority–African American (80 percent) department. And I did not find this to be the case.[8] Instead, I found the same overall pattern of intergroup dynamics, but Latinas/os' boundary-making action was less frequently and less intensely expressed. The following encounters illustrate this finding.

One January evening, four months into my job in Marination, we were seasoning pork loin filets that we had stuffed with wild rice. I was tossing filets into a tub filled with garlic and herb seasoning alongside Carmen, an older Mexican worker, Lydia, an older South American worker, and Ms. Angie, an older African American worker. Tanesha and Kim,[9] both young African American workers, and Valerie, of mixed African American and Mexican descent, were seasoning meat at a different table. Lydia had just been over there briefly when Tanesha called me over and asked, "How do you say 'Black slut' in Spanish?" She and Kim offered something like *verde negra puta* and I corrected them, saying, "not 'green black slut,' just '*negra puta*.'" Chuckling, she asked, "How do you say 'ugly Black slut'?" I asked who they were trying to call an ugly Black slut, joking as I walked away that I knew who. "We're just trying to learn Spanish," one of them replied cleverly. They called me over again and asked, "How do you say 'bad breath'?" Feeling suddenly self-conscious about the foggy air leaving my mouth, I responded that "breath" is *aliento* and before I could continue, Tanesha jumped in "*Aliento*? Well, tell Lydia she got some *aliento*," laughing mischievously. Kim walked over sneakily to Lydia and repeated the word, giggling. "*Aliento!*" "That's mean," I said to Tanesha, watching as Lydia furrowed her brows at "La Princesa," as she called Kim, an ironic nickname that referred to Kim's perceived low level of work effort and demands at having her way.

A while later, when we had finished seasoning meat at one table, Lydia and I moved to help finish seasoning tubs of meat on the rack where Tanesha and Kim were working. As Lydia tried to put a heavy tub filled with filets on the small table where Tanesha was working, Tanesha resisted, blocking her path. Lydia insisted, muttering, *"negra cabrona"* (Black bitch) loud enough for Tanesha to hear. A short while later, Tanesha turned to me and said, "Lydia be talking junk." Lydia, perhaps stinging over the breath comment, was standing at our original work area looking bitter. Throughout the night, as I walked over to ask why she was sour, she simply snapped, *"Esta negra puta me tiene harta!"* (I'm sick and tired of this Black slut!). Tanesha too seemed pretty serious the rest of the night, leaving me to wonder if she was upset about her interactions with Lydia. Lydia was cranky, but Tanesha was getting on other workers' bad sides that night by talking junk. In the locker room after work, Ms. Angie was furious because Tanesha had called her out in public after she had used the bathroom, and laughed at her: "Hey Ms. Angie, aren't you gonna wash your hands?" "I don't come looking to get dick in my ass every time I come to work!" Ms. Angie had exploded. As we walked out together, Tanesha made another comment, prompting Ms. Angie to tell me, "I don't mind jokes, but don't have a laugh at my expense, I don't like that!" I suggested she say something to Tanesha. "I might," she responded, dead serious.

"GIMME SOME OF THAT BECKY!": WORKING THE BOUNDARIES THROUGH SEX AND HUMOR

In the Marination Department, much of our time was spent at a table wrapping bacon around filets, creations formed from "tenderloin tips" that had been ground up the previous day in a giant, slow-mixing vat and filled into cylindrical plastic bags, frozen overnight, and then sliced. We hauled tubs full of filets from the racks to our table, where we prepared to add value to these mushy blobs of meat. In our first days working here, our supervisor and crew leader informed us we were to take apart each strand of bacon that came in a pack or box—this was usually bacon not suitable for market for one reason or another—and lay the slices on the table. We were then to spray three shots of thrombin and twenty-seven shots of beef fibrinogen onto the array of bacon before individually wrapping the filets and stacking the pile of them back into the tubs. Of course, the cheap plastic bottles quickly stopped spraying properly, so we took it upon ourselves to pour inordinate amounts of "blood" and "tequila," or "red stuff" and "white stuff," as we came to refer to these substances, on our bacon. After completing a layer of bacon-wrapped filets, we would season the meat with peppercorn or garlic and herb—often covering the meat with fistfuls of the dust since there was no measurement device—stacking layer after layer, tub after tub until the order was filled.

Working in Marination among predominantly young African Americans, I learned that "Becky" was a personification of oral sex, the act itself named generically after a white-girl-sounding name which, for reasons not clear to me, is eponymous with fellatio. Given our frequent bacon-wrapping tasks, workers would sometimes shout out for more bacon when we ran out at the worktable. The two words, *bacon* and *Becky,* became one and the same, especially because the rapper Plies had recently released a song called "Becky" about requesting and getting oral sex. As the only person with the bilingual fluency to cross-communicate the subtle meanings involved in this elision, the task of translating for my Latina/o coworkers fell to me. The voice of Deandra, our African American assistant to the crew leader, reverberated through the department as she piped out, "Give me some of that beckoooon!" Soon Lydia was trying to join the chorus, cracking us up by belting out the fused "beckon" in a funny, voice-breaking way that I said sounded like a rooster.

Over the course of my seven months in Marination, Lydia alternated between outbursts aimed at "that *negra*" that were usually triggered by an incident on the line (e.g., Tanesha's insistence on stuffing pockets with meat even when the steel grate that made Lydia's "wipe down" job easier could not be found) and declarations about Tanesha's essential goodness ("How can I complain? The girl has been very good with me"). Typically their relationship was playful. A month after the incident recounted above, I walked up when Tanesha was bantering with Lydia about her husband and son. "Do your husband like dark chocolate?" she asked, amid muffled laughter. Lydia responded that her son likes "*chocha negra*" (Black pussy) (he is married to a Black Puerto Rican woman, whom Lydia dislikes). Over time, Tanesha took to calling Lydia her "momma" and they developed a relationship of some affection and trust, for instance lending each other small amounts of money and making sure each got back to the floor on time from breaks. In addition, Tanesha took to switching from time to time with Lydia, doing her "wipe down" job when Lydia could no longer stand to or when Tanesha's hands were too cold to stuff pockets.

Such crude humor was a common communication device between Latina/o and African American workers, who otherwise generally lacked a shared language through which to engage one another. Sex and laughter, it seems, have a universal appeal. Indeed, folklorists, anthropologists, and cultural sociologists have studied the role of humor and jokes, as well as sexuality, as crucial mediums through which intergroup relationships are channeled (Vucetic 2004; Nagel 2003; Dundes 1987; Lowe 1996).[10] In the Loin Boning Department, almost like a sort of call-and-response mantra, an African American worker would ask a Latina coworker, or vice versa, "You like *mucho chaca-chaca?*" to which she would respond "Every day!" to everyone's giddy delight. The function of this sort of humor was also, I believed, made possible by the fact that for the most part African Americans and Latinas/os remained segregated romantically, eliminating the jealousies and fights that seemed to be a common root of conflict. Nevertheless, I did wonder at times if it really was all in good fun.

One evening in late January 2010, our workstations in the Marination Department were set up in three- to four-person groups because we had been assigned to do "re-work" from the Pork Chop Department: emptying boxes of pork chops and reweighing, sorting, and packing the chops correctly. My scale was next to Deandra and Valerie, and Tanesha packed for me as Lydia and Carmen opened boxes of overweight chops and helped empty chops into our tubs. There was constant chatter between Valerie and Deandra, and a lot of sexual banter and joking. Deandra teased Terry, telling him to "shake that ass!" and at one point, when Lydia put her tongue in her cheek to simulate oral sex, she dropped down as though to give Marvin head. Terry and Marvin both chuckled, looking somewhat embarrassed. Deandra and Jessica asked me how to translate words and phrases like "dick," "rotten pussy," and "suck on my knob," but also innocuous words like "hello," "how are you," and names of numbers and colors. Deandra said she wanted to take a class to learn Spanish so people would say, "Damn, this Black bitch speaks Spanish!" Valerie, whose mother is African American and father is Mexican, remarked on how she is terrible at Spanish, and how she should already know it.

Out of nowhere during a lull, Lydia said to me in Spanish, "I stop and think, and wonder if these *negritos* spook themselves when they wake up in the morning. Because they're ugly! Everyone looks ugly when they wake up, but them, imagine!" These comments, while not entirely at odds with other things Lydia said, were confusing because I knew that she and Carmen also flirted with some of our Black coworkers, for instance Carmen saying she thought Marvin was cute, and Lydia teasing

Marvin about his *ñaño* (penis).[11] Maybe I was especially caught off guard because just that night, as we had had dinner in the cafeteria, a television blared news of the earthquake toll in Haiti, and Lydia had remarked with pity and said she would consider adopting a Haitian child.

Throughout the night, Lydia and Tanesha worked side by side. Lydia, who knew Tanesha was carrying on an affair with Dennis, kept placing her hand on Tanesha's belly and saying she was pregnant. Tanesha turned to me and said, "I've been a very bad girl. Naughty." She joked that "your boyfriend came onto me and I couldn't resist him, and I put it in his face and he went for it." Later Lydia came back to this tease, saying, "Too much *chiqui-chiqui*," something she said a lot and the others were familiar with. "Too much chicken," Tanesha said with a giggle. But Lydia was also affectionate toward Tanesha, and Tanesha seemed genuinely to feel the same, laughing heartily and letting Lydia tug on her fingers playfully.

Just a few days later when the machine broke down as we began to run tenderloin tips, Lydia and Tanesha engaged in some banter, as usual, and summoned me as their interlocutor and translator. Lydia looked over at Tanesha and Kim and could not contain her laughter, telling me to tell Tanesha that they looked like twins. I walked over and did so, adding, "I don't know why she thinks that." Tanesha smiled and said, "Tell Lydia she and Carmen look like twins. And when they smile they got the same teeth. Tell her to go stand by Carmen and smile." I walk back to Lydia, hardly able to suppress my laughter. Lydia was cracking up herself, and she told me to tell Tanesha that when I conveyed what Lydia had said, she and Kim had looked at one another to see who was the prettier "twin." She told me to tell Lydia something else about how she and Carmen "had the same teeth." Lydia said to tell her she said the twin thing first, so her comeback didn't count. Tanesha laughed, and then said, "Tell Lydia she look just like a leprechaun." "I don't know how to say 'leprechaun' in Spanish," I confessed, and we got a good laugh.

On another evening, coming back from break, Tanesha said something to "Mom" (Lydia) and they walked back to the floor, arms around each other's shoulders. In the locker room after work, when Lydia came out saying the bathroom smelled like rat poison and I told this to Tanesha, she responded to tell Lydia, "It's her stanky-ass pussy." Tanesha quickly added, "Tell her I'm just playing," and Lydia said "*más le vale*" (she better be). A few days before this, when they were teasing each other, Tanesha said she could "smell her stanky breath all the way over here," but I did not translate this to Lydia.

Among my Latina/o coworkers in the Marination Department, where 80 percent of workers were African Americans, there was a sense that being the majority and being Black meant that they defined the rhythms of the labor process. But as often as this became a source of friction among individuals—Carmen and Maya bickering about the pace or quality of each other's work, for example—it also became the motivation for Latina/o workers to step back and follow their lead—Carmen or Lydia would frequently time their return from breaks according to when they saw "*las negras*" hurrying back down the stairs.

One night in February, I was leaving the locker room with Lydia and Carmen after changing out of our work clothes, and we discussed my impending departure to begin working in Loin Boning as well as Lydia's possible move back to Florida. Carmen said to Lydia, "You're leaving, and then Vanesa is leaving, and I'm left here alone with the vampires." Lydia said, "At least we already domesticated them a bit." Carmen responded, laughing, "*o ellas a nosotras!*" "*No, nosotras a ellas,*" said Lydia. Carmen teased her, saying that Tanesha had her "*marcando paso*" (in lockstep). Lydia laughed, and said that "Tanesha has been very good people with me. But today she wanted me to stuff pockets with meat and her do the wipe down and I said no, *mamita*, that's your business." We laughed, and when I went to the bathroom, Tanesha, whom we had been calling Tani, was looking in the mirror and said, "What ya'll sayin' about me?" as Carmen walked out of a stall. I explained that Lydia said she was "*buena gente*" (good people) to her, and what she said about her request to stuff pockets. She smiled.

By March, when I was close to leaving the Marination Department to begin working in Loin Boning and Packing, Tanesha and Lydia were tight as ever—at least when it came to working together. At several points as we ran products one night, Lydia putting stuffed filets in pockets and Tanesha doing wipe down, I walked over to their station, peeking from behind a column, and found them playing: Tanesha tapping Lydia's helmet or wiping her hands on her apron, and Lydia playing mad. "*Cabrona!*" she'll holler. Tanesha laughed heartily at these games. I walked up and chatted with Lydia, leaning over the machine, and Tanesha interjected, "Don't be talking to my momma. Momma, come on!" and pointed me back to my station with mock authority.

But Tanesha's sensitivity to being talked about in Spanish reminded me of an incident with Jaycene, a Black coworker in her thirties from New York that I had become close to early on. The mistrust African

American workers felt about Latinas/os speaking Spanish around them, which other scholars have documented as well (Waldinger 1997), was made abundantly clear one night when Jay put me on notice, texting me that "I consider you a friend, but when you are with your Spanish people I feel something is being said about me. Please don't do it again."[12] Earlier that night, as we were changing out of our work clothes in the locker room, Lydia pointed toward Jay and said that she looked like a beauty queen from her country. I translated this to Jay, who responded simply, "Oh, okay." Although in this particular instance Lydia was not bashing Blacks, she occasionally spoke negatively about Blacks in general and had a proclivity for joking about Black coworkers to their faces, clearly letting them know that she was talking about them.

In sum, whether in the majority-Latina/o Loin Boning Department or the majority–African American Marination Department, I did not observe African Americans drawing especially strong or negative boundaries vis-à-vis their Latina/o counterparts. Nor did African Americans articulate these when asked in interviews about their experiences working with Latinas/os at Swine's or when I socialized with them in informal contexts outside of work. Instead, the thrust of African Americans' discursive repertoire relating to Latinos/migrants would more accurately be characterized as ranging between ambivalent and sympathetic. Certainly, the frequency and kinds of boundaries that African Americans articulate were in stark contrast to those in Latinas/os' discursive repertoire about them. The fact that African Americans' made only weak articulations of grievances in ethnoracial terms, compared to Latinas/os' strong articulation of grievances in such terms, is strong support for viewing Latinas/os, not African Americans, as the most racially alienated group at Swine's. In contrast, comments from African American workers such as Thomas, Vincent, and Linda suggest an ethos of solidarity among workers and a sympathetic ambivalence about immigration. The data laid out in this chapter suggests that the concepts of racial alienation and linked fate may help to explain my findings, which challenge the expectations of competition theories and the conclusions put forth recently regarding African Americans' exclusionary treatment of Latinas/os (Marrow 2011). Previous research has been narrowly locked into competition models, and has suffered from methodological limitations such as a reliance on interviews with Latinas/os to gather data on African American attitudes and behavior.

RECONCILING RACIAL ALIENATION AND
LINKED FATE AT SWINE'S

A flaw in Lawrence Bobo and V.L. Hutchings's (1996) elaboration of the racial alienation concept, a measure of the degree to which group members feel enfranchised or aggrieved, is its narrow construction and application to the case of African Americans, as argued in chapter 4. While nothing in their conceptualization of racial alienation precludes it from capturing the experience of groups other than African Americans, in practice the application of the concept suggests a subtle elision between the two. As a result, it becomes difficult to envision that racial alienation motivates the attitudes and behaviors of other groups, since—by fiat—African Americans are presumed to be *the* quintessential racially alienated group. Focusing instead on the *relational* dependence of intergroup dynamics patterned through the prism of white dominance moves us away from this snare. But how does the concept of linked fate relate to the concept of racial alienation? It would seem that the former is a precondition for the latter. Yet scholars predict that having a strong sense of linked fate reduces in-group members' prejudice toward out-group members (Sánchez and Masuoka 2010), while scoring positive on racial alienation is predicted to heighten prejudice toward out-groups (Bobo and Hutchings 1996).

In the context of Swine's—*within the social organization of labor*—racial alienation is felt most acutely by Latinas/os, who perceive that their group is the most oppressively exploited and that African Americans are a privileged group. At the same time, in the context of Swine's, as in the broader American society, African Americans appear to possess a heightened sense of linked fate, the result of a historical legacy that has intensified their feelings of commonality not just with one another but perhaps also with other subordinated groups. Importantly, though, these dynamics manifest themselves in this way on the condition that Latinas/os are indeed the most aggrieved group at Swine's.

Whether or not less-intense boundary making on the part of African Americans toward their Latina/o counterparts reflects a tacit concurrence that, as a group, African Americans are relatively more advantaged than Latinas/os at work is an intriguing possibility. But there is other supportive evidence for this finding—a finding that differs substantially from the expectations and conclusions based on competition and conflict models, of which the group position model is one variant. Survey research on

African Americans' attitudes about Latina/o immigration offers evidence that suggests that their views are softer than whites' attitudes toward immigrants, and less negative about Latinas/os than Latinas/os' views of them (Mindiola, Flores Niemann, and Rodríguez 2002; McClain et al. 2006; Yancey 2003; Thornton and Mizuno 1999). Further, Vincent Hutchings and Cara Wong have examined the immigration attitudes of African Americans and whites and found that, while the two have similar overall preferences, the mechanisms that underlie their positions differ substantially. Crucially, perceptions of competitive racial threat were found to be stronger predictors of the immigration attitudes of whites than of African Americans. These authors posit that claims about inter-minority conflict might be exaggerated, perhaps "because minority group members are more concerned with the competition emanating from whites rather than from other racially marginalized groups in society" (Hutchings and Wong 2014, 436). This theme comes up again in the discussion of the concept of prismatic engagement in the concluding chapter.

Although survey research has important limitations, including social desirability bias and a reliance on the articulation of attitudes that may differ from actual behaviors, surveys that provide adequate samples of African American respondents at least make attributions about attitudes and rationales based on African Americans' own statements, rather than extrapolating their attitudes and explanations from the depictions and perceptions of Latinas/os, a fatal methodological flaw with serious substantive implications. For whatever reason, social scientists have been too quick to accept claims about African Americans' attitudes and behaviors as conclusive fact. The theories (e.g., group-based competition) and heuristic models (e.g., sense of group position) that have generally informed research on intergroup relations have contributed to this state of affairs, as have the methodological dependencies (e.g., interviews) that constrain social scientists' research designs and blind them to implicit assumptions and subtle biases in their data.

Whatever collective experience individual Latino/a migrants may have been a part of in their origin communities, their defining collective experience as migrants in the United States is a fusion of disparate national and subnational subjectivities into an aggregate identification—by others most definitely, and increasingly by themselves—as *hispanos*. In contrast, although African Americans are by no means homogenous, they nonetheless share a collective history, memory, and in many ways experience that forged them as a group a long time ago (Eyerman 2004; Dawson 1994; Gurin, Miller, and Gurin 1980).[13] This is important to recognize, and helps to explain my findings in a number of ways. If African Americans indeed possess a strong sense of linked fate, for Latinas/os, who constitute a diverse assortment of national and subnational identities, a sense of linked fate is taking shape under very different circumstances.

Beyond Swine's, survey research on Latino/a linked fate has argued that a "brown utility heuristic," or a sense of commonality among Latinas/os, is a prerequisite for them to express solidarity with other groups, such as African Americans (Sánchez 2008). And yet, survey research finds this felt commonality among Latinas/os to vary substantially by national origin. At Swine's, Hondurans, Mexicans, Salvadorans, and other Latina/os come together as *hispanos* through their shared subordination, and their shared sense that African Americans occupy a position of privilege relative to their own. The particular circumstances that shape Latino/a pan-ethnicity, and which make possible an emergent sense of linked fate among Latinas/os at Swine's, therefore cast a dubious shadow on the potential for Latina/o workers to extend solidarity to their African American counterparts but do not appear to similarly inhibit African American workers' potential for developing a sense of linked fate with Latinas/os.

Conclusion

Prismatic Engagement: Latina/o and African American Workers' Encounters in A Southern Meatpacking Plant

"The thing is that this country belongs to whites. This is the whites' country. They are the owners of this country. In other words, this is their country."

—Claudia, Salvadoran worker

"The fact is that, despite what we designate as progress wrought through struggle over many generations, we remain what we were in the beginning: a dark and foreign presence, always the designated 'other.'"

—Derrick Bell, *Faces at the Bottom of the Well*

When Claudia stared across at our African American supervisor Michael and told me that when she ever left Swine's for good, she would say to him, "Goodbye, stupid nigger," I responded with indignation. I asked why she saw the misdeeds of Blacks so clearly, and why this was always articulated in racialized terms, when she never did the same with whites, even though whites were the real power holders in society. She responded sternly that when it came to the workplace, she felt it was Blacks who were the oppressors. But beyond this, she was puzzled by my concern. "What do you have against whites? The *negros* can do anything and you defend them." I tried to explain to her that I was against racism, and that the United States had a horrific history of oppression of Black people, from slavery to segregation and beyond. I told Claudia that I thought part of the struggle against racism was denouncing the unearned privileges of whiteness that contribute to the oppression of others. "No, why not? If I was white, I mean born in this country, I would be terrible," she interjected with her characteristically mischievous humor. Later, seeing my agitation, she urged me to "calm down," saying, "It's only like two Blacks that I hate," meaning, I supposed, Michael and maybe her coworker Lauren.

Throughout this encounter, Claudia asked me such questions as why "nigger" was such an offensive term to African Americans when she would not be hurt if someone called her a wetback. During my digressions into the history of American race relations, she would suddenly interrupt with a re-declaration of her parting words to Michael. I tried to engage her in a discussion about race and power in the United States, but she accepted without much in the way of protestation that "this country belongs to whites." At least as Claudia saw it, the power wielded by whites over others in American society is in some sense legitimate: at worst an established fact one should accept with resignation, at best a prerogative to which one can aspire.

This conclusion summarizes my contributions and research findings from my study of Latina/o migrant incorporation in the New South and intergroup relations. The first section outlines the major critiques of research on Latina/o migrant incorporation and intergroup relations addressed in this book. The second section discusses the concept of prismatic engagement, explaining how it contributes to the analysis of relations among subordinated groups in the United States. To do so, it builds on the major findings and arguments presented in chapters 2 through 7, which are summarized. The final section proposes a series of legal and policy interventions that begin to address, but do not exhaust, the social implications of these findings.

ADVANCING THE STUDY OF LATINA/O MIGRANT INCORPORATION AND INTERGROUP RELATIONS IN MATURING DESTINATIONS

In this book, I have reviewed key sociological perspectives on intergroup relations as well as major findings from recent research on intergroup relations in new migration destinations in the U.S. South. I have proposed extensions to analytical frameworks and concepts, including the model of ethnic succession and the concept of racial alienation, to make these better suited to the study of relations among subordinated in this case, Latinas/os and African Americans. I have also forcefully for situating the study of intergroup relations in the crucial social domain of the workplace, a context in which Latino/a migrants and African Americans encounter one another in structured ways that are likely to be meaningfully related to how they think about and act toward each other. Further, I advance the concept of prismatic engagement to capture the mediating role of white dominance in relations among subordinated groups, an issue of which scholars have not adequately taken account. There are also myriad critiques of the extant literature, and discussions of other scholars' critiques of that literature. I briefly discuss these first, before turning to a discussion of how my research advances our understanding of intergroup relations in the New South.

Most studies of Latino/a migration to the U.S. South are purely descriptive case studies (e.g., Zúñiga and Hernández-León 2005; Arreola 2004), though recent contributions by Jennifer A. Jones (2012), Helen Marrow (2011), and Laura López-Sanders (2009) make advances toward synchronizing theory with data on Latino/a migrant incorporation in new destinations. But in general, scholars have noted insufficient efforts to construct empirical designs that are linked to theoretical frameworks, to situate research findings in the broader literatures on migrant incorporation or race relations, or to propose new conceptual tools, let alone paradigm shifts associated with changing migration patterns that are supposed to represent a dramatic departure from pre-1990 patterns (Waters and Jiménez 2005). Researchers have acknowledged the need to synthesize explanations of intra- and intergroup interaction, study interethnic relations between minority groups, recognize the importance of objective conditions as well as perceptions and discourse, and study broad social processes in local settings in new destinations (Hernández-León and Zúñiga 2005, 253). These limitations have been accompanied by a tendency to pose analyses of incorporation processes in a simplistic good-versus-bad framework, particularly in terms of the quality of intergroup relations. That is, many studies give only superficial treatment to the substance of group dynamics and discourse, instead privileging often-tentative conclusions about how "successfully" Latino/a migrants are becoming integrated into the social fabric of their new communities. As an ethnography, this book is rich in descriptions of people, scenes, and processes, but I also attempt to link these to the larger analytical questions I set out to answer. I do not seek to define relations between Latina/o and African American workers as either good or bad. Rather, I attempt to understand the conditions that motivate the thrust, rather than the totality, of their relations.

In chapter 2, I framed the macro social and economic contexts that condition Latina/o migration to nontraditional destinations in the American South and their contributions to the region's agro-industrial complex as its premier labor force at the turn of the twenty-first century. I drew attention to the stories of Latina/o migrants, the chief protagonists of the remarkable transformation of workplaces throughout the U.S. South. Within this discussion, I incorporated a gender lens, focusing especially on the migration and labor market experiences of Central American women, who have received less attention than their male and Mexican counterparts thus far in the literature on Latino/a migration to nontraditional destinations, even though they form a significant and growing component of the phenomenon in the contemporary American South. I highlighted the paths that different migrants followed to arrive in North Carolina, and developed an understanding of these women and men as a crucial component of the agro-industrial labor force of the rural U.S. South.

This chapter then situated the theoretical debates about broad shifts in the ethnic/racial composition of industries and workplaces throughout the U.S. South and beyond, a process that has been referred to as ethnic succession, by examining how these changes occurred at the micro level of a meatpacking plant in North Carolina. I laid out the context of change at Swine's Inc.—the legal-political conditions, industrial strategies, and social network mechanisms that together shaped the process of ethnic succession at Swine's and probably at workplaces throughout the agro-industrial complex of the U.S. South (Schwartzman 2013; Stuesse 2009; Smith-Nonini 2003). In the early 1970s, twenty years after the then-small, family-run meatpacking plant began operations, dozens of mostly young, African American workers went on strike to protest unfair labor practices, and launched an (ultimately unsuccessful) campaign for union representation at the plant. By the early 1990s, when the United Food and Commercial Workers launched another effort at organizing workers at Swine's, small numbers of Latinos/migrants had started to work at the plant, mostly trickling in from the broader agro-industrial complex of animal farms and poultry processing plants where they had already been working. The union won the representation election, but this victory was overturned in court.

At the same time, the transformation of the Swine's workforce from majority African American to majority Latina/o accelerated rapidly. By the late 1990s, the shift was complete, and growing numbers of Honduran, Mexican, and Salvadoran women joined the ranks of workers after 2000. Throughout this period, employers' hiring preferences regarding workers were realigned to favor Latina/o migrants. But the 1990s was also a period when the animal production and processing industries in the area saw significant growth, and, coupled with a declining availability of African American workers, labor control through displacement of the incumbent African American workforce likely coincided with replacement and simple growth mechanisms. Critically, management's ability to enact its preferences regarding workers was subject to the broader sociopolitical environment, and manipulable through its own Human Resources policies that artificially expanded or contracted the pool of eligible workers.

In the latter part of the first decade of the twenty-first century, management found its ability to enact its preferences highly circumscribed by the dramatic shifts in U.S. workplace immigration law enforcement and the larger exclusionary legislative trend this was embedded in. The pendulum began to swing in the other direction, as the precarious position of unauthorized Latina/o workers was fully exposed. A noticeable shift in hiring toward African American and older, more established, or second-generation Latinas/os occurred, with very few Latina/o migrants gaining entry and many unauthorized workers finding themselves part of a grand, if gradual, purge. Yet management was not prepared to fully relinquish control in securing the kinds of workers it had the greatest taste for, and crafted Human Resources policies that restricted the eligibility of many potential hires. A new stage of ethnic succession at Swine's took all workers, Latinas/os and African Americans, by surprise as Haitian refugees, steered by company officials in Virginia, began to take positions on the line at a staggering pace in January 2011, less than a month after I left my job at Swine's. I argue that the ethnic succession model's built-in assumptions about the relationship between mechanisms of compositional change—displacement versus replacement—and the likelihood of intergroup conflict are perhaps better suited to studying large-scale aggregate change but unnecessarily limit analysis of the actual social relations between workers at Swine's. Actual social relations may or may not be determined primarily by the mechanisms that drive compositional change, but factors beyond these mechanisms may also play as important a function or more. I propose that the shifting preferences of employers for Latina/o migrant workers positioned this group at an advantage at the hiring phase, but at a disadvantage relative to other groups, such as African Americans, within the social organization of labor once they were hired. The very feature that makes immigrants attractive to employers, in this case the capacity for subordination, is also likely to be the basis for their disadvantage relative to other groups of workers within the social organization of labor on the shop floor.

In chapter 3, I began to develop the analysis that forms the crux of this book, calling attention to the symbolic expression of group boundaries. This third chapter traced the categories and meanings of shop-floor racial talk with parallel attention to the diverse ethnoracial panoramas in Latina/o migrants' origin countries. How are the terms *moyo, negro,* and *moreno* used at work? What does this suggest about how Latinas/os view African Americans as a group? And how does this language relate to pre-migration ideas about Blacks and blackness? Immersed participant observation over an extended period of time at Swine's permitted analysis of how work—as a setting that brings together multiple groups and subjectivities, as a structure that organizes the positions these groups and subjectivities occupy, and as a process that mediates the experience of oppression and exploitation—conditions the articulation of symbolic boundaries between groups that are meaningfully engaged with one another.

I showed that Latina/o workers rely on a variety of symbolic resources that communicate understandings and representations of African Americans that are held in common. An important but insufficiently studied type of symbolic resource involves language, namely, the forms of ethnoracial identification that designate understandings of African Americans as a group. I showed how the use of such categorical language is much more prevalent among Latinas/os toward African Americans than the other way around, and examined the features of one particularly salient designation of African Americans as *moyos,* a term whose valence is indefinite and situational, but frequently acquires pejorative significance. I traced the transnational origins of this identification, finding that its adaptation and propagation occurs within the transnational "third spaces" that Latina/o migrants occupy.

I also probed the ethnoracial panoramas of diverse Latina/o migrants' origin countries, searching for precursors to the self-understandings and representations of groups marked racially as "other" in the American South where they now find themselves. For example, I argued that the ethnoracial panorama of Honduras may predispose Honduran migrants (as opposed to Mexicans or Salvadorans) to a more fluid, "friendly" posture toward groups marked as "other" despite the universal devaluation of blackness itself. However, the subordinating experience of being migrants who are "not from here" brings together Honduran and other Latina/o workers in a common position as *hispanos,* as they most often refer to themselves collectively. Their direct class proximity to African Americans and the imperatives of the rigid American racialization system create the conditions for strong symbolic boundaries to be drawn. Because symbolic boundaries reflect social boundaries, even as they strive to create, reinforce, or transform these, I considered how the strong symbolic boundaries Latina/o workers draw with their African American counterparts, which frequently assume a negative valence, are tied to these groups' positions within the social organization of labor, and to their emergent sense of group position more broadly.

In chapters 4 and 5, I exposed the character of social relations among workers at Swine's, showing how the symbolic boundaries Latinas/os express are rooted in their perception that they are the most oppressively exploited workers and that African Americans occupy a privileged place within the social organization of labor. These chapters elaborate my study findings about intergroup relations and develop their intersection with labor relations and dynamics, particularly exploitation, subordination, and resistance. In chapter 4, I called attention to the most important social distinction that Latina/o workers make vis-à-vis their African American counterparts: their perception that African Americans occupy a privileged position within the social organization of labor and that Latinas/os are the most oppressively exploited workers. The strong symbolic boundaries that Latina/o workers draw against African American workers, discussed in chapter 3, reflect this crucial distinction. In encounters with African American workers, and in comments about them, Latinas/os express their resentment in hyperbolic declarations, such as that they are "going to come in painted black so they don't have to work." In casting African American workers as "lazy," they attempt to even out their statuses, at least symbolically, filling in the initial boundary that was outlined through bold and persistent ethnoracial identification. I drew on Lawrence Bobo and V.L. Hutchings's (1996) concept of "racial alienation," which refers to the degree to which group members feel enfranchised or aggrieved, to explain my findings about strong and substantially negative boundary making by Latina/o workers at Swine's. In the context of Swine's, Latinas/os rather than African Americans feel the greatest sense of racial alienation. At the same time, this suggests that scholars have too narrowly focused on direct competition for resources as the primary motivator of intergroup conflict. In doing so, they have mostly looked at the incumbent group—African Americans—as the group likely to feel a competitive threat and therefore to react in exclusionary ways that spur intergroup conflict. Although this focus is consistent with conventional theories of ethnic competition and conflict, I showed that other deprivations can drive intergroup conflict. In this case, Latinas/os' conviction that they are especially disadvantaged relative to African Americans in the workplace is the primary source of intergroup conflict. At the same time, it is important to remember that playfulness and banter is a common communicative device in interactions between Latina/o and African American workers, one that sometimes reinforces but often bridges boundaries between them.

At times, Latina/o workers attempted to challenge oppressive exploitation at Swine's, but this resistance tended to succumb to an acceptance of super-exploitation itself, and proceeded to challenge instead African Americans' perceived ability to escape its most oppressive elements (e.g., "*Morenos* should have to work like we do"). In chapter 5, I delved into the experience of super-exploitation and subjugation to a brutal labor discipline regime and described the social organization of labor, laying out the ethnoracial makeup of various jobs. It is the *perception* of relative privilege and disadvantage that shapes how Latinas/os view African American workers' and their own group's position in the workplace. I argued that the vulnerabilities of "illegality" that objectively mark only unauthorized migrants bleed onto the group as a whole, *hispanos*, because supervisors on the shop floor use the group as a shorthand for the qualities that make the former so tractable. I further argue that, whereas scholars have drawn attention to the mechanism of "deportability" that undergirds the vulnerabilities of unauthorized migrants, in a more proximate sense for the unauthorized migrant workers, their vulnerabilities stem from their special "disposability." But it should not be surprising if, for a variety of reasons—including the distinct vulnerabilities of "illegality" that mark all Latina/o migrants regardless of authorization status and bring them together as *hispanos*, but also the native-born advantages of being "from here," having citizenship, and speaking English—native-born workers really do occupy a position of relative privilege. The critical point, however, is that these advantages are viewed by Latinas/os to accrue to Black Americans as Blacks, rather than as Americans more generally.

In chapter 6, I showed how the composition of the authority structure affects the intergroup dynamics explained in chapters 4 and 5.

Latina/o workers view an African American–dominated authority structure as contributing to the perceived privileged position of African American workers (e.g., "since they're the same color"), while viewing white authority as impartial in applying labor discipline to all workers ("He treats everyone the same"). I had the opportunity to study these dynamics when, after seven months of working in the Loin Boning and Packing Department, the African American superintendent was forced out and replaced with a white superintendent. Thus, I had a chance to observe these dynamics before, during, and for two months following the transition. For some Latina/o workers, this shift caused them to redirect their resentment away from the perception of unequal treatment between Latina/o and Black workers, and toward a repudiation of the deterioration of working conditions for *all* workers, which many attributed to the new, white superintendent. For other workers, this change in the authority structure, and what it was believed to represent for the erstwhile privileged African American workers, presented an opportunity to rejoice in the loss of perceived Black privilege, and even to benefit from alliance with white authority, whose goodwill was now achieved on individualistic terms (e.g., "Goodbye, nigger!"). Yet, even for those few Latina/o workers whose resentment was redirected, their attribution was never articulated in racial terms as it was toward the African American supervisor.

On the other hand, the comparatively weaker symbolic boundaries that African Americans draw vis-à-vis their Latina/o counterparts must be explained. In chapter 7, I questioned whether the modal tendency can be characterized as exclusionary, as other scholars have argued, or whether ambivalence is a more fitting description. First, I suggested that, as a group, African Americans at Swine's do not articulate strong boundaries against Latinas/os because they do not feel resentment rooted in a sense of relative deprivation vis-à-vis Latinas/os. This is the logical corollary to an understanding that Latina/o workers, not African Americans, feel the greatest sense of racial alienation at Swine's. Second, although Latinas/os and African Americans are both convinced that some members of the other group dislike them in ethnoracial terms, among Latinas/os especially rumors about the ill intentions of out-group members are fostered by in-group mistrust, making for sharper intergroup boundaries. Third, race and immigration scholars' expectation that economic competition leads African Americans to feel their sense of group position threatened runs into problems when African Americans' views about immigrants are compared to those of whites, and when African Americans' attitudes about Latinas/os are considered alongside Latinas/os attitudes about them. Studies show that African Americans' views are more favorable of Latinas/os than whites', and more favorable of Latinas/os than Latinas/os' views of them.

Yet another explanation should be obvious, but seems to have been overlooked thus far because research has tended to focus on only one dimension of intergroup relations—African Americans' supposed attitudes and behavior toward Latinas/os stemming from competitive threat—rather than the complex interplay of relations that shape Latina/o migrants' social incorporation as an active and ongoing process. Whatever collective experiences individual Latina/o migrants may have been a part of in their origin communities, their defining collective experience as migrants in the United States is the fusion of disparate national and subnational subjectivities into an aggregate identification—by others most definitely, and increasingly by themselves—as *hispanos*. In contrast, although African Americans are by no means homogenous, they nonetheless share a collective history, memory, and experience that forged them as a group a long time ago. Hence, the forceful boundary making on the part of Latina/o workers reflects the flurry of activity typical of a group *as yet in formation,* whose position in the American stratified system of belonging is uncertain and characterized by multiple pathways. Further, I built on the concept of linked fate, which refers to the degree to which group members feel their individual fortunes to be tied to that of the group as a whole (Dawson 1994). Scholars hypothesize that groups with a high sense of linked fate—such as African Americans, whose solidaristic policy preferences have been explained with reference to this concept—will also be more likely to display solidarity with other subordinate groups. I proposed that linked fate may play a role in accounting for my findings, a possibility that scholarship narrowly focused on competition perspectives has not sufficiently considered.

The big story that brings together these chapters is that while Latinas/os' encounters with African Americans at work contribute to their negative perceptions about Blacks, it is, beyond other factors, Blacks' objective status as Americans that actually creates the conditions of relative advantage and disadvantage that Latinas/os deem unfair. Latinas/os' boundary-work vis-à-vis African Americans often implicates whiteness, while rarely identifying it directly. Neither historically nor in the present have African Americans been the principal sponsors of exclusionary immigration legislation or the promulgators of anti-immigrant movements. In fact, African

American political and civic organizations have staunchly opposed these measures and strongly aligned themselves with the civil and human rights positions of immigrant-rights organizations and immigrant communities. While some suggest that the African American masses may feel differently, leadership across the spectrum of religion and politics has actively fought the wave of exclusionary measures that swept across Southern legislatures in the wake of Arizona's SB 1070 (Bacon 2012; Eaton 2011). It has neither actively nor directly articulated the exclusionary positions that have locked migrants into an unrelenting state of persecution, and my research shows that at the workplace level, African Americans do not encounter Latinas/os as if they feel particularly threatened.

I propose that by conceptualizing Latina/o–African American relations as prismatic engagement, we recognize that whiteness not only mediates relations between subordinated groups, but also that subordinated groups view one another very differently through the prism of white dominance. Although I have discussed limitations to my research in each chapter, several potential limitations deserve some consideration here. This is, after all, a study of one meatpacking plant in North Carolina. As such, some readers may question how generalizable my findings may be. This is a valid concern, but I argue that my research design, which involved working in multiple departments of different sizes, compositions, and kinds of work, bolsters the reliability and potential generalizability of my findings to other working-class contexts with similar compositional features and structural conditions in which Latina/o migrants are embedded in the American South. A related and equally valid challenge involves a counterfactual. Would the prevalence of racialized resentment on the part of Latinas/os be similar in a context in which their main counterparts were native-born whites rather than African Americans? Undoubtedly, this is a fascinating question, and one that future research may attempt to address. Given the differences in the content of Latinas/os' discursive repertoire aimed at white and African American workers and supervisors at Swine's, I would not expect this to be the case. Still, it poses an interesting avenue that future research may wish to pursue.

PRISMATIC ENGAGEMENT: SUBORDINATE GROUP RELATIONS IN A SYSTEM OF BELONGING CHARACTERIZED BY WHITE DOMINANCE

Immigration and race/ethnicity scholars have been eager to evaluate the effect of the massive immigration from Latin America that began in

1965 but expanded significantly in the late 1980s on the American system of racialized stratification (Marrow 2011; Frank, Akresh, and Lu 2010; Lee and Bean 2007; Haney López 2006 [1996]; Bonilla-Silva 2004; Gans 1999). Several different propositions of an emerging order that transforms the Black-white binary stand out, including the possibility of a white-nonwhite divide, a Black/non-Black divide, and a tri-racial divide. If not precipitated, attempting to adjudicate between these propositions—which correspond to outcomes—at a time when the process of incorporation is very much still under way would benefit from attention to the dynamic conditions that are contributing to this transformation. This book sheds light on these dynamics, viewing the incorporation of Latina/o migrants as a process of mutual adjustment by which groups both achieve and are ascribed social positions in a stratified system of belonging. Indeed, the dynamics and contours of Latina/o migrant incorporation in the American South of today will weigh heavily in the future reconfiguration of systems of racial and class stratification in the United States as a whole. Some scholars and many pundits have suggested that Latina/o–African American relations in the American South are somewhat strained and may foreshadow the emergence of a new Black/non-Black racial fault line in the United States (Marrow 2011; Lee and Bean 2007; Gans 1999). My findings are not entirely at odds with these appraisals, but the data and arguments I advance present a robust counterpoint to the theoretical and empirical roads other scholars have taken to reach these rather pessimistic conclusions. This is no mere academic debate, for the political implications turn out to be quite different.

Claire Jean Kim's (1999) racial triangulation theory posits that Asian Americans inhabit dual roles in the American "field of racial positions," being valorized relative to Blacks but simultaneously devalued as civic outsiders and perpetual foreigners. Drawing on Kim's theory, Helen Marrow has argued that Latinas/os experience discrimination in the American South along two dimensions—one related to race and one related to citizenship—dimensions that parallel those outlined by Kim. Marrow (2011; 2007) argues that Latino/a migrants feel the greatest discrimination along the citizenship dimension, and that they point to African Americans rather than whites as the group that treats them in the most exclusionary ways. My findings, based on sixteen months of participant observation totaling more than five thousand hours on the production lines of a Southern meatpacking plant, and supplemented by twenty-three in-depth interviews with Latinas/os and African Americans, question these conclusions. I suggest that methodological flaws and theoretical tunnel vision, both with substantive implications, have produced misguided and misleading conclusions.

Scholars rightly point out that discrimination and exclusion can occur along several axes, and Latinas/os interviewed by researchers may very well report that they feel greater discrimination from African Americans than from whites. But it is methodologically problematic to extrapolate actual attitudes and behaviors of African Americans from Latinas/os' accounts. It is also theoretically myopic to limit the possible range of grievances that can motivate intergroup relations and conflict to competition. This book, which combines immersed participant observation and interviews with an analytic lens that considers sources of grievance other than competition, presents a very different picture of relations between Latinas/os and African Americans. And by situating the study in the workplace, the context that most defines the lives of working-class migrants and native-born groups alike, I uncover important conditions that shape relations between these groups.

First, I argue that the concept of prismatic engagement incorporates the centrality of white dominance to analyses of relations between subordinate groups, a feature that too often disappears from accounts of relations among minority groups (Lie and Abelmann 1999). White dominance mediates subordinated group relations in a number of ways, as I have shown in the preceding chapters. Latina/o migrants enter the American field of racial positions already predisposed to view blackness negatively, based on the racialization schemes of their communities of origin. In Southern workplaces such as Swine's, African Americans are the main group they encounter in similar class positions as workers. Whites are almost entirely absent from the workforce, but it is the "invisible weight of whiteness"—to borrow a phrase from the sociologist Eduardo Bonilla-Silva (2012)—that undergirds the system into which their groups are stratified.[1] Even some Latina/o workers who are certain that Blacks are "more racist" toward Latinas/os than whites acknowledge that there are hardly any whites working at Swine's (and thus insufficient data on which to make such a generalization). Furthermore, these workers acknowledge that their perceptions about discrimination and intergroup relations are shaped almost entirely by their experiences at work, where they spend the majority of their time.

Because African American workers are seen as having the less difficult or strenuous jobs, and as more able to escape the most oppressive elements of exploitation at Swine's, Latinas/os develop resentment toward them. In a context where white workers are scarce (except in managerial, supervisory, and office positions, where they are highly concentrated), and preconditioned to view blackness negatively, perceptions of difference in the positions occupied by Latinas/os and African Americans within the social organization of labor produce a resentment that is racialized, and which paradoxically assigns value to being Black in this micro context. The perception that African Americans in positions of authority augment African American worker privilege, while whites in positions of authority are viewed as fair and neutral (or as oppressive, but never *because* they are white), demonstrates how white dominance mediates the encounters between Latinas/os and African Americans at Swine's. Indeed, this finding manifests as the mirror image of what has been termed the transparency phenomenon: "the tendency of whites not to think about whiteness, or about norms, behaviors, experiences, or perspectives that are white-specific" (Flagg 1993, 957). Transparency is not a quality of whites per se but rather a property of whiteness. As such, it is not *just* whites who are subject to it, but all who have a place within the system of racialized stratification (though not in identical terms). In this sense, the "possessive investment in whiteness," as the historian George Lipsitz puts it, is a question of relational and relative terms rather than absolutes. According to Lipsitz, "All communities of color suffer from the possessive investment in whiteness, but not in the same way" (2006 [1998], 185). This is why Latinas/os and African Americans gaze through the same prism of white dominance yet see different realities and possibilities. The latter is reminiscent of W. E. B. Du Bois's poignant contemplations on what he called the "double consciousness": "The Negro is a sort of seventh son, born with a veil, and gifted with second-sight in this American world,—a world which yields him no true self-consciousness, but only lets him see himself through the revelation of the other world. . . . It is a peculiar sense, this double-consciousness, this sense of always looking at one's self through the eyes of others, of measuring one's soul by the tape of a world that looks on in amused contempt and pity" (Du Bois 1995 [1903], 45).

Claudia's comments in the encounter that opens this chapter suggest that, in any case, she views the power wielded by whites over other groups as being in some sense legitimate. This raises a second issue that has not adequately been considered by scholars, and which is also captured by the analogic concept of prismatic engagement. African Americans are not necessarily, as some scholars too easily presume, "insiders" along the axis of citizenship—at least not in the same way as white Americans are. Claudia's comments at the beginning of this chapter suggest precisely this point: that African Americans—like Latinas/os—in some sense do not "own" this country as do whites. And the common elision in Latinas/os' discursive repertoire between "Americans" and "whites" or *bolillos*, but rarely between "Americans" and "Blacks" or *moyos*, is also suggestive of African Americans' marginal inclusion along this dimension. In fact, African American and Latina/o workers each accuse the other of "looking down" on them.

While Latinas/os perceive their exclusion to be predicated on their not being "from here," African Americans perceive their marginalization as that much more degrading precisely because they *are* "from here." However, like other subordinated populations (e.g., unauthorized migrants), African Americans, especially poor and working-class African Americans, wage a losing battle in the "politics of entitlement" that characterizes contestations over mere access to the pie—"the right to have rights"—let alone the size and flavor of the slice (Cacho 2012). Most compellingly, popular slogans for social movements on behalf of African Americans and unauthorized migrants—"Black Lives Matter" and "No Human Being Is Illegal"—encapsulate the peripheral position from which these communities make claims to full personhood. In turn, the rallying cry of Tea Party organizations composed of and supported almost entirely by white, middle-class Americans—"Take it back, take our country back!"—epitomizes the insurrectionary resentment of those who feel their entitlement as the rightful owners of the pie under siege (Burghart and Zeskind 2010; Parker and Barreto 2013).

While scholars have usefully drawn on racial triangulation theory to explain Latina/o-African American relations, I call into question the idea that disadvantage along both the racial and civic exclusion dimensions extends to Latinas/os, while only the racial dimension extends to African Americans. Indeed, the pitfall in recent applications of racial triangulation theory to relations among subordinated groups is that these do not properly incorporate the mediating role played by white dominance in conditioning how these groups encounter one another in a field of racial positions.[2]

The determining role of white dominance is precisely what Claire Jean Kim (2000; 1999) emphasizes in explaining Asian Americans' dual position in the "field of racial positions" as valorized relative to Blacks and devalued as perpetual foreigners. But where Kim's racial triangulation perspective most clearly illuminates the interests and actions of whites in constructing the relative positions that subordinate groups occupy and the common discursive frames that represent them, it does not properly describe the dynamics by which subordinated groups themselves construe interests and exercise agency vis-à-vis one another, and do so not as isolated minority groups but rather from within the field of racial positions that are their reference points, and therefore inevitably through the prism of white dominance. I argue that the axis of civic exclusion does not unequivocally place African Americans as insiders precisely because of the mediating role of white dominance in the United States *and* in Latina/o migrants' communities of origin. Ultimately, when African American and Latina/o workers encounter one another at Swine's, they do so looking through the refractory lens of white dominance, giving relations between these groups the qualities of prismatic engagement. The nature of each group's experience means that African Americans and Latinas/os view one another rather differently through the distorting optic of this prism. The diagram below gives an illustration of the attributes (and their values) crucial to understanding relations between Latinas/os and African Americans at Swine's, and summarizes the insights derived from applying a prismatic engagement perspective to the study of social relations among subordinate groups.

And yet, perhaps at times, Latina/o workers at Swine's, even those who most vehemently articulate strong and negatively valenced boundaries vis-à-vis their African American counterparts, glean the group struggle in the American racialized system of belonging in ways that intuit some solidarity across subordinate group boundaries. I asked Claudia over lunch one afternoon at McDonald's if there was racism in this country. She responded with her usual mix of seriousness and dark humor:

> In the country? I think so, same as everywhere. We're not from here. They don't want us. [I asked on whose part, and toward whom?] The *hispanos* and the *negros*. It's that we're not from here. From the Americans, the *bolillos* you could say. We come to invade their country, they don't want us! Sorry, I don't care! If they don't like it, they can go to El Salvador. They can go and I'll stay here.

Unlike much of Claudia's previous commentary, her response to my questions about whether racism exists in the United States, who is subject to it, and who perpetrates it suggests that at some level, she views Latinas/os and African Americans as sharing a similar subordinate, outsider position relative to whites. These subsequent reflections introduce the faint hum of a different sort of awareness, one that is requisite for the development of lasting solidarities.

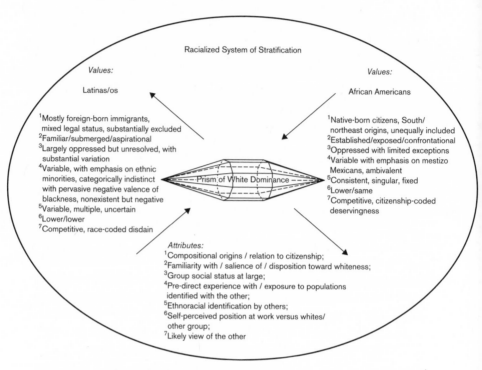

FIGURE 11. Attribute-value diagram of prismatic engagement: Latinas/os and African Americans at Swine's.

In accepting Latinas/os' perceptions about African Americans' attitudes and behaviors toward them as *fact*, rather than attempting to understand how these groups encounter one another in a setting, structure, and process that molds their relationship to one another and conditions Latina/o migrants' emergent sense of group position within the broader American stratified system of belonging, we fall short as researchers. We contribute to the invisibility of white nativism in current anti-immigrant movements and increasingly powerful political blocs, and we erase its historical legacy of de jure and de facto racism. We also reinforce Latinas/os' blindness to its determining role in producing their subordinate status, while missing altogether the factors that may both compel and motivate them to attain incorporation as non-Blacks—perhaps someday as whites for some, but for now most certainly as *hispanos*—as well as *how* they do so. It is in this sense that the familiar racial specters, which have been conjured in the orchestration of dominant-subordinate group social positions, and which have most recently been articulated in the coded terms of what the legal scholar Ian Haney López (2014) calls "dog whistle politics," are retooled to serve as what I call racial foils in the stories told about social relations among subordinated groups.[3] We also neglect what may be the most important point: that by improving the labor protections and working conditions of *all* workers regardless of authorization status, a virtue in itself, we also diminish the bases for employers' preferences and disparate treatment, and therefore also for conflict among Latina/o and African American workers, and the perpetuation into the indefinite future of racialized forms of group-based inequality.[4]

THE SOCIOLEGAL FOUNDATIONS FOR UNIVERSAL LABOR PROTECTIONS

"Janet, antes de que te vayas por qué no nos dejas la unión" (Janet,
before you go, why don't you leave us the union)."
—Leticia, Honduran worker

As you might imagine if you have read up to this point, slaughterhouse work is physically, psychologically, and emotionally grueling. The environmental conditions of the workplace overwhelm every bodily sense. Given all of this, and considering that a typical workday often lasts fifteen hours, all workers at Swine's labor under extraordinary duress. Yet most Americans that I have talked to about this project do not even realize that being forced to work that many hours in a day is perfectly legal in the United States. And the challenges and vulnerabilities immigrant workers face adds a dimension of powerlessness that not only crushes spirits and bodies, but drives a wedge between Latina/o and African American workers, making it difficult for them to unite in their common interest of improving their work-life existence.

My objective as an entrenched researcher was to gain a deep understanding of the social and economic incorporation experiences of Latina/o immigrants in the American South, a region where immigration was until recently a rare, rather than large-scale, phenomenon, and a region that has been characterized by white social, economic, and political domination over African Americans. Today, the South is being recreated and reimagined, as new immigrant destinations within it have blossomed, dramatically altering the historic ethnoracial panorama.

FIGURE 12. Photo of the author, Vanesa Ribas, at a rib trimming and bagging table on her last day of work at Swine's.

Among other questions, scholars have debated what impact Latina/o immigration is having on social relations among groups in the South, and what this might tell us about the emerging racialized system of stratification in the United States more broadly. An issue that scholars have been particularly concerned with is whether Latina/o immigrants and African Americans experience economic competition, and if so, whether there is growing social conflict rooted in African Americans' perceptions of economic threat. My findings point to a different reality. While African American workers did not seem especially threatened, Latina/o workers expressed a profound resentment, their grievances rooted in their perception that they are the most oppressively exploited workers. The implications of my findings are that improving working conditions of all workers—and this includes extending equal rights and remedies to unauthorized immigrant workers as well as raising the floor of working conditions at the bottom of the labor market—offers a necessary course of action for relieving inequalities now and impeding them from arising in the future.

Proposed immigration reforms, as too few have noted, lack any interventions in labor laws. And worse, as a *New York Times* editorial points out, proposed guest-worker programs might only add new dimensions and volume to immigrant workers' vulnerabilities (*New York Times* 2013). Executive orders by the Obama administration—Deferred Action for Childhood Arrivals (DACA) in 2012 and Deferred Action for Parents of Americans and Lawful Permanent Residents in 2014—provide for some unauthorized migrants to receive temporary relief from deportation concerns and the possibility of temporary work authorization. These measures are, of course, welcome respite for a beleaguered population, but nevertheless perpetuate its uncertain and precarious status. Politicians have been too busy planning ways to build ever-more-militarized borders to notice or care that their wars over symbolic domination of the U.S.-Mexico border in no way address the fuel for "migration outside the law" (Motomura 2014). So long as employers can count on a sociopolitical playing field that generates a perfectly exploitable type of worker, demand for immigrant labor—unauthorized or otherwise—will continue or resurface down the line, maybe during the next economic boom. It should be our urgent task to propose and evaluate efforts to mitigate the most oppressive elements of this system, advance reforms that enhance workers' well-being in the workplace, and ensure that all workers have equal rights and remedies, recognizing that all workers deserve dignity and a voice on the job. To do so, the cynicism of current labor laws and corresponding legal precedents must be exposed and changed.

First, a serious assessment of the labor-market dynamics that produce and perpetuate demand for immigrant labor must consider how and why such workers come to represent solutions to employers' labor needs—not because this will limit future flows, though this may be a by-product of policy crafted in light of such an assessment, but because a serious assessment will force us to see the built-in inequalities in the regime of worker rights and remedies that allow immigrant labor to occupy such a precarious position within the social organization of labor, not only at the slaughterhouse where I conducted research, but in workplaces throughout the country.

Since the passage of the Immigration Reform and Control Act in 1986, there has been a growing validation of the equal rights of unauthorized workers to the protections guaranteed under the National Labor Relations Act (e.g., to join labor organizations and be protected from unfair labor practices during organizing campaigns) and Fair Labor Standards Act (e.g., to recoup unpaid wages), but a simultaneous narrowing of the scope of remedies afforded to them upon the infringement of their rights. In 2002, the Supreme Court ruled that unauthorized workers are not entitled to back pay or reinstatement on the grounds that such a holding contradicted the aims of IRCA, which for the first time enacted sanctions for the employment of unauthorized workers. Some legal scholars posit that the majority in the *Hoffman Plastic Compounds, Inc. v. NLRB* decision misconstrued the statute, and therefore ruled in error (García 2012). After all, IRCA's main teeth—employer sanctions—were intended to deter *employers'* hiring of unauthorized workers. As the dissent of Justice Breyer expresses, the finding that such workers were not eligible for remedies for the infringement of their rights under the NLRA effectively nullifies those rights. The Hoffman decision actually magnifies the incentives for employers to hire unauthorized workers, then dispose of them at their convenience, for instance when those workers dare to uphold their workplace rights in an effort to improve their conditions of employment. Although thus far in practice the substantive ramifications of *Hoffman* have been delimited rather than cascading, the symbolic consequences of the decision have been enormous (Gleeson 2012).

These are the very issues at the heart of immigrant workers' vulnerabilities, as their disposability in the workplace is premised on their deportability at large. Any immigration legislation must very clearly restate the subjection of all workers, without distinction of status, to the rights and remedies afforded under the National Labor Relations Act—hence invalidating the *Hoffman* decision. Legal scholars of labor and immigration issues have proposed the dismantling of the employer sanctions regime altogether (Wishnie 2007), or in more limited fashion, the suspension of employer reporting requirements during the course of a labor dispute (Decker 2006). Still others propose enlisting the cooperation of undocumented workers in employer sanctions cases, an approach that has not been seriously considered but is applied in other areas of civil and criminal justice law (Heydari 2010).

The paradox on which the *Hoffman* Court predicated its decision, and judges' stated imperative to obliterate it, is thus a mystification. But it is a mystification that thrives because—based on the seemingly irrefutable logic of common sense—it represents itself as merely stating the obvious. Such a reading misconstrues both the nature of law as a metastructure of American society as well as the letter and spirit of particular laws. Indeed, at present the treatment of unauthorized workers reflects the "fractured membership" that increasingly characterizes their subjection to various spheres of law in the United States (Núñez 2010).

Individuals' subjection to law in the United States is moderated by fire-walls that exist throughout the vast system of legal codifications and bureaucratic governance. Institutional bodies with firewalls include the Social Security Administration and the Census, agencies with strict regu-lations on the sharing and public disclosure of individual-identifying information. And contrary to the notion that the law operates in a neat, unambiguous fashion to declare norms, regulate behaviors, and sanction offenses, law in practice is sometimes contradictory, even giving rise to perverse outcomes and paradoxes anathema to common sense.[5] Michael Walzer's (1983) argument for "complex equality" can be viewed as a legal rationale for adjudicating claims where firewalls have been eroded or do not yet exist, leading to a standoff between conflicting interests.

Although the legal scholar Linda Bosniak (2006) is wise to point to the limits of "normative nationalism" among liberal political theo-rists—that the tensions inherent to the condition of alienage make it impossible to maintain separate spheres—this orientation is preferable to the "nativist nationalism" of both the political right and left.[6] And there is certainly an abundance of opportunities to enhance noncitizens' conditions of existence before the notional bases of governance dissolve into irreconcilable contradiction. At the same time, there is a strong claim to be made that any law that systematically limits the rights and remedies of a class of workers diminishes the First Amendment protec-tions not just of those persons, but of *all* persons. Going to the heart of the matter, other legal scholars have proposed challenging the constitu-tionality of this regime on the grounds that the Thirteenth Amendment prohibits systems of slavery or involuntary servitude (Zeitlow 2012; Ontiveros 2007; Pope, Kellman, and Bruno 2007; Goluboff 2001).[7]

The parallel impoverishment of labor protections on other fronts deserves mention as well. Despite what would seem to be the political and deliberative value inherent in much labor speech, appeals to First Amend-ment protections have tended to advance the claims of employers and businesses as opposed to workers and their organizations (Garden 2011). Indeed, for decades, conservatives have cultivated legal rationales for lim-iting the collection of union dues as "compelled speech" (e.g., so-called right-to-work laws), curbing the informational efforts of union compre-hensive campaigns as "extortionary speech" (e.g., civil RICO cases), and attacking the self-presentations of would-be workers as "commercial speech" (e.g., anti–day laborer ordinances). At the same time, the Supreme Court has developed expansive constructions of free speech that safeguard the interests of economic elites and treat corporations alternately as rights-bearing individuals (e.g., *Citizens United v. FEC*) and as unwieldy, unsanctionable entities (e.g., *Wal-Mart Stores Inc. v. Dukes*). Given these tendencies, it might seem wise to abandon free-speech arguments in favor of progressive causes. Quite the opposite, I suggest redoubling and expanding the scope of such efforts. Recently, legal scholars have argued forcefully for the enhancement of First Amendment protection of labor speech (Fisk 2014; Garden 2011). There are, in sum, several rationales on which to stake a claim to universal labor protections in the United States. Each of these involves distinct but interconnected aspects of labor and employment law on the one hand, and immigration law on the other, while reconciling the clashing interests according to the trumping mandates of the American Constitution. No doubt, the law serves as the repressive arm of the state (Lowe 1996), but it must be harnessed whenever possible in the interests of justice. As Kimberlé Williams Crenshaw (1995, 111–12) soberly cautions: "People can demand change only in ways that reflect the logic of the institutions they are challenging. . . . In sum, the potential for change is both created and limited by legitimation."

Unfortunately, given the current composition of the Supreme Court—the most conservative in decades—there are likely to be few victories for workers or immigrants in this domain. But because Congress is likely to initiate reforms to immigration and naturalization law in the coming years, the domain of legislation—not litigation—may prove a more fruitful avenue of action. As the renowned labor scholar Ruth Milkman (2011) puts it, the emancipatory promise of the National Labor Relations Act desperately needs renewing, and this must occur more broadly within an employment, labor, and immigration law reform agenda.[8]

Second, cross-national studies of the labor market position and conditions of bottom-level workers are sorely needed, with the objective of identifying key legal and policy areas to target for improvement. These might include maximum working hours, mandated breaks, paid lunches, et cetera. Why should workers—immigrants or native-born citizens—have to choose between not having a job and having one that turns them into wage slaves? These efforts would inform the urgently needed initiative to reform employment law to better align the legally acceptable conditions of employment with the conditions average Americans imagine already exist, and would bring the American workplace into the mainstream of workplaces throughout the world of advanced capitalist democracies.

Third, we should pursue studies of human resources policies and practices at the level of firms. Employers often complain that they lack sufficient pools of eligible labor, but they manipulate the pools by contracting or expanding criteria for eligibility according to their whims. Objective—and conservative—projections of labor needs must be developed, figures that do not come solely from the horse's mouth. The laissez-faire approach of some scholars who advocate for the rights of migrants and against punitive enforcement measures is not a solution, either. All too often, enforcement programs are condemned but the valid underlying concerns about working conditions are not addressed. Sometimes, the "hardworking" character of migrants and their acceptance of substandard conditions of employment are extolled as virtues that benefit the U.S. economy, contributing to the foreigner-featuring scripts that instrumentalize immigrants and impel "national mythmaking" (Mendelson 2010; Cacho 2012; Honig 2001). Calls for reform that narrowly focus on legalization serve the interests of capital very well, and in a cynical way those of the desperate and hardworking migrant supposedly eager to accept subordination in American workplaces, while deferring to the future the repetition of current struggles surrounding employment of unauthorized migrants and their conditions of existence. The horse's mouth reeks of self-serving entitlement to consume the lives of workers at any cost.

Tom Hensley, the president of Fieldale Farms Corp. in northern Georgia and former chairman of the National Chicken Council, recently addressed lawmakers at a Senate Special Committee on Immigration and Georgia's Economy, opposing statewide legislation targeting immigrants (HB 87 passed in May 2011, following Arizona's lead with SB 1070, and South Carolina and Alabama have since passed similar legislation with SB 20 and HB 56, respectively). Hensley told lawmakers: "We were 67 percent Hispanic in 2004. Our turnover was 25 percent. Our workers' compensation cost was $50,000 a month. Our health care cost for the whole year was $8 million. It was about that time that the federal, state, and local governments let it be known that these folks are not welcome. Fast forward to 2010, we're about 33 percent Hispanic now. Our turnover is 75 percent. Workers' comp costs are $150,000 a month. Our health care last year was $20 million. Those are staggering numbers, but that's the economic reality" (Galloway 2011).

Let us say we believe Mr. Hensley that as the company's Latina/o workforce was cut in half in the span of six years, turnover and workers' compensation costs tripled, and health care costs more than doubled. Without a doubt, these are the distressed cries of employers all over the United States who have found their once nearly unfettered access to migrant workers significantly curtailed. What are we to conclude from this? One could conclude that Latina/o (probably much of it unauthorized) labor saved the company loads of money. But who is this a good thing for? Workers' compensation costs are real; the fact that they tripled shows that these costs were kept artificially low, probably because company personnel dissuaded, misinformed, or outright unlawfully prevented injured workers from filing claims. Even tripled, these costs are surely on the lower end of where they would be if the repetitive motion injuries many workers suffer were included (Ames, Hall, and Ordonez 2008). As for health care costs, assuming that many Latina/o workers were unauthorized, many enroll in but rarely if ever use their employer-sponsored insurance out of fear that they will get in trouble (because many work under assumed identities), and some workers are too afraid to sign up at all. Even low turnover, usually attributed to the work ethic of migrants, is kept artificially low by the limited mobility of workers who lack authorization status, making it risky to change jobs. In explaining why they see native-born workers as less likely to stay on at Swine's, many such workers say it is "because if they leave this job, they can go get a job anywhere else, or they can collect unemployment." If even I, a fluently bilingual, PhD-educated woman, had a very difficult time navigating workers' compensation and health claims, we can only imagine what the experience is for a migrant who speaks very limited English and has a low level of education—especially if he or she lacks authorization status. It is hard to align with the position of business leaders such as Mr. Hensley because it requires complicity with their destructive exploitation of migrant workers' vulnerabilities.

At a time when business and its political allies have launched the most massive coordinated assault on labor in decades—made all the more egregious because they seized the opportunities created by the economic crisis they engineered in the first place—it may seem incongruous, even impossible, to insist on the expansion of worker protections (Milkman 2013). But this is the only avenue that has the potential for greatly diminishing the bases of employers' appetite for unauthorized migrants—and with it, the problematic aspects for all workers that are associated with the creation of a caste of denizens on the line.

Notes

PREFACE

1. Throughout this book, I use *Latino/a* to refer to that group in general, and *Latina/o* when specifically talking about my research and research subjects, to reflect the fact that unlike most contexts in which immigration is studied, women made up a substantial share of the people in my setting. For the plural, I consistently use *Latinas/os*. For the possessive plural, I use *Latinas/os'*. For simplicity, I use simply *Latinos* in the term *Latinos/migrants*.

2. I explain my usage of the term *ethnoracial* in chapter 3.

3. All of the people's names in this volume are pseudonyms, as are the names of places that pertain to my field site. The descriptions of Perry, North Carolina, and Swine's are true, as well as my evocations of nearby towns and other companies; only the names are of my invention.

CHAPTER I

1. I adapt this term from Raymond Williams (1977).

2. In chapter 2, I build on the work of Roger Waldinger (1997) regarding the process of ethnic succession, showing how compositional shifts at Swine's have been conditioned by the legal and political environment dealing with unauthorized migration; industrial strategies pursued by packers to secure steady, super-exploitable labor; Human Resources policies that shrink or expand the eligible pool of labor; and migrant social-network mechanisms that ensure progressive succession. Ethnic succession at Swine's, I argue, is characterized by multiple mechanisms that are difficult to untangle. These consist of displacement of the incumbent African American majority with the purpose of quashing labor organizing through disproportionate and preferential hiring of Latina/o migrants given their share of the applicant pool, the replacement of the incumbent African

American majority through differential attrition, and the replacement of the incumbent African American majority through the aforementioned hiring practices in the context of growth (the workforce at Swine's in 2009 was double what it had been in the early 1990s).

CHAPTER 2

1. Durand, Massey, and Capoferro (2005) refer to four key periods of Mexican migration to the United States. The classic era preceded the restrictive immigration quotas of the 1920s, and Mexican migrants were concentrated in Texas (about 50 percent in 1920). There was some diversification in destinations (California especially, and Chicago to a lesser extent), but the Great Depression brought a halt to this diversification. The bracero era of 1942–64 made California a prominent destination; in 1960, 42 percent of Mexican immigrants lived in California, and about 6 percent in Illinois and Indiana. The undocumented era ran through the 1986 Immigration Reform and Control Act (IRCA) and marked the full ascent of California as the preeminent destination, with 57 percent of Mexican migrants living in California by 1990 (16). Post-IRCA is the fourth and current era.

2. Curiously, both McDonald's establishments in Perry hired substantial numbers of Latinas/os by 2009, while Burger King and Wendy's were staffed almost entirely by African Americans.

3. I estimate that at Swine's, at least 50 percent of Latinas/os were Hondurans, 25 to 35 percent Mexican, 10 percent Salvadoran, and the rest other Central American, Caribbean, and South American. In the Loin Boning and Packing Department, I estimate that 75 percent of the approximately two hundred workers were Latina/o, and most of the rest African American. Out of approximately 150 Latinas/os in this department, 50 to 60 percent were Honduran, 20 to 30 percent were Mexican, and about 7 to 10 percent were Salvadoran. The remainder included a handful of Dominicans, two or three Puerto Ricans, two or three Guatemalans, and one or two Nicaraguans.

4. Years earlier, researchers from the University of North Carolina and the North Carolina Committee on Occupational Safety and Health (NCOSH) conducted interviews and surveys of poultry workers in Duplin County, North Carolina, and came to the same conclusions (Smith-Nonini 2003).

5. Crucially, more than one third of households in the Olancho region (81,201 households) receive remittances, which average 3,470 lempiras or close to $200 per month (Flores Fonseca 2008a). This may seem like a small amount, but not when observed in the context of the country's extensive poverty. The GNI per capita in Honduras was $1,040 in 2004 (World Bank Indicators), making it one of the poorest countries in the Americas (Gindling and Terrell 2010). A striking contrast in basic levels of well-being between households that receive remittances and those that don't is that the former are substantially more likely to have electricity, running water, and access to sewage disposal systems. At the national level, remittances exceed the income generated by the maquiladora industry and made up 20 percent of the total GDP in 2007, though this figure decreased somewhat following the economic recession in the United States

(Endo, Hirsch, Rogge, and Borowik 2010). In short, much as in Mexico and El Salvador, migrant remittances are a crucial source of economic sustenance in Honduras. Although Boston, Miami, New York, and Saint Louis are considered important destinations for Honduran migrants, Hondurans have also formed enclaves in the rural Midwest and the South.

6. Unlike "the city," Cristina says, Olancho is the kind of place where people offer you food when you visit their homes, even considering how little they may have for themselves. Olancho is the kind of place where a horde of men will chase you down and rape you if you turn them down, Adriana, another Honduran worker, retorts. I doubt that either of these depictions is entirely true, but my worker-friends who described Olancho in these ways were perhaps conveying certain grains of truth about the place. Over a twenty-four-hour period in January 2010 in this department with a population of less than five hundred thousand, sixteen people were found dead as a result of what was thought to be feuding between organized crime's powerful families in the region (La Prensa 2010).

7. The pervasiveness of everyday violence from above and from below, and how the two converge in the lives of Hondurans, is captured by the anthropologist Adrienne Pine (2008). There wasn't much that sounded appealing from the stories my worker-friends told me about their hometowns. "Ernesto is not like that, though." Cristina told me time and again how he had never hit her, and that this was a remarkable accomplishment considering the ordinary violence displayed by the other men in his family and the control they exerted over their women. "Julio won't even let his wife go anywhere without his permission," Cristina told me about Ernesto's adopted brother. The time she and Ernesto brought Julio's wife to my house for dinner, they had been sure to get Julio's blessing. Ernesto had even worked under Cristina's supervision at the Korean maquila in Choloma where she had worked since she was a teenager, she told me with glee. But he made sure she understood that even though she was his boss there, at home he was the boss. Still, though, he had never hit her.

8. But by early 2014, Bubu had arrived in North Carolina and reunited with his family, surviving the dangerous journey and a month in a detention center for unaccompanied minors in South Texas after ICE transferred him and other children out of the "icebox" he said they were initially held in.

9. This was the case for Ileana, Cristina's in-law. Ileana is from Potrerillos, in the department of Cortés on the north coast. Mitch destroyed banana plantations there belonging to the Tela Railroad Company. There is also sugarcane, but only men work there, she tells me.

The *maquilas* began arriving—the *chinos* [meaning Asians] who went to Honduras—in Villa Nueva [but she did not work in factories]. I was like a secretary to a *diputado* for Cortés department. When my kids were entering the regular school, I decided to come to the United States because I didn't earn enough to put them through school. Now my daughter is in university and the others are still in school. I've been here three years. Someone told me they would help me get here. It costs a lot of money. I earned enough to feed us, but no more. I earned 100 lempiras [$5.50] a day. Someone told me they could send me $50 a month, or they could bring me. I came with the help of a couple I knew, and arrived in Virginia. I wanted to work quickly, because my kids would call me and ask me to send them money. So I had my brother here. And he said, come.

10. The reader may be interested to know how I came to be an employee at Swine's. On a balmy Sunday night in July 2009, I got in line outside its gates. The week before, I had driven up to a worker in the parking lot and asked how to go about applying for a job there. The worker, an older African American woman I later recognized as a Quality Assurance employee named Janine, told me to go to the unemployment office and fill out an application. "Is that how you got hired?" I asked naively. "No, but I've been working here for eighteen years!" The next morning, I arrived at the local ESC office but was told they were taking applications directly at the plant. An older Black woman and I made our way to the factory, where the guard at the gate told us we were too late to apply. He instructed us to show up at night and wait for a security guard to hand out numbers at four in the morning to the first twenty people in line so we could come back later in the morning to fill out applications for production jobs. As we walked back to our cars, the woman protested that she wasn't going to do all that; she would come back at seven in the morning. I told her she wouldn't make the cut, if what the guard said was true. "We'll see, then." I would later come to know this woman as Ms. Angie, a no-nonsense kind of woman who enjoyed sipping on a few "Buttweisers," which she also referred to as "Clydesdales," after getting off work from the night shift in the Marination Department.

I returned to the plant that same night, but by the time I arrived, there were already twenty-two people in line ahead of me. I waited, hoping I would get a number anyway. There appeared to be an equal number of Black and Latino men applying (approximately five to eight and six to eight, respectively) and four Latinas, at least two of whom I guessed were second generation. Some weeks later, I learned that two of the Latinas, who were bilingual and in their early twenties, had failed the drug test and were not hired. I found this out when I ran into them at Walmart and they recognized me, but not as the woman who had loaned them jumper cables to start their friend's car; they mistook me for the woman who had sold them a "drink" that "didn't work" and so "they found the marijuana." Close to four in the morning, the security guard came out to the gate and handed out numbers to the first twenty people in line, and much to my disappointment told the rest of us we would have to come earlier next time.

So that Sunday night I arrived earlier, and there were only around thirteen already in line. On this night most of them were African American men and a few women, along with two white (or Indian) young men and two Latin Americans (one man and one woman). I had brought coffee, a bottle of water, and a magazine, and I squatted against the chain-link fence. A Black man and woman at the front of the line had removed a seat from their car and brought a red blanket for the woman to wrap herself in and a rolling desk chair for the man to sit in. An old Black man had brought a crossword-type magazine and a cushion to rest against. I chatted with Germán, who is Honduran, and Isabel, who is from Michoacán, to pass the time. It turned out Germán had worked here in 1996 and was returning to see if they'd hire him despite his "bad record" (getting fired for fighting) and despite being told in 2002 that he would not be rehired. Isabel and her husband, who had moved their family from California to North Carolina to escape the high cost of living, both worked at the Pig Corporation plant in Davis, North Carolina, but that facility was in the process of shutting down. Her husband followed the company here while she picked up a job at a textile factory. We talked about which are the bad jobs here—pulling out intestines, sticking the pigs to bleed them. Around midnight, trucks started delivering hogs for the early-morning slaughter. Each time a truck passed by, everyone in line paused to watch, and someone made a comment about the hogs' fate, usually with dry humor. Isabel exclaimed, "Poor little pigs. But *carnitas* are so tasty!" And then, "Poor things, the little pigs. It's their last night!" And finally, "Poor things, the little pigs. We'll all have to become vegetarians so they don't get slaughtered!"

Isabel's commentary then extended to the African Americans in line in front of us, and later behind us, and to Blacks in general. As we discussed our experiences trying to apply thus far, and affirmed our belief that the company was hiring a lot right now, Isabel explained, "*Es que éstos no duran. Se quedan uno o dos días y ya. No aguantan. Huevones que son*" (It's that these people don't last. They stay one or two days and that's it. They can't take it. Lazy-asses that they are). A short time later, she made a similar remark, saying, "*Son flojos*" (They're lazy). When I asked who, she said, "*los morenos.*" She maligned the work ethic of "*éstos*" (these people), adding that "*Piden de todo. Estampillas, welfare, housing. Todo quieren que se lo den*" (They ask for everything. Food stamps, welfare, housing. They want everything handed to them). She was baffled that so many were getting hired. She mentioned that there were purges at the Davis plant of workers whose social security numbers did not match, and suggested that more Blacks come in then to take their places. I was astonished at her casual remarks as we sat and stood shoulder to shoulder with African Americans in line. I voiced no agreement or disagreement, but just casually nodded along to her remarks. Although I was initially quite surprised and uncomfortable at the brazenness with which Isabel made such comments, this experience was just the first of many like it.

On this Sunday, the guard emerged as dawn approached and handed out numbers to those of us in line. I returned to the plant at nine o'clock to fill out the application, and I was interviewed by the "recruiter," a woman who I already knew was Puerto Rican thanks to Isabel. We went into the back office and she looked over my application quickly, asking next to nothing about my work experience or education. She asked where in Puerto Rico I was from, and I asked her if she was from there as well (she replied that her parents were from Vieques). When something about my knowing English came up, she attributed this to schooling in Puerto Rico, and I added that at home we spoke both. She got a checklist and started reading off questions, including, "Are you afraid of working with knives? Would you have a problem working in hot or cold environments? Is this a long-term or short-term job for you? Why do you want to work for us? Why should we hire you? Do you prefer to work in hot or cold? Do you prefer first or second shift?" To all, I answered "correctly." I am a hard worker, responsible, able to learn quickly, motivated, committed, and bilingual. It's a good-paying job. Long-term, I mean at least a year. Either shift; if I have the option, night shift. Cold. Myrna gave me a form—a conditional offer of employment to work in a new department (Marination), starting Monday, August 3, with an orientation (she said it used to be two days but was now one) on Friday, July 31. She gave me an appointment note to come back at one in the afternoon for my drug test and physical, and some medical forms to fill out. Carla, a Honduran woman in her late thirties, was waiting to speak with Myrna before starting her shift in the Pork Chop Department. She told me she started three weeks ago, and couldn't understand why they had assigned her to Pork Chop, where it is mostly *morenas*, and she is practically the only *hispana*. I hadn't imagined it would be so easy for me to get hired. I walked out stunned, knowing this would be one hell of an experience. A few days later, the Human Resources manager told those of us new hires who had arrived for orientation on time: "You will be the successful ones."

11. It is likely that segregation patterns are the result of multiple factors: steering by Human Resources personnel, differential attrition, and artifact resulting from the changing composition of eligible applicants at different periods.

12. Gabriel Thompson (2012) of *The Nation* brought much-needed attention to this issue in his criticism of the debate over poultry processing-line speeds, which the USDA had recently allowed industry to increase, and food safety: "The way food safety has dominated this debate highlights how, in a country obsessed with food, we still fail to appreciate the people whose work brings the food to our table. While the government has responded to public demands for better inspection processes, tens of thousands of poultry workers may soon find their already dangerous job becoming much more so, with almost no public debate. We consider a food product safe if it's something we can feed our children. But what if producing the food does so much damage to the hands of workers that they are unable to hold their own?" Indeed, an article in the *Washington Post* described in gory detail the likelihood that increasing line speeds will "increase risk of bird abuse" but made no mention of the guaranteed immiseration of workers' lives under these new provisions (Kindy 2013). For those interested in how the physical organization of killing and the politics of (not) seeing converge in the modern slaughterhouse, see Timothy Pachirat's (2011) inside account in *Every Twelve Seconds: Industrialized Slaughter and the Politics of Sight*.

13. When I was hired at the plant in August 2009, I was assigned to work in the Marination Department. This was a "further processing" department, where activities included seasoning, stuffing, and bacon-wrapping loin filets and tenderloins. Once workers prepared the product, usually working in groups at tables, they took positions on a line that ran the product through an individual packaging and sealing process. My usual position on the line was near the end, boxing the packaged product. This department was small (approximately twenty-five employees), predominantly African American (approximately 80 percent), with a white-dominated authority structure (African American crew leader, white supervisor, white superintendent). After working in Marination for seven months, I requested a transfer to the Loin Boning and Packing Department, which was a large (approximately two hundred) "core production" department situated in the same area as the Cut Floor (approximately 175 employees), majority Latino/a (75 to 80 percent), with an African American–dominated authority structure (two Latino crew leaders, one Native American

crew leader, one African American crew leader, one African American supervisor, one Puerto Rican supervisor, and an African American superintendent). I worked in Loin Boning and Packing for nine months, until December 2010. My transfer was purposeful and strategic, as I wanted to experience and observe departments where the composition of workers, authority structure, and working conditions differed significantly.

14. An excerpt from field notes I recorded during my first month in Loin Boning conveys the gravity of the working conditions I encountered on the packing lines, and my gloomy state of mind at the time:

This shit sucks, my third week working over here in Loin Boning and Packing. It's awful, it's god-awful. My back breaks at work, it's just killing me! My hands hurt, my fingertips are numb, my shoulder feels like it's down to the bone, and I'm feeling depressed, not feeling like I'm making any connections with any of the people I work with. This is probably one of the hardest things I'll ever do in my life. The best way I can describe it is as super-exploitation, wage slavery, these are the kinds of terms that come to mind when I think of what we're doing. Since I've started it's been a regular thirteen-and-a-half to fourteen-and-a-half hours, ranging from twelve to fifteen hours. You would never have thought the difference between thirteen and fourteen hours could be felt so acutely, but it is. Workers expect to be leaving later and later, whenever work is done as far as the bosses are concerned. In a resigned, delirious way, they will say, "We're not leaving until ten o'clock!" or "We're not leaving tonight!" or "We're not going home tonight!" It speaks volumes to me about the way in which exploitation has been internalized as there being no choice, no way out of the situation.

We're located alongside the Cut Floor, and Packing is set off from Loin Boning at the end of that line. Packing bags of loins that usually range between ten to thirty pounds, tenderloins, and ribs, thrown back on the line to be vacuum sealed (by *la tortuga*) and boxed for shipping. In ribs you work either in partners or by yourself bagging ribs (e.g., FoodMart extra meaty), "Louisiana" ribs that are boxed eighteen to a box, two scales/scalers, several tables where workers trim ribs. . . . I had started to both place myself and be placed at the loins. I thought the more interesting people were there, and I wanted to figure out where I hurt the least. Tenderloins are bagged using *cucharas* [spoons] where, usually, two tenderloins are placed for bagging—not as easy as you think. At least three people work at this station. Some loins are meant for export to Japan, these are the motherfuckers because the bags are smaller. Tenderloins drop down a chute, and workers can push a lever to move the line (with piles of tenderloins) forward. Loin lines are two—one usually for bagging "Japanese" loins, often with a padding that is placed over the meat which is taken off the line and laid on a stand for bagging. Sometimes two people work each stand, but usually just one both grabs loins and bags them. The other line is typically worked by several pairs, one who pulls loins off the line and the other who wrestles with bagging loins.

Loins are cold, fingers freeze, back throbs and burns, shoulders hurt. For the person bagging, fingers feel like falling off, numbness in fingers from bagging, I'm worried about my fingers. [I go into more detail in the recordings.] Sometimes small hams come down the loin lines. Quantity of work is difficult to gauge relative to Marination. Depends on kill amount, Cut Floor orders, number of lines running, whether there is a "test" and how much (a mysterious portion of the work falls under these special orders). At different points in the day people report the combo count [of whole loins left to debone] on the floor and people begin to get a real sense of how much longer we will work. A typical count is forty-two or forty-five after the test is done. People will consider thirty-two or so a decent count, meaning we will get out around seven thirty. Loin boning line can do between twelve and sixteen combos an hour running two lines. The work is intense, at a speed that is almost unsustainable, the number of hours is brutal, and the work itself is heavy and strenuous. This creates a mood of generalized anxiety, cynicism, negativity, pessimism, desperation, a really bad mood. I've noticed that my mood is like a rollercoaster throughout the day, plummeting after four or five in the afternoon. I think this mood contributes to relations among workers.

15. LaGuana Gray (2014) documented similar sentiments among the African American women poultry-processing workers she interviewed in Arkansas and Louisiana.

16. Charlie LeDuff (2000) reported that at the world's largest hog processing plant, in Tar Heel, North Carolina, the composition had reversed itself between 1997 and 2000, from 50 percent African American and 30 percent Latino/a to 60 percent Latino/a and 30 percent African American. By 2008, when a third representational election was held and a union victory secured, the composition had shifted again to majority African American, a result of company-collaborated ICE raids. While much has been made of Latinas/os' alleged reluctance to support the union (but see Milkman 2006; Gabriel 2008; Terriquez 2011), Ernesto hung his union badge proudly from a nail on the wall by the front door of their trailer, as he had been working there at the time. His brother Heriberto, and his wife, Celia, still work there. Heriberto has Temporary Protected Status (TPS).

17. See Kathleen Schwartzman's (2013) *The Chicken Trail* for an extended discussion of the role of refugees in the latest of three "ethnic successions" in the meatpacking and poultry industries. The first refers to the relocation and restructuring of meatpacking away from the Midwest (primarily white workers) and into the South (primarily African American workers); the second refers to the shift from a predominantly African American workforce to a majority Latino/a and migrant workforce; and the third refers to the growing reliance on refugee resettlement programs that service Somalis, Hmong, Laotians, et cetera. See Stuesse and Helton (2013) for a history of the intersection between labor struggles, racial domination, and immigration in Mississippi chicken processing plants.

18. Mexican immigration into coastal communities in the mid-Atlantic was sponsored by the blue crab industry, when three employers, two of them based in North Carolina, sought H-2 workers (Griffith 2005). By the end of the 1990s, and following restructuring in the seafood industry, fewer than 10 percent of the workers were African American women, mostly "elder women for whom the processors attempt to find as much work as possible" (Griffith 2005, 69). In eastern North Carolina's blue crab processing industry, the response to ethnic transition in late 1980s was "uneven," with some African Americans sensing that they had been pushed out and others saying that they simply took the opportunity to find alternative employment. Yet it seems that as Mexican workers arrived, available work (a set amount determined by the number of workers and crabs to pick on any given day), and thus income, declined, perhaps making these jobs even less attractive (67–68). On the other hand, Griffith claims that this period coincided with increased opportunities for young African American women at community colleges, in the growing tourism industry, and in the expanding health care services sector.

19. This simple yet common story of vacancy and shortage (e.g., "immigrants take jobs no one else wants" and "there aren't enough workers to fill all available positions") has been challenged by Kathleen Schwartzman in her (2013) study of the poultry processing industry in the U.S. South.

CHAPTER 3

1. Anani Dzidzienyo and Pierre-Michel Fontaine coined the term "Afro-Latin America" to designate all regions of Latin America where significant groups of people of known African ancestry are found. George Reid Andrews unpacks this definition, explaining that it is localized, rather than disaporic, and requires self-identification or identification by others as "Black" in order to be counted as such. For him, it also requires a threshold above which such a region/population should be included under the umbrella of Afro-Latin America. But the basic problem underlying the idea of Afro-Latin America is identifying the population that is to be considered Afro-Latin American: "How then do we 'know' who is of African ancestry and who is not? We 'know' simply by accepting what natives of the region tell us" (Andrews 2004, 5). Unfortunately, such a definition excludes those three countries that are of primary interest to my study—Mexico, Honduras, and El Salvador—especially if the unit of analysis for passing Andrews's threshold is the country one comes from. All is not lost, though, as these countries, despite their much smaller Afro–Latin American populations as defined by Andrews, nevertheless reveal enough about their socio-racial hierarchies to understand the position of blackness (and whiteness) in the dominant society.

2. Afro-Hondurans represent a diversity of histories with respect to "arrival to Honduras, levels of assimilation to mestizo society, and current configurations of culture and language" (England and Anderson 2004, 6).

3. Cristina: Between us and them, they're called *morenos*.
Vanesa: Who calls them that?
Cristina: We do. A los *negros*—those of black color. *Morenos* is dark skin. We call people of black color *morenos*. They speak Spanish and their own language. But we don't get along badly. Actually, we like it because when we go to the beach they play music and dance *punta*. *Punta* comes from them!
Vanesa: But what about within your own communities, like where you lived with Ernesto's family. There's people who are really dark, and other people who are really light. Is that acknowledged there in some form?
Cristina: Yes. In Olancho?
Vanesa: Outside of the Garifuna communities.
Cristina: Yes, the person who is as white as I am is rare there. Maybe because of their parents' origins. But not the majority, nor their hair.
Vanesa: And what name do they give that person?
Cristina: Just the place. Olanchanos, if they're from Olancho.
Vanesa: No, I mean, like here in this country, people talk about *blancos, negros, hispanos*. So in Honduras, are there less distinctions between groups?
Cristina: No, there are Koreans, Turks, and Americans. But we don't look at them like, "Who are these people that come here?"
Vanesa: But what about among Hondurans themselves? Do people talk about different groups? Or are there different words to describe people who look different?

Like someone from Olancho who was dark skinned, is there a word to describe them?

Cristina: No.

Vanesa: So people don't talk of *negros, morenos*? Or do they?

Cristina: Well, of the *negros*, just *morenos*. But if we're on the bus and they're speaking in their language . . . [interruption]. But there in San Pedro there is a *colonia* that is just theirs. Only *negritos* live there. The *colonia* of the *morenos*, of the Garifunas. I don't know why they made that *colonia* just for them.

Vanesa: And so what do they call someone like you over there?

Cristina: Over there? Just my name, normal. Just that they know, if I get to a place and there aren't people like this, then they know I'm not from there. Because when I got to Olancho, people said, "Right that you're not from here?" Because of the way I talk and the physical, the color. Because the place where I'm from people are like this. It borders Guatemala. Because people were more related with the *indios*. So to them my hair is *indio*. It's just that I have more *indio* in me than . . .

Vanesa: Than what?

Cristina: Than . . . It's that we're all *indios*. All of us are *indios*, mixed with Spaniards. Because Spaniards arrived in Honduras, but *indios* were the ones who lived there. The Spaniards arrived and they mixed. We wouldn't be this way, but we're mixed. Our hair is more *indio* than Spaniard.

Vanesa: And the Africans?

Cristina: The Africans?

Vanesa: They're there too, right? I mean, they got there too.

Cristina: Yes. The *negritos*? They're not from there, either. They got there too. But we wouldn't be this way . . . the *indios* are different. The *indio* hair is like this, and the African hair is *colochito* [curly]. So it doesn't get confused. The places where it's like this, in Honduras it's just two places. They're called Copán and Santa Bárbara. Just that in Santa Bárbara, people are white but rosy [*coloradita*]. Now, in the city of San Pedro, you will find all types. Since people arrive there from all over. People aren't distinguishable, since people are from all over. But if I go to a specific place, outside of the city, people know I'm not from there.

Vanesa: And in Honduras, do people talk about racism against darker-skinned people?

Cristina: No. Actually, they like to make coconut bread. They peel the coconuts by hand. Fast.

Vanesa: Who?

Cristina: The *negros*. They have a specialty of peeling them [coconuts] like this, and putting a straw in them. We can't do it. They are the Garifunas.

Vanesa: And who are "we"?

Cristina: We are . . . of the other color, not *negros*. Because they're Honduran too. They're born there. If they sell things, we buy them.

4. Ileana, like her in-law Cristina, had a peculiar response when I asked her about the ethnic or racial distinctions that were common in Honduras. Ileana had her own interpretation of the popular ethnoracial language in Honduras. Her mention of "Americans" or "gringos" who backpack in Honduras, and whom she first refers to as *bolillos,* shows the elision between national and racial identification (i.e., being American means being white). Her response shows that within the strictly Honduran ethnoracial landscape, "Blacks" are almost automatically associated with Garifuna.

Vanesa: In Honduras, maybe on the north coast they talk more about this, like here in the United States where people talk about *negros, blancos, bolillos, hispanos, moyos.* How do people in Honduras describe people in that racial sense? What words do they use? How are the people distributed?

Ileana: Actually, in the area where I'm from, when a *bolillo* arrives—because sometimes they go there, carrying their backpacks—over there when people see a *bolillo* it's like it makes them happy they came.

Vanesa: But over there they don't call them *bolillos.*

Ileana: No, *Americano.* Or *gringo.* They call them *gringos.* People love them there.

Vanesa: But what about among Hondurans, not the Americans who vacation there, I mean black Hondurans, or Garifuna, or *morenos?*

Ileana: Over there we call them *morenos. Morenos* we call them.

5. Lest we forget that subordinate groups in non-U.S. contexts, like those in the United States (Lipsitz 2006 [1998]), also encounter one another through the prism of white dominance, an example from Honduras provides a sharp reminder. Political ecologists studying land struggles on the north coast of the Honduran Mosquitia between indigenous Miskito and Afro-indigenous Garifuna have shown these to be intertwined with "racial struggles," as both subordinate groups deploy dominant ideologies that resonate with the region's socioracial hierarchies in order to support the primacy of their position and disparage the other group and its claims (Mollett 2006). Whereas the Miskito mobilize ideologies that characterize Garifuna as "savage" and "violent," the Garifuna propel ideologies that depict Miskito as "ignorant" and "backward." Thus, much as is the case for relations among subordinate groups in the United States, subordinate groups in other contexts—in this case the Honduran north coast—also encounter one another through the refractory prism of dominant groups.

6. Noting that Leticia was using the term *hispano* to refer to ethnoracial categories in the Honduran context, I asked if this term was used there. "No, the most common term is *ladino.*" I asked if Hondurans also say *moyolo,* a term another Honduran worker had mentioned to me, and whether that is the source of *moyo.* She responded that it is not the source of *moyo,* since "you can call any *hispano* a *moyolo.*"

7. Cristina, for her part, disputed that *gringas de cerro* is a designation for people "like me or her" in Honduras and found the proposition rather funny.

8. Sometimes Hondurans and Salvadorans refer to themselves as *negros,* but never in the sense of belonging to Blacks as group. Rather it means being somewhat dark in skin tone, illustrating the distinction between race and color labels that some scholars have studied in the Latin American context (Golash-Boza 2010). On one occasion, I was driving through downtown with Sara when she remarked in a tone of disgust about all the Blacks out on the street. When I gave her a look of disapproval, she shot back, in an ironic tone, "I am *negra.*" Sitting in Cristina's living room one afternoon, as we discussed the ethnoracial panoramas of Honduras and the United States, her brother-in-law Heriberto proclaimed "I am *negro!*" as he outstretched his arms to show his skin tone. But the chuckles of Cristina and her husband Ernesto betrayed the hyperbolic character of his comment.

9. This speculation has the support of the renowned linguist Fritz Hensey (Hensey 2012).

10. There is growing evidence of transnational racialization processes whereby international migrants communicate or transport understandings, beliefs, values, and experiences from and to origin and host communities (Jones 2013; Lewis 2012; Zamora n.d.; Roth 2012).

11. I do not seek to make definitive attributions of primacy with respect to whether "race" or "ethnicity" should be considered the "master" category. This debate is long-standing and unwieldy, and resolving it here is neither necessary nor intended. Some important works on either side of this debate include Roediger (2005), Wade (1997), and Steinberg (2001 [1981]). Barrera (2008) and Golash-Boza (2006) examine this debate with respect to Latinas/os specifically. Throughout this book I refer to "ethnoracial" as opposed to one or the other to capture the fact that, regardless of which scheme is considered the broader one, it is how these schemes intersect as particular *groups* that matters for my analysis. In other words, *moyo* is not an exclusively racial category, because individuals who would be identified as Black in Mexico or Honduras are not called *moyos* there. *Moyos, bolillos,* et cetera are not transferable categories, but rather refer specifically to African Americans and American whites. Thus, I employ the term *ethnoracial*.

12. Fittingly, perhaps, linguists have undertaken fascinating studies of the emergence of "Hispanic" as an ethnoracial construct, and on the variety, origins, and meanings of ethnonymy surrounding this U.S. group. Unfortunately, this research has not been sufficiently integrated into the contemporary race or immigration literature (see Stephens 2003 for an excellent example).

13. Survey research has found that African Americans have less negative views of Latinas/os than Latinas/os have of African Americans (Mindiola, Flores Niemann, and Rodríguez 2002).

14. When Marcos, a Chicano boning line worker, was given some off-line supervisory functions as a regular worker, and he approached La Madrina's workstation to bark orders about the work she was putting out, La Madrina told him in no uncertain terms: "Listen *pendejo,* turn around and walk the other way because the next time you yell at me like that I'm going to give you the blow job of your lifetime [*te voy a dar la mamada de tu vida*]." She didn't mean it would be a pleasurable experience.

15. Not long after this incident, Lydia and Carmen were at my apartment drinking Coronas and tequila one night after work. We talked about whether I had told Black workers of my research. Both thought it was a bad idea for me to do so: "The *negros* are very traitorous, in my experience," Carmen said. Lydia concurred. Carmen gave the example of two Black coworkers with whom they sometimes had run-ins about setting the terms of the work process on the line.

16. Recall that earlier, Cristina told me Vincent had asked her to explain *moyo* to him, when he confronted her after she referred to *moyos* in his presence.

17. Wendy Roth (2012) examines the commonalities and differences in the ways in which Puerto Rican and Dominican migrants, as well as nonmigrants in origin communities, articulate ethnoracial self-understandings. She traces

processes of transference and diffusion of "racial schemas" from Latin American contexts to American contexts and vice versa, as well as the convergence of national identities into pan-ethnic forms of identification. Nadia Kim (2008) has advanced Claire Jean Kim's (1999) "racial triangulation" perspective by considering the imposition and constitution of Western, American, and white supremacist ideals and practices beyond the physical borders of the United States into Korea.

CHAPTER 4

1. A few days after this, Jeremy and Vincent were sitting together in the cafeteria when I walked by their table. A group of workers had collected money to buy Mother's Day pizza. Vincent protested that I hadn't invited him to participate. "Sorry, it was a last-minute thing," I told him. As I walked away, Jeremy called out, "She doesn't like Black men!" perhaps associating me with Cristina's remarks. I protested that that wasn't true, that I had never said that. At that point, Vincent laughed and jumped in. "No, that's not true, 'cause she went to the Onyx Lounge!" Jeremy and Vincent laughed heartily at this. Some months earlier, when I first transferred to Loin Boning, I was bagging ribs at a table where Vincent and Gary were trimming ribs. Vincent was asking me lots of questions about what I did when I wasn't at work, teasing me that I was like an "old lady" for staying home all the time. I told him about my recent trip to the Onyx Lounge, a Black nightclub in Bennettsburg, to see rapper OJ da Juiceman with my coworkers Tanesha and Deandra from the Marination Department. He and Gary both got a kick out of this, asking me if I was "scared" because "only dope boys go there."

2. These perceptions had already surfaced among Latino/a poultry processing workers in North Carolina by the early 2000s (Smith-Nonini 2003; Marrow 2011), and Angela Stuesse (2009) has noted similar perceptions among Latinas/os working in Mississippi poultry plants. Shannon Gleeson (2010) has noted similar views among Latino/a (mostly Mexican) restaurant workers in San Jose (California) and Houston, despite the fact that these workers rarely encounter African Americans in their workplaces.

3. Throughout the chapter, in referring to "racialization" I favor Nicholas De Genova's (2005, 2) definition: "the dynamic processes by which the meanings and distinctions attributed to 'race' come to be *produced* and continually reproduced, and more important, are always entangled in social relations and conflicts, and thus retain an enduring significance because their specific forms and substantive meanings are eminently historical and mutable."

4. This field of study includes what Nicholas De Genova (2005) would call the liberal nativist wing of immigration scholarship, applying a literal denotation of "nativism" to mean the presumption of primacy of the interests of the native-born. But this is perhaps an oversimplification, since frameworks for understanding intergroup relations have long noted the importance of competition over resources as a condition for the presence or absence of conflict. Nevertheless, liberal and right-wing nativist nationalist scholarship on the economic "consequences" of immigration for Americans, particularly less-skilled workers and African Americans, abounds, and these debates inform the U.S. political

establishment. For a sampling of these views, see *The Impact of Illegal Immigration on the Wages and Employment Opportunities of Black Workers* (a 2010 briefing report on testimony delivered before the United States Commission on Civil Rights 2010).

5. Even before such a relationship between the dynamics of workplace compositional shifts and intergroup relations can be tested, whether compositional shifts are attributable to displacement or replacement dynamics must first be empirically established. Usually, though, scholars assume that one or the other dynamic is at work by either drawing on indirect suggestive indicators or by employing a reverse logic that confirms their assumptions (i.e., if there is conflict in intergroup relations, then displacement must be at work, and if there is not, then replacement must be at work).

6. Employing the less-than-ideal reverse logic laden with assumptions identified earlier, they interpret their evidence, drawn from interviews with Los Angeles employers, as more suggestive of ethnic succession through replacement than of displacement.

7. Other variants of threat-based explanations of prejudice emphasize aggregate-level compositional factors, such as the size of the minority group, economic conditions, and niche overlap (Quillian 1995, drawing on Blalock 1967; Olzak 1992, drawing on a strand of Fredrik Barth's work).

8. Interestingly, though the authors are silent about the race of the perpetrators, it is implicit that they are white.

9. This is an interesting aside to Roger Waldinger and M. I. Lichter's explanations for why network recruitment aids immigrants in achieving niches through replacement, and supports the argument in chapter 2 about the difficulty of untangling replacement-displacement dynamics.

10. In the mid-1990s, an organization called Citizens Against Illegals formed and organized demonstrations in collaboration with the Ku Klux Klan. Around the same time, a series of carpet mill raids were conducted via Operation South-PAW, and an INS office was established with the support of local government. According to Victor Zúñiga and Rubén Hernández-León (2005), anti-immigrant and anti-Latino/a letters to the editor flooded the local newspaper, but then the newspaper shut this down and local industrialists "began to articulate a public discourse recognizing the importance of immigrants and their various contributions to the region" (265). The authors seem to recognize the self-serving ends to which this was directed: "By extolling the virtues of immigrants, the industrial elite seemed to undermine all other workers that were not like them" (265). This, in turn, brought forth the class divisions among whites (266).

11. Though Steve Striffler (2005) does not specify this, it is implicit that the members of this task force, and the county commissioner in question, were all white.

12. Helen Marrow (2007, 223) proposes several hypotheses regarding the effects of Black population size. First, a higher proportion of Blacks may reduce tensions because the sense of threat will be mitigated by "strength in numbers," and this in turn may provide more opportunities for contact (implying cooperation). Second, a higher proportion of Blacks will intensify tensions because of more opportunities for contact (implying competition and conflict).

13. See also Helen Marrow (2011, 149–54). Like Marrow's respondents, David Griffith (2005) cites turkey and meatpacking workers around Newton Grove, North Carolina, who claimed that "African Americans were the most unfriendly toward them and the most likely to treat them with disrespect" (66). See also Steve Striffler (2005) for similar comments from Latinas/os in Arkansas.

14. This is a paradox that Helen Marrow does not adequately explain. Conflict models typically postulate one group as an incumbent, and another as an incoming, potentially threatening group. While the relative size of the groups is important, it is assumed that the size and rate of growth of the *incoming*, potentially threatening group is of crucial importance. In contrast, Marrow assumes that the size of the *incumbent* group (African Americans) is the variable of importance, not the size of the incoming, potentially threatening group (Latinas/os). Her findings that Latino/a–African American relations are less conflictive in the county with a higher Latino/a population, and more conflictive in the county with a smaller Latino/a population and a majority African American population, run counter to the expectations of conflict models where the variable of importance for gauging African American response is assumed to be the size and rate of growth of the Latino/a population.

15. Helen Marrow's conclusions are just as plausibly a reflection of Latino/a migrants' negative projections about African Americans through which they articulate and reinforce social boundaries as they are an indication that African Americans feel their group position threatened and therefore display an exclusionary posture toward Latinas/os. While Marrow (2007) buttresses her findings in Paula D. McClain's (2006) preliminary review of 2003 Durham survey data that suggests Blacks are more "concerned" about immigration than whites (14–16), McClain also reviews a 1996 survey (cited in Johnson, Johnson-Webb, and Farrell 1999) that showed that fewer Blacks held negative views about Latinas/os. McClain et al. (2006) found that Latinas/os view African Americans far more negatively than African Americans see them, and view whites more favorably than whites view them. (See also McClain et al. 2007 for a complete analysis of white and Black attitudes toward Latino/a immigrants.) In sum, given that much of Marrow's own interview data is restricted to Latinas/os (fourteen out of 129 interviews were with African Americans and twenty-seven with whites), and that survey data on individual attitudes is not unambiguous, a more tentative conclusion is warranted. Finally, as Marrow acknowledges even as she argues that conflict between African Americans and Latinas/os is more pronounced in neighborhoods and schools than in workplaces (2007, 248), "a more thorough and nuanced understanding of intergroup relations in large, low-wage industries" is needed (2007, 115). Specifically, I would add that such studies should examine relations at the level of particular workplaces, not just at the level of industries or occupations.

16. For a similar critique of media coverage and framing of African American–Korean relations, see Lie and Abelmann (1999).

17. David Griffith (2005, 70), looking at North Carolina and other nontraditional destinations for Mexican immigration, notes that recent decades have not seen population stagnation or declines, and that the South in general has a

large population of low-skilled African Americans, "many of whose jobs have either been undermined by or abandoned to Mexicans."

18. The flip side of group-based attributions that Blacks are "lazy" is Latinas/os' implied self-assessment of being "hardworking," a moralized claim to worthiness discussed in depth by Ruth Gomberg-Muñoz (2010).

19. Later, I thought about whether I should have brought up the potential offensiveness of this to her, but decided it was best for the time being to keep my mouth shut to avoid alienating any more Latina/o coworkers. I had recently gotten into tiffs with Doris and Tania, two very cantankerous Honduran women. Jeremy certainly could have said a lot more to her, and opted not to for whatever reason (perhaps because he felt that Leticia had affection for him and was ignorant of the inappropriateness of her comparison). In any event, a few months later, Jeremy quit his job at Swine's to run a bar he had recently purchased, and Leticia was hurt that he had not said goodbye.

20. In my first days working in Loin Boning, several Latina/o workers expressed surprise that I was Puerto Rican, saying they thought I was a *bolilla*, and teasing that Daniel and I looked like siblings because we were both *güeros*. I later found out that Daniel was *indígena*. Claudia told me this once we became friends, after Daniel had quit and returned to Mexico, but she never knew his true identity—either that he was *indígena* or his real name, which apparently marked him as *indio*—while they were romantically involved.

21. Rosa and Cristina could dish it out, too. At the end of July, we were all hurriedly bagging ribs as we got ready to finish the workday. Perhaps Vincent was mouthing off at one of them, because Rosa muttered, "*pendejo huevón.*" "You too," Vincent shot back. Then out of nowhere Cristina said to me, "*Él se molesta cuando le preguntan si es gay*" (He gets mad when people ask him if he's gay). "People ask him if he's gay?" I asked. "It's just that he looks gay, don't you think?" she replied. "Hmm, I don't know." I said to Vincent, "She says you get mad when people ask you if you're gay." "Gay, me? I ain't a faggot." Cristina was kind of chuckling. Vincent said, "Your husband got a *sancho*! [Honduran slang for male lover]" She laughed and said, "Yeah, *tú eres el sancho!*" I told Vincent, "She said you're his *sancho.*" Cristina howled, "I don't care, *a mí no me importa!*"

22. Only once did I hear an African American worker—a cranky woman named Constance—impugn the work ethic of Latinas/os as a group. And in this instance, the valence of the banter involved was not clear to me. In general, African Americans assessed Latinas/os' work ethic as a group positively, or, more commonly, they insisted that among Latinas/os, as in all groups, there are hard workers and lazy workers.

23. Some of the ideas in this chapter are hinted at in comments from Latinas/os interviewed by Helen Marrow, who suggested that Blacks are advantaged at their workplaces, too. The appearance of these comments among Marrow's interviewees suggests that these findings are not limited to social relations at Swine's but may extend across many American workplaces, certainly in the South. In fact, similar clues surface in the data collected by Roger Waldinger and M.I. Lichter (2003) on Los Angeles low-wage workplaces. But the most direct acknowledgment that the social organization of labor may be an impor-

tant factor mediating Latino/a–African American relations comes from Angela Stuesse (2009).

CHAPTER 5

1. Leticia had been teased mercilessly by Latina coworkers when she first started working at Swine's. These women referred to her as *payula* (washed-out complexion) and made fun of what they viewed as her unkempt appearance. They also gossiped about her husband, who suffered from an incapacitating respiratory disease and was unable to work, making Leticia the sole breadwinner.

2. When Hurricane Mitch struck Honduras in 1998, Hondurans in the United States became eligible to apply for Temporary Protected Status. However, once the application period elapsed, no new TPS applications were allowed, and only renewals have been issued since. Salvadorans, whose status as refugees in the United States during the country's decadelong civil war became the subject of intense litigation (Coutin 2000), became eligible for Temporary Protected Status in the immediate aftermath of an earthquake that struck the country in 2001.

3. Roberto Gonzáles and Leo Chávez (2012) theorize abjectivity—a concept that combines *abject* and *subjectivity*—as describing the state of being of those who are cast out by the nation and then defined through that expulsion as having been outcasts all along.

4. Some readers may draw the conclusion that employer sanctions "work." I reject this interpretation on several grounds, and in the concluding chapter I suggest a different course of action.

5. On a lighter and more uplifting note, one episode of collective action between African Americans and Latinas in the Marination Department culminated in a race to the smoking room. My field notes for January 7, 2010 tell the story:

Clock out at 1:53 a.m.

As we arrive, we get on the line and finish about 25 boxes of teriyaki tenderloins from first shift. Then we run 128 boxes of peppercorn tenderloins (also from first shift?), move to 210 garlic and herb filets, 210 portobello filets, then wrap a bit (Ms. Angie, sometimes Dilmer and Deandra and Tina and Avery had been wrapping throughout the night), end up running about 40 boxes.

Although we end up running only 40 boxes, originally it got around that there were 6 racks, and we all wondered how the hell we were going to get all this work done.

At different points in the night, Clyde told people that we were not going home until we finished all the product "or we wouldn't have a job." He also announced that we would stay until two o'clock in the morning if we had to, but this was ridiculous since no matter what we were going to stay that late, as the night proved.

Valerie calls Macy out on the line about how she gets mad, likening her to Clyde. Macy seems upset by Valerie's remarks (the next day at start of work she comments that she "hates when people pretend to be your friend then talk behind your back").

Clyde is in an awful mood tonight, and Joe barely walks through our floor. Early on, Edrick asks me if we've been scolded yet and I tell him we've been scolded plenty in the last couple of days. He says the boxes we reworked from Pork Chop the other night (from Tuesday or Wednesday?) were no good. I explain to him about Tuesday and how we had been told to just weigh the boxes with one or two of the pallets. Then I tell him about yesterday's training log bullshit and we agree that that was Joe and Clyde's responsibility, not ours. Edrick says they always look for someone to wipe their asses with, and that's us. A little while later, Edrick comes by and holds his fists up. I ask does he want to fight, and he says he just did. He took Joe to HR because he yelled at him unnecessarily in front of everyone in Pork Chop, and HR told Joe to calm down. Joe, he says, is stressed out (probably because of the 80 or so pallets of chops that have had to get reworked and are losing shelf life) and shouts when he's in that state.

Joe and especially Clyde's attitude definitely contributed to workers' wondering about our third break. For a while now, I have brought this up to people, and especially this week I have ranted about it several times. Tonight, we are prepared to stay until 2 a.m., and are going to try to get our break. I notice Edrick talking to Kim and Valerie and I walk up, asking him, "Isn't it true we're supposed to get a break?" Edrick confirms this (they may have already been talking about it) and I say that we're the *pendejos* [assholes] who let them get away with it for five months. He says we have to ask for it, or go to HR. Then separately I ask Edrick if we can get what we're owed if we go to HR. He hesitates, chuckling, avoiding an answer, saying that the company will lose money that way. Close to 11, Kim asks me when should we ask Clyde about our break. I suggest around 11:30 or 11:45. Kim and Macy have both asked him, and he has not given an answer, saying he doesn't know, and another time saying, "There's a truck waiting on this product [the portobello order]."

Once we finish the order, Clyde begins to instruct us to go wrap, when I walk up to him as Joe is walking up as well, and ask, "What about our break?" Clyde walks off with a wave of the hand, leaving me with Joe, who feigns a look of confusion and asks, "What break? Didn't you get your breaks already?" "The break we're supposed to get now," I say. "You get another break if you're going to work 8 hours and 20 minutes or more," he says. "Right, and aren't we?" "I don't know that yet," he says lamely. I shake my head and furrow my brow, releasing a chuckle, and walk away to the prep table. There, Kim, Tanesha, and Lydia ask what he told me, and I rant that he's an asshole acting like he's stupid. Edrick walks up and we are all ranting about the break issue.

At the other table, Deandra or Macy has shouted something to Clyde, and I hear Clyde shout to Deandra, "Maybe you should go to the nurse and get your hearing checked." She is pissed and shouting ensues. At my table, Kim says we should get here early tomorrow so we can go to HR. Lydia insists, and I translate that it can't be just one of us, it has to be a group of us. Shortly, I begin to hear subversive shouts of "break!" like a cacophonous chorus. I join in, shouting, "Where's our break!" repeatedly, and Lydia shouts, "Break!" This persists for less than a minute, but it has Clyde clearly rattled. Soon after it dies down, Joe appears and chats with Clyde, who probably tells him we're demanding our break. Lydia notes that now, when it really counts, everyone is scared and doesn't say anything. But neither does she. Then Joe calls out, "You guys have ten minutes." We are elated and run upstairs. My adrenaline is pulsing and I can tell others are excited. The locker room is buzzing. In the smoke room, we also buzz, and Kim is across from me. "That was awesome!" I say. "Yeah, it was!" she says with a smile.

Back on the floor after break, Clyde shouts for Deandra to do spec, and she does, but an argument ensues. She returns to bacon wrap, and I go up, asking what happened: "He's just doing that to fuck with you." "Oh yeah, well, I got something for him. He done fucked with the wrong bitch." And a little while later, as we are about to leave, chatting with Macy and me, she says, "My brother kills people just for fun."

Macy also had an altercation with Clyde, and Clyde called Joe to the floor.

We stop by the supervisor's office to pick up our paystubs and end up waiting for Joe for about ten minutes. When he does show up, apologizing because he had to do something, he is jokey, telling some of us how we had given him dagger eyes tonight.

6. This episode of collective action, rare as it was, presented a serious dilemma for me, both as a researcher and as a person committed to equality. On the one hand, I was initially excited that workers felt driven to act together to protest conditions of work, even if it took the form of a letter rather than some more radical tactic. But as their concerns shifted from asking for changes to the labor process to denouncing Black workers' supposedly advantaged position and demanding that they be equally subordinated, my enthusiasm plummeted. I mulled over my response to the Latina/o workers about this issue, even as the letter I drafted omitted any mention of Black workers. Ultimately, I did not have to face the dilemma—either by silencing Latina/o workers' claims of Black privilege or somehow perpetuating a problematic dynamic involving Latina/o and African American workers—because the collective effort collapsed. The Latina/o workers could not agree on what else the letter should ask for, or whether they should sign it, and talk of submitting the letter soon fizzled, despite my follow-up.

7. Latinas/os at Swine's, as elsewhere, represent a diversity of nationalities and other subjectivities. But with few exceptions, most of them deemphasize internal heterogeneity. For example, a Honduran worker explained: "I think we're all the same [*hispanos*]. But the Mexicans and the Hondurans don't get along too well, I don't know why. But I've never had problems with anybody." Clara, one of the minority of Mexican workers at Swine's, was among the few Latina/o workers I spoke with who made any substantial reference to within-group boundaries:

> I get there and I'm Mexican, and the majority of them are from Honduras. Someone comes by and says, "Ah, you can tell she's Mexican." Hilda was my friend and she is Honduran. But in that first month that I was alone, I only talked with Cristina. Then Hilda started working there and we have been friends. But there's always that talk among them about Mexicans. Because Mexican women don't wear makeup, and they say we're more Indian. So sometimes you're just better off staying quiet. We're *compañeras* at work but sometimes it's better if you just keep your distance. Even the way we talk is different among *hispanos*. I didn't say anything because my need was greater. I felt discrimination, but from the Hondurans.

8. Turnover rates are notoriously misleading, in part because different researchers measure them differently, but also because it is possible to have very high turnover rates despite a majority of workers remaining employed (Grey 1999). That is the case somewhat at Swine's. For industries such as this, a year can be a relatively long time.

9. Employers may prefer to hire immigrants over native-born workers because they are viewed as the ideal subordinates. But for the same reason, it could be hypothesized that *once hired*, native-born workers are situated relatively more favorably than immigrants within the social organization of labor.

CHAPTER 6

1. Claudia asked me what the word "nigger" meant. I said that it was a horrible word, with a terrible history of oppression. But what was the story behind it? she pressed. I said it wasn't about a particular story, but rather about a long

history of oppression of Blacks in this country. Claudia knew it was a hurtful slur, which was why she had uttered it in reference to our African American floor supervisor Michael, whom she couldn't stand. But she did not understand why "nigger" was such a violently unspeakable slur. I told her there was not really an equivalent term for Latinas/os. She countered, "But people can call me wetback, illegal, undocumented, and I don't care, it doesn't hurt me." As others have found (Marrow 2011), Latino/a immigrant workers seem to have little knowledge of the tumultuous racial history of the American South. On Martin Luther King Jr. Day in 2011, I was cooking dinner with Claudia and Sara when they thanked King for "freeing the slaves," as it meant a holiday from work. I tried to clarify that King did not free the slaves, but they showed no interest in a history lesson. On the same holiday in 2012, I was again with Claudia and Sara, at Claudia's trailer. I noticed a catered cake on the table when I arrived, and asked what it was for. The two of them joked that it was in celebration of Martin Luther King Jr.'s birthday. Their banter then deteriorated, returning to the slave theme in the context of turning the authority relations at work on their head: "I wish they were still slaves. I would whip the hell out of Michael!" At other times, though, Claudia seemed more sympathetic to the idea that African Americans in positions of authority face resistance in the white-dominated echelons of power at Swine's. On separate occasions, she noted that George seemed marginalized by the white superintendent and supervisors of the Cut Floor, and thought this was because he is Black.

2. Much of the research on the composition of the authority structure in workplaces studies its effects on outcomes such as the wages of workers of particular racial or gender status (see for example Cohen and Huffman [2007] on women in managerial positions).

3. The department superintendent was African American, and one of two floor supervisors was as well. The other, Luis, was Puerto Rican, but he quit shortly after I transferred. The position was vacant until January 2011 (after I had left), when Javier was hired. Javier is Mexican and had worked as a supervisor at Berkshire Chicken alongside Don, the white superintendent who took over when the African American superintendent, George, was pushed out in October 2010. Word was that Don got the plant to hire his buddy Javier—the two live together as well—and that Don got hired because he is friends with Larry Mendosa, the Human Resources manager. Before the Puerto Rican supervisor, Luis, there was a Mexican supervisor named Carlos, who is married to the Salvadoran boning line worker Emma, ex-sister-in-law of my buddy Claudia, but Carlos was let go when his papers "turned out bad." Emma befriended Don (as did Claudia, in a way, since he had a crush on her), and Don spent practically every weekend socializing with Emma and Carlos, and frequently attended Claudia's parties, or invited her to his. None of the crew leaders on the main boning floor were Black. (Jim, an African American, was crew leader in the "little boning room" that mostly trimmed jowls, located in a different part of the plant.)

4. Clara said, "The *morenos* that you see on the line now are from Haiti. I see that the people from Haiti are very solidaristic [*unidos*], they stick together, unlike what I see with either Mexicans or Hondurans. And between us and

them there's no communication because neither of us speaks English and they speak French."

5. Natalia noted that at Leslielac, a factory where she previously worked, things were different. "At Leslielac, there were more Americans. Things were *parejo* there because there weren't many *hispanos*, so who was going to do all the work?"

6. This was how Elsie put it. One afternoon, I was called upstairs to translate for Elsie and Don, who were in Don's office. He berated her for supposedly throwing backbones into the inedible vat without properly shaving every last particle of meat from them with her small whizard knife. She tried to defend herself, in vain. Don told her she would do as she was told or turn in her knives. Elsie turned to me and exclaimed with outrage, "He talks to us like we're animals!"

7. Unlike most Latina/o workers, Vincent liked Michael, saying that Michael "does me pretty good" and was responsive to his needs and requests. I asked him why, and he said, "We have a lot in common." In particular, he mentioned that they grew up in the same area and that Michael went to school with his uncle. With respect to the changes wrought by Don, Vincent said, "I can't stand Don. I had to cuss him out the other day!" Don had told Vincent to do some task, and Vincent said okay but did not move immediately because the materials he needed to do the task had not yet arrived. Don proceeded to yell at him, and Vincent responded, "I'm not your fucking kid so don't yell at me." Don sent him upstairs to the supervisor's office, where they argued over whether Don had yelled at him. Vincent thought he could have gone to Human Resources to report the incident and that Don would have gotten in trouble for yelling, but he preferred to handle the situation "like grown men" and not "be a snitch." Vincent judged George as "more person-oriented" and someone "you could talk to if you had a problem." Don, he said, "doesn't care about you. Don cares about making himself look good, and the only way he can make himself look good is getting that work done."

8. Indeed, there was no certain affinity between Black workers and Black supervisors. Lawrence, an African American supervisor on the Hamboning afternoon shift who was widely disliked by workers, told an African American new hire who was having trouble keeping up with work on her line to "stop acting like a nigger." Shortly after this incident, another new hire was fired and then arrested for punching Lawrence in the face and knocking his glasses to the ground after Lawrence berated him on the line.

9. According to Philip Cohen and Matthew Huffman (2007), research to date has been unable to operationalize models of the effects of minority access to authority positions on minority employees' status because of data limitations, but see Smith and Elliott (2002) for an analysis of the effects of ethnic concentration on employees' access to authority.

CHAPTER 7

1. If Vincent's preoccupation with what he termed "the tissue issue" suggests a view of Latinas/os as dirty and unhygienic, on other occasions Black workers articulated a view of Latinas/os that suggested quite the opposite, but just as

comically. One evening, I picked up take-out Chinese food with Jaycene, an African American worker in her thirties who worked in the Marination Department. As we left the restaurant, we walked past a laundromat. Jaycene remarked that it "smelled like Mexicans." I laughed, and asked what she meant. She explained that "Spanish people" always smell strongly of clean laundry, muffling a chuckle at her own comment.

2. Vincent taunted Latina/o workers as well from time to time. But, importantly, his taunts were not characterized by criticisms of their work efforts as a group, nor were they expressed through ethnoracial language or slurs. Instead, he usually employed homophobic taunts, bantering with Latinas/os by calling them *jotos* (faggots).

3. Despite the preponderance of diverse evidence to support my findings, some readers will wonder if how I was perceived ethnoracially by others in the field colored the data I gathered, yielding biased results. Most factory workers and managers initially identified me as white. Many came to know I was from Puerto Rico and spoke Spanish as well as English, and was highly educated. Some forgot these attributes from time to time and reverted to the assumption that I was a white American local to the area (e.g., "How do you know Spanish?" or "Do you go with a Black boy?"), while others may never have known about them. I was never identified by anyone as Black, though some Latina/o workers thought I defended African Americans too much. Some Black workers seemed to test me, making derogatory statements about Black people or "jokingly" accusing me of disliking Black people, presumably to gauge my response. In short, given this experience, I'm not sure what would be a logical hypothesis of respondent bias.

4. Felicia was among the few African American women I met who was in a relationship with a Honduran migrant fellow worker. She was eagerly learning Spanish but told me that she gets a bad reaction about her relationship from "Hispanic women" at work.

5. Such a conspiracy theory might explain away my analysis, but it depends on an impossibly mystical notion of African Americans' unknowability.

6. If readers still question the robustness of the findings I report, Yanira's experience lends strong support to major features of my analysis. Yanira, a young Dominican packer in the Loin Boning and Packing Department, whose ambiguous ethnoracial status was commonly misidentified by Latinas/os and African Americans alike, also blurred group boundaries by socializing with Latina/o, African American, and white workers outside of Swine's. In fact, soon after she started working there around October 2010, Yanira moved in with Candace, a rare white recent hire in Loin Boning and Packing. Yanira also became friends with Vincent outside of work, visiting him at home and drinking with him. Her ambiguous ethnoracial status gave her a view of intergroup relations from where the peripheries converge, that is, from a self-identified Latina subjectivity frequently first encountered as Black by others:

> Most people get along most of the days. But I think they're kind of prejudiced—the Mexicans—a little bit, when other people from other places come in. Like with me, at the beginning, they wouldn't really talk to me. Until I started talking Spanish. And I didn't even want to talk Spanish. But somebody didn't know how to speak English, so

I thought, why am I being a jerk, I'll speak Spanish. And I started speaking Spanish. I started saying I was Dominican. And then they started being nice to me. I didn't say it right away, but around the third day I started saying it. More of them talk to me now.

With me it's kind of weird because I'm Hispanic but my skin is dark. Not all of them do, but I specifically notice it. Because, like I said, now I speak Spanish to everybody. At the beginning, the Black people were friendly and nice to me. I wouldn't speak Spanish, not a lick, nothing. I thought, there's no need. These people speak English. I wasn't around the Spanish people then. They kept putting me with the English-speaking people. Then Alma started speaking to me. She doesn't know English. The Mexicans—not all of them are Mexicans—but the Spanish-speaking people started to help me. And they tell me I'm not Black, just dark-skinned. "*Tu moya no eres*," Rosa tells me that. And they just treat them weird [Blacks in general, Haitians in particular]. They make fun of them. "Look how Black they are. And some of them, you don't know if they're a boy or a girl" [Haitians]. Sometimes I'm like, God, if I hadn't spoken Spanish. The native Mexicans and those types, because us Dominicans and the little Puerto Ricans that are there, they don't treat people like that. But the Mexicans, they're just prejudiced. Because I've noticed—you know Lina [Indian worker identified as white]? She talked to me. And Emily [white worker]. So it's not the white people. "I thought you was a *moya*. Look at this nigga trying to speak Spanish." I said shut up, nigga. I be an ass. You know who treated me a little different? Michael. He's a sweetheart, he helps everyone. One day he heard me speaking English, and he said, "Where'd you learn English?" I'm thinking, "Hello, we're in America." I told him I came here when I was six years old, so that's how I know English. And at first, Don was trying to intimidate everybody. And I was thinking, "I have my papers."

I know that the white people, they talk to whoever and anybody. Some Black people are racist, too. They don't talk to everybody. Some of them. Some of them do talk to everybody. Some say, "Oh my god, you talk Spanish?" and they look at you with a face like, "Oh, I thought she was one of us." In the shipping area, the guys. Mostly when people found out that I speak Spanish, some people treated me not the same, and some people treated me better, and some people didn't care. They're like, "Oh cool, you're bilingual."

Truth is, the white people are just free. That's how I see it. They speak and talk to anybody and everybody. The Black people—they hold off, sometimes. They're not exactly prejudiced, but they hold off to who they speak to, sometimes. And mainly, in my opinion, it's the Mexicans. Not the Mexicans because they're not all Mexicans so I can't be prejudiced either. But most of them—Spanish-speaking people—they're, in my opinion, the most prejudiced. That's what I saw. Because they've never been anywhere but their place [Latinas/os]. 'Cause some of them are like, "The Dominican Republic, what is that?"

In the end, Yanira pointed to the imperative to get along when your job hinges on brute interdependence. But her more refined analysis is as profound as it is unique, given her ambiguous ethnoracial status. It shows that group boundaries are sharp and mutually exclusive, and invested with affective significance. Moreover, as Yanira saw it, Latinas/os—not African Americans—draw the boldest and most negatively inflected boundaries vis-à-vis other groups.

7. Although Helen Marrow (2011) took into account the relative size of groups in the two North Carolina counties that she studied, recall from chapter 4 that her findings—stronger exclusionary boundary-making action attributed to African Americans toward Latinas/os in the majority-Black county that had

only a small Latino/a minority—runs counter to the typical hypotheses derived from competition models (Olzak 1992). In such formulations, it is the size and growth rate of the incoming group (in this case, Latinas/os) rather than the incumbent group (in this case, Blacks) that would be the crucial variable accounting for competitive threat.

8. A different challenge that readers might raise regarding my findings is worthy of some consideration here. If competition theories would expect intergroup prejudice and conflict to arise from an incumbent group's direct competition for resources, such as jobs, then perhaps African Americans *not already employed* at Swine's would articulate very different views about Latinas/os and migrants than those I report here. This is certainly a possibility, but whether it is the case does not alter the validity of my argument about *intergroup* relations, since Latinas/os' primary means of engaging with African Americans is in the workplace. Moreover, African American new hires, who might then be expected to articulate a stronger and more negative discursive repertoire vis-à-vis their Latina/o counterparts, did not appear to do so. Recall from chapter 4 that Aisha, the young African American new hire, was taunted incessantly by Latina/o coworkers in ethnoracial terms, but this was not paralleled in her actions toward them. In fact, Aisha appeared to enjoy flirting with Latinos, and remarked about the numerous handsome Latinos working at Swine's. Recall as well that Adrienne, to whom Cristina had said she was going to come to work painted black so she didn't have to work, reacted with remarkable restraint. Finally, and more importantly, getting a job is not the only aspect of economic competition to be considered. Status within the social organization of labor is certainly a potential resource over which groups may be in competition. My findings about African Americans' weak and more ambivalent boundary-making action could be interpreted to suggest that they perceive a low level of competition for status in the workplace. This, in turn, bolsters my argument that the crucial factor motivating Latina/o–African American relations at Swine's is Latinas/os' perception that they are the most oppressively exploited workers and that African Americans occupy a privileged position—a motivating grievance quite distinct from the one competition models typically propose.

9. Kim is Vincent's cousin.

10. Of the four "humor mechanisms" that K. A. Neuendorf (2010) identifies (superiority/disparagement, incongruity, arousal, and social currency), the crude sexual humor that was prevalent in exchanges between Latinas/os and African Americans is best thought of as a combination of arousal and social currency mechanisms. That is, such crude humor serves to relieve psychological tension through sexual humor (arousal) while building relationships through playful interaction (social currency). Nicholas De Genova (2005) refers to the comically surreal aspects of Latinas/os' workplace humor as *relajo*. Throughout this book, the element of humor—perhaps especially in the form of disparagement—is a persistent theme.

11. Several months later, I became aware that Lydia was involved, perhaps romantically, with an African American supervisor in another department.

12. Jaycene's husband Troy worked in the Hamboning Department on the later shift, and recounted overhearing two Latina coworkers talking about him,

leading to a confrontation in which he warned them that he knows what *negro* means.

13. Perhaps related to the strong sense of linked fate resulting from the "black utility heuristic" (Dawson 1994), the assumption of homogeneity among African Americans was strong. This took a comical twist one October day as I chatted with Vincent as we emptied a combo, throwing the bagged bellies and ribs on the line. Following up on his usual sexual banter, he asked me, "So which one are you today? The virgin or the other one?" "Probably the virgin." "Why?" "I'm feeling kind of in a funk." "A funk, what's that?" "In a bad mood or whatever." "Is that some white-people slang?" "Dude, just because you haven't heard of some slang word doesn't mean it's white-people talk. There's lots of places in this country, not just Perry, North Carolina." He replied, "Whatever, I'm Black and we're all the same." I said, "No, that's not true. Black people are *not* all the same, there's lots of subcultures among Black people." He said, "No, we're all the same, it's all the same thing." I said, "No, I know plenty of Black people who belong to lots of different subcultures." Vincent said something about Puma sneakers: "That's getting really popular among Hispanic people, right?" I was like, "What do you mean? When I was a teenager and trying to be all alternative in Puerto Rico, that's what I would wear." "That's 'cause you're Hispanic." "No, that's because I was trying to be alternative." "Like goth?" "I wasn't goth, I was alternative, or punk rock. But yes, I've known Black goth people, and even Black men who are in the gay bear subculture." "Yeah, but there's faggots in every race." "Huh?" "Like this guy right here," he said, referring to Gerardo, a young Honduran guy who worked at the ribs station. "Right, faggot?" I was in a bad mood now. I said, "I don't like that kind of language," waved him off, and walked away. Gerardo asked me, "What's he saying to me, that I'm a faggot [*culero*]?" I went back to my "Louisiana" table. A few minutes later Vincent came up to me and said, "Yo, come on, did that offend you? I told him I was sorry. I'm just playing with him. That's how I joke with him. I didn't mean anything by it. You didn't have to get angry and walk off and come hide over here, acting all like the trick. I was like, damn, she *is* a girl." I said, "No, I just didn't want to be involved in that. I just don't like that talk." "Well, do you accept my apology?" "Yes, I accept your apology." "Then can I have a piece of gum?"

CHAPTER 8

1. For the beginnings of an empirical assessment of whiteness theories, including the tenet regarding its "invisibility," see Hartmann, Gerteis, and Croll (2009). For an excellent review of the state of "whiteness" studies, see also McDermott and Samson (2005).

2. Recent work by Jennifer Anne Meri Jones (2013) moves in this direction. Drawing on research carried out in Winston-Salem, North Carolina, Jones proposes that Latinas/os (mostly mestizo and Afro-Mexicans) and African Americans develop a common identification as minorities through their shared experience of discrimination, which they attribute to whites and white-dominated organizations. These understandings lead some to expressions of solidarity between the groups.

3. Indeed, the analysts Jorge Chavez and Doris Marine Provine (2009) have found that "conservative citizen ideology" is the primary determinant of immigrant-related restrictionist legislation at the state level. Robin Jacobson (2006) also finds racial motives in her analysis of immigration restrictionists' efforts to abolish or restrict birthright citizenship in the United States.

4. Some readers may draw the conclusion that employer sanctions "work." I would reject this interpretation on several grounds, and suggest a different course of action. Undoubtedly, the threat of government investigation and sanctions may push some corporate bosses to direct their human resources minions to comply with work authorization verification requirements. But employers are *rarely* sanctioned, despite the fact that they frequently knowingly hire workers lacking authorization either as a strategy to create a super-exploitable workforce or because the pool of available workers with authorization is insufficient to meet labor demand (Wishnie 2007). When employers are sanctioned, as in the Postville, Iowa, raid, workers and the broader community often suffer the most. In Postville, the costs and disruption to production that the raids exerted left the company unable to carry on business, and the entire economy of a small town was dealt a crippling blow by the plant closing and the mass exodus of people. In contrast, a years-long investigation into Tyson, where the company faced accusations of actual involvement in human smuggling (such charges are even more rarely brought against employers), ended in acquittal. Some will argue that the audit style pursued by the Obama administration is less disruptive and more humane, but it is really just a polite way of wrecking lives and communities while preserving the basis for a subclass of workers. Others have supported the E-Verify program, including making employer participation obligatory. But numerous problems have arisen in the implementation of this program. Even when employers participate in E-Verify, it is clear that they are apparently allowed to dispose of unauthorized workers essentially at their leisure and convenience, robbing them of paid vacations and bonuses that are accrued over time through hard work and self-negation, and, again, preserving the basis for a subclass of workers. Further, when a worker loses their job because it is suddenly discovered that their papers are of questionable authenticity, they frequently end up taking a job at a firm in a similar industry that operates at a subperipheral level. Now, instead of working a Swine's knife job at $12.50 per hour with good health benefits, they do the same work for $8 per hour, without benefits. Does this seem like it "works"? And if yes, for whom?

5. As an obvious example, double-jeopardy clauses under the Fifth Amendment can be considered one such instance. The "fruit of the poisonous tree" doctrine under the Fourth Amendment, guaranteeing protection against unlawful searches, is more broadly illustrative of the extent to which the American legal system not only tolerates but is built upon deep paradoxes resolvable only by relenting to the eminent domain of the Constitution. In these examples, procedural considerations of significance to the protection of guarantees under the Constitution quash even common knowledge of guilt.

6. Linda Bosniak (2006, 140) writes: "The quest for unmitigated inclusion within the community can therefore serve as a regulative ideal, but in actuality, such inclusion is a fantasy."

7. Note that these arguments operate within a nationalistic-universal labor rights framework. Beyond these arguments, I support a fundamental human right to migrate, particularly so when the free mobility of capital is a major contributing cause of people's need to do so, and especially when the United States has deep and long-standing asymmetrical ties to the country from which people are migrating, as is the case in Mexico and Central America. Because the debates about controlling migration are so often transparently about defining who belongs, and the chief sponsors of movements and measures targeting immigrants pander to white lower-middle-class conservatism—not the working-class African Americans who are supposed to be most threatened economically by unauthorized migrants—we need to lay bare the issues for what they are: nativist reaction in the service of (white) nativist nationalism.

8. See Cynthia Estlund (2002) on the "ossification" of labor law in the United States.

Bibliography

Alba, Richard, Ruben Rumbaut, and Karen Marotz. "A Distorted Nation: Perceptions of Racial/Ethnic Group Sizes and Attitudes Toward Immigrants and Other Minorities." *Social Forces* 84, no. 2 (2005): 901–19.

Alexander, Ames, Kerry Hall, and Franco Ordonez. "The Cruelest Cuts: The Cost of Bringing Poultry to Your Table." *Charlotte Observer*, February 10–15, 2008. http://www.charlotteobserver.com/poultry/.

Allport, Gordon. *The Nature of Prejudice*. Reading, MA: Addison-Wesley Pub. Co., 1954.

Almaguer, Tomás. "At the Crossroads of Race: Latino/a Studies and Race Making in the United States." In *Critical Latin American and Latino Studies*, 206–22. Minneapolis: University of Minnesota Press, 2003.

American Community Survey, 2010. [Additional details redacted]

Andreas, Carol. *Meatpackers and Beef Barons: Company Town in a Global Economy*. Niwot, CO: University Press of Colorado, 1994.

Andrews, George Reid. *Afro-Latin America, 1800–2000*. New York: Oxford University Press, 2004.

Anrig, Greg, T.A. Wang, and P.D. McClain. *Immigration's New Frontiers: Experiences from the Emerging Gateway States*. New York: Century Foundation Press, 2006.

Arreola, D.D. *Hispanic Spaces, Latino Places: Community and Cultural Diversity in Contemporary America*. Austin: University of Texas Press, 2004.

Bacon, David. "How Mississippi's Black/Brown Strategy Beat the South's Anti-Immigrant Wave." *The Nation*, April 20, 2012. http://www.thenation.com/article/167465/how-mississippis-blackbrown-strategy-beat-souths-anti-immigrant-wave.

Barrera, Mario. "Are Latinos a Racialized Minority?" *Sociological Perspectives* 51, no. 2 (2008): 305–24.

Barrett, James R., and David Roediger. "Inbetween Peoples: Race, Nationality, and the 'New Immigrant' Working Class." *Journal of American Ethnic History* 16, no. 3 (1997): 3–44.

Barth, Fredrik, ed. *Ethnic Groups and Boundaries: The Social Organization of Culture Difference* (results of a symposium held at the University of Bergen, February 23–26, 1967). Bergen, Norway: Universitetsforlaget; London: Allen & Unwin, 1969.

Bean, F.D., and S. Bell-Rose. "Introduction: Immigration and Its Relation to Race and Ethnicity in the United States." In *Immigration and Opportunity: Race, Ethnicity, and Employment in the United States*. New York: Russell Sage Foundation, 1999.

Bell, Derrick. *Faces at the Bottom of the Well: The Permanence of Racism*. New York: Basic Books, 1992.

Berg, Justin Allen. "White Public Opinion Toward Undocumented Immigrants: Threat and Interpersonal Environment." *Sociological Perspectives* 51, no. 1 (2009): 39–58.

Blalock, Hubert M. *Toward a Theory of Minority Group Relations*. New York: Capricorn Books, 1967.

Blumer, Herbert. "Race Prejudice as a Sense of Group Position." *The Pacific Sociological Review* 1, no. 1 (1958): 3–7.

Bobo, Lawrence, and V.L. Hutchings. "Perceptions of Racial Group Competition: Extending Blumer's Theory of Group Position to a Multiracial Social Context." *American Sociological Review* 61, no. 6 (1996): 951–72.

Bobo, Lawrence D., and Devon Johnson. "Racial Attitudes in a Prismatic Metropolis: Mapping Identity, Stereotypes, Competition, and Views on Affirmative Action." In *Prismatic Metropolis: Inequality in Los Angeles*, 81–166. Edited by Lawrence D. Bobo, Melvin L. Oliver, James H. Johnson Jr., and Abel Valenzuela Jr. New York: Russell Sage Foundation, 2000.

Bonacich, Edna. "Abolition, the Extension of Slavery, and the Position of Free Blacks: A Study of Split Labor Markets in the United States, 1830–1863." *American Journal of Sociology* 81, no. 3 (1975): 601–28.

———. "Advanced Capitalism and Black/White Race Relations in the United States: A Split Labor Market Interpretation." *American Sociological Review* 41, no. 1 (1976): 34–51.

———. "A Theory of Ethnic Antagonism: The Split Labor Market." *American Sociological Review* 37, no. 5 (1972): 547–59.

Bonilla-Silva, Eduardo. "From Bi-Racial to Tri-Racial: Towards a New System of Racial Stratification in the USA." *Ethnic and Racial Studies* 27, no. 6 (2004): 931–50.

———. "The Invisible Weight of Whiteness: The Racial Grammar of Everyday Life in Contemporary America." *Ethnic and Racial Studies* 35, no. 2 (2012): 173–94.

Bonilla-Silva, Eduardo, and Karen S. Glover. "'We Are All Americans': The Latin Americanization of Race Relations in the United States." In *The Changing Terrain of Race and Ethnicity*, 149–84. Edited by Maria Krysan and Amanda E. Lewis. New York: Russell Sage Foundation, 2004.

Borjas, George J. "Do Blacks Gain or Lose from Immigration?" In *Help or Hindrance? The Economic Implications of Immigration for African Americans*, 51–74. Edited by Daniel S. Hamermesh and Frank D. Bean. New York: Russell Sage Foundation, 1998.

Bosniak, Linda. *The Citizen and the Alien: Dilemmas of Contemporary Membership*. Princeton, NJ, and Oxford: Princeton University Press, 2006.

Bourdieu, Pierre. *Distinction: A Social Critique of the Judgment of Taste*. Cambridge, MA: Harvard University Press, 1984.

Bourgois, Philipe. "One Hundred Years of United Fruit Company Letters." In *Banana Wars: Power, Production, and History in the Americas*, 103–44. Edited by Steve Striffler and Mark Moberg. Durham, NC: Duke University Press, 2003.

Briggs Jr., Vernon M. *Illegal Immigration: The Impact on Wages and Employment of Black Workers*. Testimony before the United States Civil Rights Commission, Ithaca, New York, 2010. Accessed June 9, 2015. http://digitalcommons.ilr.cornell.edu/briggstestimonies/26/.

Broadway, Michael J., and Terry Ward. "Recent Changes in the Structure and Location of the U.S. Meatpacking Industry." *Geography* 75, no. 1 (1990): 76–79.

Brodkin, Karen. *How Jews Became White Folks and What That Says About Race in America*. New Brunswick, NJ: Rutgers University Press, 1998.

Brown, Hanna. "Race, Legality, and the Social Policy Consequences of Anti-Immigration Mobilization." *American Sociological Review* 78, no. 2 (2013): 290–314.

Brubaker, Rogers, and F. Cooper. "Beyond Identity." *Theory and Society* 29, no. 1 (2000): 1–47.

Brueggemann, John, and Cliff Brown. "The Decline of Industrial Unionism in the Meatpacking Industry: Event Structure Analysis of Labor Unrest, 1946–1987." *Work and Occupations* 30 (2003): 327–60.

Burawoy, Michael. *Manufacturing Consent: Changes in the Labor Process Under Monopoly Capitalism*. Chicago: University of Chicago Press, 1979.

Burghart, Devin, and Leonard Zeskind. *Tea Party Nationalism: A Critical Examination of the Tea Party Movement and the Size, Scope, and Focus of Its National Factions*. Institute for Research and Education on Human Rights, 2010.

Burns, Peter, and James G. Gimpel. "Economic Insecurity, Prejudicial Stereotypes, and Public Opinion on Immigration Policy." *Political Science Quarterly* 115, no. 2 (2000): 201–25.

Cacho, Lisa M. *Social Death: Racialized Rightlessness and the Criminalization of the Unprotected*. New York: New York University Press, 2012.

Calavita, Kitty. "Immigration, Law, and Marginalization in a Global Economy: Notes from Spain." *Law & Society Review* 32, no. 3 (1998): 529–66.

CEDOH. 2005. [Additional details redacted]

Centeno Garcia, S. *Historia del Movimiento Negro Hondureño*. La Ceiba, Honduras: José Hipolito Centeno Garcia, 1997.

Champlin, Dell, and Eric Hake. "Immigration as Industrial Strategy in American Meatpacking." *Review of Political Economy* 18, no. 1 (2006): 49–69.

Chavez, Jorge M., and Doris Marine Provine. "Race and the Response of State Legislatures to Unauthorized Immigrants." *Annals of the American Academy of Political and Social Science* 623 (2009): 78–92.

Chavez, Leo. *The Latino Threat: Constructing Immigrants, Citizens, and the Nation.* Stanford, CA: Stanford University Press, 2008.

Chavez, Sergio, Ted Mouw, and Jacqueline Hagan. "Occupational Enclaves and the Wage Growth of Latino Immigrants" (under review).

Chomsky, Noam. *Turning the Tide: U.S. Intervention in Central America and the Struggle for Peace.* Boston: South End Press, 1985.

Cohen, Philip N., and Matthew Huffman. "Working for the Woman? Female Managers and the Gender Wage Gap." *American Sociological Review* 72, no. 5 (2007): 681–704.

Coutin, Susan Bibler. "Being en Route." *American Anthropologist* 107, no. 2 (2005): 195–206.

———. "Cultural Logics of Belonging and Movement: Transnationalism, Naturalization, and U.S. Immigration Politics." *American Ethnologist* 30, no. 4 (2003): 508–26.

———. *Legalizing Moves: Salvadoran Immigrants' Struggle for U.S. Residency.* Ann Arbor: University of Michigan Press, 2000.

Cravey, Altha. "The Changing South: Latino Labor and Poultry Production in Rural North Carolina." *Southeastern Geographer* 37, no. 2 (1997): 295–300.

Crenshaw, Kimberlé Williams. "Race, Reform, and Retrenchment: Transformation and Legitimation in Antidiscrimination Law." In *Critical Race Theory: The Key Writings That Formed the Movement,* 103–22. New York: The New Press, 1995.

Cuadros, Paul. *A Home on the Field: How One Championship Soccer Team Inspires Hope for the Revival of Small Town America.* New York: Harper-Collins, 2007.

Dawson, Michael. *Behind the Mule: Race and Class in African-American Politics.* Princeton, NJ: Princeton University Press, 1994.

Decker, Annie. "Suspending Employers' Immigration-Related Duties During Labor Disputes: A Statutory Proposal." *The Yale Law Journal* 115, no. 8 (2006): 2193–201.

De Genova, Nicholas. *Working the Boundaries: Race, Space, and Illegality in Mexican Chicago.* Durham, NC: Duke University Press, 2005.

Desmond, Matthew, and Mustafa Emirbayer. "What Is Racial Domination?" *Du Bois Review* 6, no. 2 (2009): 335–55.

Dixon, Jeffrey C. "The Ties That Bind and Those That Don't: Toward Reconciling Group Threat and Contact Theories of Prejudice." *Social Forces* 84, no. 4 (2006): 2179–204.

Donato, Katherine M., and Amada Armenta. "What We Know About Unauthorized Migration." *Annual Review of Sociology* 37 (2011): 529–43.

Donato, Katherine M., and Carl L. Bankston III. "The Origins of Employer Demand for Immigrants in a New Destination: The Salience of Soft Skills in a Volatile Economy." In *New Faces in New Places: The Changing Geography of American Immigration,* 124–48. Edited by Douglas S. Massey. New York: Russell Sage Foundation, 2008.

Du Bois, W. E. B. *The Souls of Black Folk.* New York: Penguin Books, 1995 [1903].

Dundes, Alan. *Cracking Jokes: Studies of Sick Humor Cycles and Stereotypes.* Berkeley: Ten Speed Press, 1987.

Dunn, Timothy, Ana Maria Aragonés, and George Shivers. "Recent Mexican Migration in the Rural Delmarva Peninsula: Human Rights Versus Citizenship Rights in a Local Context." In *New Destinations: Mexican Immigration in the United States,* 155–86. Edited by Victor Zúñiga and Rubén Hernández-León. New York: Russell Sage Foundation, 2005.

Durand, Jorge, Douglas S. Massey, and Chiara Capoferro. "The New Geography of Mexican Immigration." In *New Destinations: Mexican Immigration in the United States,* 1–22. Edited by Victor Zúñiga and Rubén Hernández-León. New York: Russell Sage Foundation, 2005.

Eaton, Susan. "A New Kind of Southern Strategy." *The Nation,* August 29–September 5, 2011. Accessed June 9, 2015. http://www.thenation.com/article/162694/new-kind-southern-strategy.

Elliott, James R., and Ryan A. Smith. "Race, Gender, and Workplace Power." *American Sociological Review* 69, no. 3 (2004): 365–86.

Emirbayer, Mustafa. "Manifesto for a Relational Sociology." *American Journal of Sociology* 103, no. 2 (1997): 281–317.

Endo, Isaku, Sarah Hirsch, Jan Rogge, and Kamil Borowik. "The U.S.-Honduras Remittance Corridor." World Bank Working Paper no. 177. Washington, DC: The International Bank for Reconstruction and Development/The World Bank.

England, Sarah. *Afro-Hondurans in New York City: Garifuna Tales of Transnational Movements in Racialized Space.* Gainesville: University Press of Florida, 2006.

England, Sarah, and Mark Anderson. "Auténtica cultura africana en Honduras? Los afro-centroamericanos desafían el mestizaje indo-hispánico hondureño." In *Memorias del mestizaje.* Edited by Charles Hale, Dario Euraque, and Jeffrey Gould. Antigua, Guatemala: CIRMA, 2004.

Environmental Investigation Agency (with support from the Center for International Policy). "The Illegal Logging Crisis in Honduras: A Report." 2005.

Estlund, Cynthia L. "The Ossification of American Labor Law." *Columbia Law Review* 102, no. 6 (2002): 1527–612.

Euraque, Darío A. *Reinterpreting the Banana Republic: Region and State in Honduras, 1870–1972.* Chapel Hill: University of North Carolina Press, 1996.

———. "The Threat of Blackness to the Mestizo Nation: Race and Ethnicity in the Honduran Banana Economy, 1920s and 1930s." In *Banana Wars: Power, Production, and History in the Americas,* 229–52. Edited by Steve Striffler and Mark Moberg. Durham, NC: Duke University Press, 2003.

Eyerman, Ron. "The Past in the Present: Culture and the Transmission of Memory." *Acta Sociologica* 47, no. 2 (2004): 159–69.

Fantasia, Rick. *Cultures of Solidarity: Consciousness, Action, and Contemporary American Workers.* Berkeley: University of California Press, 1988.

Feliciano, Cynthia, Rennie Lee, and Belinda Robnett. "Racial Boundaries Among Latinos: Evidence from Internet Daters' Racial Preferences." *Social Problems* 58, no. 2 (2011): 189–212.

Fink, Deborah. *Cutting into the Meatpacking Line: Workers and Change in the Rural Midwest.* Chapel Hill: University of North Carolina Press, 1998.

Fink, Leon. *The Maya of Morganton: Work and Community in the Nuevo New South.* Chapel Hill: University of North Carolina Press, 2003.

Fisk, Catherine. "Worker Voice and Labor Speech After *Harris v. Quinn and Citizens United*: Why Unions Should Have the Same Free Speech Rights as Corporations and Why the Supreme Court Thinks They Do Not." Presented at the Race, Labor, and the Law Conference, Institute for Labor Relations, UCLA, 2014.

Fisk, Catherine, and Michael J. Wishnie. "The Story of *Hoffman Plastics Compounds Inc. v. NLRB*: The Rules of the Workplace for Undocumented Immigrants." In *Immigration Stories.* Edited by David Martin and Peter Schuck. New York: Foundation Press, 2005.

Flagg, Barbara J. "Was Blind But Now I See: White Race Consciousness and the Requirement of Discriminatory Intent." *Michigan Law Review* 91 (1993): 953–1017.

Flores Fonseca, Manuel Antonio. "La Experiencia Hondureña en Materia de Medición Censal de la Migración." Paper presented at the Conferencia Estadística de las Américas, CEPAL, Santiago, Chile, December 10–12, 2008 [2008b].

———. "Migración y Remesas en Olancho, Honduras." Paper presented at the III Congreso de la Asociación Latinoamericana de Población, Córdoba, Argentina, September 26–28, 2008 [2008a].

"Fortune Fellows of the United States." 1990. [Additional details redacted]

Frank, Dana. "In Honduras, a Mess Made in the U.S." *New York Times,* January 26, 2012.

Frank, Reanne, Ilana Redstone Akresh, and Bo Lu. "Latino Immigrants and the U.S. Racial Order: How and Where Do They Fit In?" *American Sociological Review* 75, no. 3 (2010): 378–401.

Frederickson, George M. *White Supremacy: A Comparative Study in American and South African History.* Oxford: Oxford University Press, 1981.

Gabriel, Jackie. "Sí, Se Puede: Organizing Latino Immigrant Workers in South Omaha's Meatpacking Industry." *Journal of Labor Research* 29 (2008): 68–87.

Galloway, Jim. "Poultry Company President: Georgia's Anti-Immigration Climate Has Made Latino Workers Scarce." *Atlanta Journal-Constitution,* February 23, 2011.

Gans, Herbert J. "The Possibility of a New Racial Hierarchy in the Twenty-First-Century United States." In *The Cultural Territories of Race: Black and White Boundaries.* Edited by Michele Lamont. Chicago: University of Chicago Press, 1999.

García, Ruben J. *Marginal Workers: How Legal Fault Lines Divide Workers and Leave Them Without Protection.* New York and London: New York University Press, 2012.

Garden, Charlotte. "Labor Values Are First Amendment Values: Why Union Comprehensive Campaigns Are Protected Speech." *Fordham Law Review* 79, no. 6 (2011): 2617–68.

Gill, Hannah. *The Latino Migration Experience in North Carolina.* Chapel Hill: University of North Carolina Press, 2010.

Gindling, T.H., and Katherine Terrell. "Minimum Wages, Globalization, and Poverty in Honduras." *World Development* 38, no. 6 (2010): 908–18.

Gleeson, Shannon. *Commitments: The Politics of Enforcing Immigrant Worker Rights in San Jose and Houston.* Ithaca, NY: Cornell University Press, 2012.

———. "Labor Rights for All? The Role of Undocumented Immigrant Status for Worker Claims-Making." *Law & Social Inquiry* 35, no. 3 (2010): 561–602.

Golash-Boza, Tanya. "Does Whitening Happen? Distinguishing Between Race and Color Labels in an African-Descended Community in Peru." *Social Problems* 57, no. 1 (2010): 138–56.

———. "Dropping the Hyphen? Becoming Latino(a)-American Through Racialized Assimilation." *Social Forces* 85, no. 1 (2006): 27–55.

———. *Immigration Nation: Raids, Detentions, and Deportations in Post-9/11 America.* Boulder, CO: Paradigm Publishers, 2012.

Goluboff, Risa L. "The Thirteenth Amendment and the Lost Origins of Civil Rights." *Duke Law Journal* 50, no. 6 (2001): 1609–85.

Gomberg-Muñoz, Ruth. "Willing to Work: Agency and Vulnerability in an Undocumented Immigrant Network." *American Anthropologist* 112, no. 2 (June 2010): 295–307.

Gonzáles, Roberto G., and Leo R. Chávez. "'Awakening to a Nightmare': Abjectivity and Illegality in the Lives of Undocumented 1.5-Generation Latino Immigrants in the United States." *Current Anthropology* 53, no. 3 (2012): 255–81.

Gordon, Jennifer, and R.A. Lenhardt. "Conflict and Solidarity Between African American and Latino Immigrant Workers." Prepared for the Chief Justice Earl Warren Institute on Race, Ethnicity, and Diversity, University of California, Berkeley Law School, 2007.

Gould, Jeffrey L. *To Die in This Way: Nicaraguan Indians and the Myth of the Mestizaje, 1880–1960.* Durham, NC: Duke University Press, 1998.

Gozdziak, E.M., and S.F. Martin. *Beyond the Gateway: Immigrants in a Changing America.* Lanham, MD: Lexington Books, 2005.

Gray, LaGuana. *We Just Keep Running the Line: Black Southern Women and the Poultry Processing Industry.* Baton Rouge: Louisiana State University Press, 2014.

Grey, Mark. "Immigrants, Migration and Worker Turnover at the Hog Pride Pork Packing Plant." *Human Organization* 58, no. 1 (1999): 16–27.

———. "Marshalltown, Iowa and the Struggle for Community in a Global Age." In *Communities and Capital: Local Struggles Against Corporate Power and Privatization.* Edited by Thomas W. Collins and John D. Wingard. Athens: University of Georgia Press, 2000.

———. "Pork, Poultry and Newcomers in Storm Lake, Iowa." In *Any Way You Cut It: Meat Processing and Small-Town America*, 109–27. Edited by Donald D. Stull, Michael J. Broadway, and David Griffith. Lawrence: University Press of Kansas, 1995.

Griffith, David. "Hay Trabajo: Poultry Processing, Rural Industrialization, and the Latinization of Low-Wage Labor." In *Any Way You Cut It: Meat Processing and Small-Town America*. Edited by Donald D. Stull, Michael J. Broadway, and David Griffith. Lawrence: University Press of Kansas, 1995.

———. *Jones's Minimal: Low-Wage Labor in the United States*. Albany: State University of New York Press, 1993.

———. "Rural Industry and Mexican Immigration in North Carolina." In *New Destinations: Mexican Immigration in the United States*. Edited by Victor Zúñiga and Rubén Hernández-León. New York: Russell Sage Foundation, 2005.

Gurin, Patricia, Arthur H. Miller, and Gerald Gurin. "Stratum Identification and Consciousness." *Social Psychology Quarterly* 43, no. 1 (1980): 30–47.

Hagan, Jacqueline. *Deciding to Be Legal: A Maya Community in Houston*. Philadelphia: Temple University Press, 1994.

———. *Migration Miracle: Faith, Hope, and Meaning on the Undocumented Journey*. Cambridge, MA: Harvard University Press, 2008.

Hagan, Jacqueline, Karl Eschbach, and Nestor Rodríguez. "U.S. Deportation Policy, Family Separation, and Circular Migration." *International Migration Review* 42, no. 2 (2008): 64–88.

Hagan, Jacqueline, Nichola Lowe, and Christian Quingla. "Skills on the Move: Rethinking the Relationship Between Human Capital and Immigrant Economic Mobility." *Work and Occupations* 38, no. 2 (2011): 149–78.

Hagan, Jacqueline, Nestor Rodríguez, and Brianna Castro. "Social Effects of Mass Deportations by the United States Government, 2000–2010." *Ethnic and Racial Studies* 34, no. 8 (2011): 1374–91.

Hall, Kerry, Ames Alexander, and Frank Ordonez. "The Cruelest Cuts: The Human Cost of Bringing Poultry to Your Table." *Charlotte Observer* (September 2008).

Hamamoto, D. Y., and R. D. Torres. *New American Destinies: A Reader in Contemporary Asian and Latino Immigration*. New York: Routledge, 1997.

Hamermesh, D. S., and F. D. Bean. "Introduction." In *Help or Hindrance?: The Economic Implications of Immigration for African Americans*. New York: Russell Sage Foundation, 1998.

Haney López, Ian. *Dog Whistle Politics: How Coded Racial Appeals Have Reinvented Racism and Wrecked the Middle Class*. New York: Oxford University Press, 2014.

———. "Race on the 2010 Census: Hispanics and the Shrinking White Majority." *Daedalus* 134, no. 1 (2005): 42–52.

———. *White by Law: The Legal Construction of Race*. New York: New York University Press, 2006 [1996].

Harrison, Jill Lindsey, and Sarah E. Lloyd. "New Jobs, New Workers, and New Inequalities: Explaining Employers' Roles in Segregation by Nativity and Race." *Social Problems* 60, no. 3 (2013): 281–301.

Hartmann, Douglas, Joseph Gerteis, and Paul R. Croll. "An Empirical Assessment of Whiteness: Hidden from How Many?" *Social Problems* 56, no. 3 (2009): 403–24.

Hensey, Fritz. Personal communication with Thomas Stephens, 2012, as related by Stephens to Vanesa Ribas.

Hernández-León, Rubén, and Victor Zúñiga. "Appalachia Meets Aztlán: Mexican Immigration and Inter-Group Relations in Dalton, Georgia." In *New Destinations: Mexican Immigration in the United States*, 244–73. Edited by Victor Zúñiga and Rubén Hernández-León. New York: Russell Sage Foundation, 2005.

Heydari, Farhgang. "Making Strange Bedfellows: Enlisting the Cooperation of Undocumented Employees in the Enforcement of Employer Sanctions." *Columbia Law Review* 110, no. 6 (2010): 1526–73.

Hill, Carole E., and Patricia Beaver. *Cultural Diversity in the U.S. South: Anthropological Contributions to a Region in Transition*. Athens: University of Georgia Press, 1998.

Holzer, Harry. *Immigration Policy and Less-Skilled Workers in the United States: Reflections on Future Directions for Reform*. Washington, DC: Migration Policy Institute, 2011.

———. *What Employers Want: Job Prospects for Less-Educated Workers*. New York: Russell Sage Foundation, 1996.

Hondagneu-Sotelo, Pierrette. *Domestica: Immigrant Workers Cleaning and Caring in the Shadows of Affluence*. Berkeley: University of California Press, 2001.

Honig, Bonnie. *Democracy and the Foreigner*. Princeton, NJ: Princeton University Press, 2001.

Howard, Judith. "Social Psychology of Identities." *Annual Review of Sociology* 26 (2000): 367–93.

Hunt, Larry L., Matthew O. Hunt, and William W. Falk. "Who Is Headed South? U.S. Migration Trends in Black and White, 1970–2000." *Social Forces* 87, no. 1 (2008): 95–119.

Hutchings, Vincent, and Cara Wong. "Racism, Group Position, and Attitudes About Immigration Among Blacks." *Du Bois Review* 11, no. 2 (2014): 419–42.

Itzigsohn, Jose, and Carlos Dore-Cabral. "Competing Identities? Race, Ethnicity, and Panethnicity Among Dominicans in the United States." *Sociological Forum* 15, no. 2 (2000): 225–47.

Izcara Palacios, Simon Pedro. "La Adicción a la Mano de Obra Ilegal: Jornaleros Tamaulipecos en Estados Unidos." *Latin American Research Review* 45, no. 1 (2010): 55–75.

Jacobson, Matthew. *Whiteness of a Different Color: European Immigrants and the Alchemy of Race*. Cambridge, MA: Harvard University Press, 1998.

Jacobson, Robin. "Characterizing Consent: Race, Citizenship, and the New Restrictionists." *Political Research Quarterly* 59, no. 4 (2006): 645–54.

Johnson, James H., Karen D. Johnson-Webb, and Walter C. Farrell Jr. "A Profile of Hispanic Newcomers to North Carolina." *Popular Government* (Fall 1999): 2–12.

Johnson-Webb, K.D. *Recruiting Hispanic Labor: Immigrants in Non-Traditional Areas*. New York: LFB Scholarly Publications, 2003.

Jones, Jennifer Anne Meri. "'Mexicans Will Take the Jobs That Even Blacks Won't Do': An Analysis of Blackness, Regionalism, and Invisibility in Contemporary Mexico." *Ethnic and Racial Studies* 36, no. 10 (2013): 1564–81.

Jones, Jennifer A. "'Blacks May Be Second Class, but They Can't Make Them Leave': Mexican Racial Formation and Immigrant Status." *Latino Studies* 10, nos. 1–2 (2012): 60–80.

———. "Who Are We? Producing Group Identity Through Everyday Practices of Conflict and Discourse." *Sociological Perspectives* 54, no. 2 (2011): 139–62.

Jones, Richard C., ed. *Immigrants Outside Megalopolis: Ethnic Transformation in the Heartland.* Lanham, MD : Lexington Books, 2008.

Juravich, Tom, and Kate Bronfenbrenner. "Bringing the Study of Work Back to Labor Studies." *Labor Studies Journal* 30, no. 1 (2005): i–vii.

Kalleberg, Arne. *Good Jobs, Bad Jobs: The Rise of Polarized and Precarious Employment in the United States, 1970s–2000s.* New York: Russell Sage Foundation, 2011.

Kandel, William, and Emilio Parrado. "Hispanics in the American South and the Transformation of the Poultry Industry." In *Hispanic Spaces, Latino Places: Community and Cultural Diversity in Contemporary America.* Edited by D.D. Arreola. Austin: University of Texas Press, 2004.

Karjanen, David. "Gender, Race, and Nationality in the Making of Mexican Migrant Labor in the United States." *Latin American Perspectives* 35, no. 1 (2008): 51–63.

Kasarda, John, and James H. Johnson Jr. *The Economic Impact of the Hispanic Population on the State of North Carolina.* Chapel Hill, NC: Frank Hawkins Kenan Institute of Private Enterprise, 2006.

Kaufmann, Karen M. "Cracks in the Rainbow: Group Commonality as a Basis for Latino and African-American Political Coalitions." *Political Research Quarterly* 56, no. 2 (2003): 199–210.

Kim, Claire Jean. *Bitter Fruit: The Politics of Black-Korean Conflict in New York City.* New Haven, CT: Yale University Press, 2000.

———. "The Racial Triangulation of Asian Americans." *Politics and Society* 27, no. 1 (1999): 105–38.

Kim, Nadia Y. *Imperial Citizens: Koreans and Race from Seoul to LA.* Stanford, CA: Stanford University Press, 2008.

Kindy, Kimberly. "USDA Plan to Speed Up Poultry-Processing Lines Could Increase Risk of Bird Abuse." *Washington Post,* October 29, 2013.

King, Ryan D., and Melissa F. Weiner. "Group Position, Collective Threat, and American Anti-Semitism." *Social Problems* 54, no. 1 (2007): 47–77.

Kirschenman, Joleen, and Kathryn Neckerman. "'We'd Love to Hire Them, But . . .': The Meaning of Race for Employers." In *The Urban Underclass.* Edited by Christopher Jencks and Paul E. Peterson. Washington, DC: The Brookings Institution, 1991.

Kochhar, Rakesh, Roberto Suro, and Sonya Tafoya. "The New Latino South: The Context and Consequences of Rapid Population Growth." Report prepared for the Pew Research Center, Washington, DC, July 26, 2005.

Krissman, Fred. "Sin Coyote Ni Patron: Why the 'Migrant Network' Fails to Explain International Migration." *International Migration Review* 39, no. 2 (2005): 4–44.

Laínez, Vilma, and Victor Meza. "El enclave bananero en la historia de Honduras." *Estudios Sociales Centroamericanos* 5, no. 154 (1973): 187–225.

Lamont, Michèle. *The Cultural Territories of Race: Black and White Boundaries.* Chicago: University of Chicago Press, 1999.

———. *The Dignity of Working Men: Morality and the Boundaries of Race, Class, and Immigration.* New York: Russell Sage Foundation, 2000.

Lamont, M., and M. Fournier. *Cultivating Differences: Symbolic Boundaries and the Making of Inequality.* Chicago: University of Chicago Press, 1992.

Lamont, M., and V. Molnar. "The Study of Boundaries in the Social Sciences." *Annual Review of Sociology* 28 (2002): 167–95.

La Prensa. "Se desborda violencia en Olancho y deja 16 muertos." January 18, 2010.

LeDuff, Charlie. "At a Slaughterhouse, Some Things Never Die." *New York Times,* June 16, 2000.

Lee, Jennifer, and Frank D. Bean. "Reinventing the Color Line: Immigration and America's New Racial/Ethnic Divide." *Social Forces* 86, no. 2 (2007): 561–86.

Leidner, Robin. *Fast Food, Fast Talk: Service Work and the Routinization of Everyday Life.* Berkeley: University of California Press, 1993.

Leiter, Jeffrey C., Leslie Hossfeld, and Donald Tomaskovic-Devey. "North Carolina Employers Look at Latino Employees." Paper presented at the Annual Meeting of the Southern Sociological Society, Atlanta, April 2001.

Leiter, Jeffrey C., Corre Robeson, and Sheryl Skaggs. "Displacement or Replacement? Changes in the Occupational Distributions and Wages in the North Carolina Industries Where Latinos Went to Work in the 1990s." Paper accepted for presentation at the Annual Meeting of the Southern Sociological Society, Baltimore, April 2002.

Lewis, Laura A. "Blacks, Black Indians, Afromexicans: The Dynamics of Race, Nation, and Identity in a Mexican 'Moreno' Community (Guerrero)." *American Ethnologist* 27, no. 4 (2000): 898–926.

———. *Chocolate and Corn Flour: History, Race, and Place in the Making of "Black" Mexico.* Durham, NC, and London: Duke University Press, 2012.

Lichter, Daniel T., and Kenneth M. Johnson. "Immigrant Gateways and Hispanic Migration to New Destinations." *International Migration Review* 43, no. 3 (Fall 2009): 496–518.

Lie, John, and Nancy Abelmann. "The 1992 Los Angeles Riots and the 'Black-Korean Conflict.'" In *Koreans in the Hood.* Edited by Kwang Chung Kim. Baltimore: Johns Hopkins University Press, 1999.

Lieberson, Stanley. *A Piece of the Pie: Blacks and White Immigrants Since 1880.* Berkeley: University of California Press, 1980.

Light, Ivan. *Deflecting Immigration: Networks, Markets, and Regulation in Los Angeles.* New York: Russell Sage Foundation, 2006.

———. "Immigration and Ethnic Economies in Giant Cities." *International Social Science Journal* 181 (2004): 385–398.

Light, Ivan, et al. "Globalization Effects on Employment in Southern California, 1970–2000." In *Globalization and the New City: Migrants, Minorities, and Urban Transformations in Comparative Perspective*, 51–167. Edited by Malcolm Cross and Robert Moore. New York: Palgrave, 2002.

Lipsitz, George. *The Possessive Investment in Whiteness: How White People Profit from Identity Politics*. Revised and expanded edition. Philadelphia: Temple University Press, 2006 [1998].

López-Sanders, Laura. "Trapped at the Bottom: Racialized and Gendered Labor Queues in New Immigrant Destinations." Paper presented at UCLA Migration Conference, October 23, 2009.

Loveman, Mara. "Is 'Race' Essential?" *American Sociological Review* 64, no. 6 (1999): 891–98.

Loveman, Mara, and Jeronimo O. Muñiz. "How Puerto Rico Became White: Boundary Dynamics and Intercensus Racial Reclassification." *American Sociological Review* 72, no. 6 (2007): 915–39.

Lowe, Lisa. *Immigrant Acts: On Asian American Cultural Politics*. Durham, NC, and London: Duke University Press, 1996.

Mahler, Sarah. *American Dreaming: Immigrant Life on the Margins*. Princeton, NJ: Princeton University Press, 1995.

Malkin, Elisabeth. "In Honduras, Land Struggles Highlight Post-Coup Polarization." *New York Times*, September 15, 2011.

Mantero, J. M. *Latinos and the U.S. South*. Westport, CT: Praeger, 2008.

Marrow, Helen. *New Destination Dreaming: Immigration, Race, and Legal Status in the Rural American South*. Stanford, CA: Stanford University Press, 2011.

———. "Southern Becoming: Immigrant Incorporation and Race Relations in the Rural U.S. South." Unpublished PhD diss., Harvard University, 2007.

Massey, D. S. *New Faces in New Places: The Changing Geography of American Immigration*. New York: Russell Sage Foundation, 2008.

Massey, D. S., J. Durand, and N. J. Malone. *Beyond Smoke and Mirrors: Mexican Immigration in an Era of Economic Integration*. New York: Russell Sage Foundation, 2002.

Massey, Douglas, Rafael Alarcón, Jorge Durand, and Humberto Gonzalez. *Return to Aztlan: The Social Process of International Migration from Western Mexico*. Berkeley: University of California Press, 1987.

McClain, Paula D. "North Carolina's Response to Latino Immigrants and Immigration." In *Immigration's New Frontiers: Experiences from the New Gateway States*. Edited by Greg Anrig Jr. and Tova Andrea Wang. New York: Century Foundation, 2006.

McClain, Paula D., Niambi M. Carter, Victoria M. DeFrancesco Soto, Monique I. Lyle, Jeffrey D. Grynaviski, Shayla C. Nunnally, Thomas J. Scotto, J. Alan Kendrick, Gerald F. Lackey, and Kendra Davenport Cotton. "Racial Distancing in a Southern City: Latino Immigrants' Views of African Americans." *The Journal of Politics* 68, no. 3 (2006): 571–84.

McClain, Paula D., Monique L. Lyle, Niambi M. Carter, Victoria M. DeFrancesco Soto, Gerald F. Lackey, Kendra Davenport Cotton, Shayla C. Nunnally, Thomas J. Scotto, Jeffrey D. Grynavisky, and J. Alan Kendrick. "Black

Americans and Latino Immigrants in a Southern City: Friendly Neighbors or Economic Competitors?" *Du Bois Review* 4, no. 1 (2007): 97–117.

McDermott, Monica. "Black Attitudes and Hispanic Immigrants in South Carolina." In *Just Neighbors? Research on African American and Latino Relations in the United States,* 242–66. Edited by Edward Telles, Mark Q. Sawyer, and Gaspar Rivera-Salgado. New York: Russell Sage Foundation, 2011.

———. *Working-Class White: The Making and Unmaking of Race Relations.* Berkeley: University of California Press, 2006.

McDermott, Monica, and Frank L. Samson. "White Racial and Ethnic Identity in the United States." *Annual Review of Sociology* 31 (2005): 245–61.

Mendelson, Margot K. "Constructing America: Mythmaking in U.S. Immigration Courts." *The Yale Law Journal* 119, no. 5 (2010): 1012–58.

Menjívar, Cecilia. "Liminal Legality: Salvadoran and Guatemalan Immigrants' Lives in the United States." *American Journal of Sociology* 111, no. 4 (2006): 999–1037.

Menjívar, Cecilia, and Leisy Abrego. "Legal Violence: Immigration Law and the Lives of Central American Immigrants." *American Journal of Sociology* 117, no. 5 (2012): 1380–421.

———. "Parents and Children Across Borders: Legal Instability and Intergenerational Relations in Guatemalan and Salvadoran Families." In *Across Generations: Immigrant Families in America,* 160–89. Edited by Nancy Foner. New York: New York University Press, 2009.

Milkman, Ruth. "Back to the Future? US Labour in the New Gilded Age." *British Journal of Industrial Relations* 51, no. 4 (2013): 645–65.

———. "Immigrant Workers and the Future of American Labor." *ABA Journal of Labor and Employment Law* 26, no. 2 (2011): 295–310.

———. *LA Story: Immigrant Workers and the Future of the U.S. Labor Movement.* New York: Russell Sage Foundation, 2006.

Mindiola, Tatcho, Yolanda Flores Niemann, and Nestor Rodríguez. *Black-Brown Relations and Stereotypes.* Austin: University of Texas Press, 2002.

Mohl, Raymond. "Globalization and Latin American Immigration in Alabama." In *Latino Immigrants and the Transformation of the U.S. South,* 51–69. Edited by Mary E. Odem and Elaine Lacy. Athens: University of Georgia Press, 2009.

———. "Globalization, Latinization, and the Nuevo New South." In *Globalization and the American South.* Edited by James C. Cobb and William Stueck. Athens, GA, and London: University of Georgia Press, 2005.

Mollett, Sharlene. "Race and Natural Resource Conflicts in Honduras: The Miskito and Garifuna Struggle for Lasa Pulan." *Latin American Research Review* 41, no. 1 (2006): 76–101.

Moore, Thomas S. "The Locus of Racial Disadvantage in the Labor Market." *American Journal of Sociology* 116, no. 3 (2010): 909–42.

Morawska, Ewa. "Structuring Migration: The Case of Polish Income-Seeking Travelers to the West." *Theory & Society* 30, no. 1 (2001): 47.

Moss, Philip, and Chris Tilly. *Stories Employers Tell: Race, Skill, and Hiring in America.* New York: Russell Sage Foundation, 2001.

Motomura, Hiroshi. "Immigration Outside the Law." *Columbia Law Review* 108, no. 8 (2014): 2037–97.

Murphy, A. D., C. Blanchard, and J. A. Hill. *Latino Workers in the Contemporary South*. Athens: University of Georgia Press, 2001.

Nagel, Joane. *Race, Ethnicity, and Sexuality: Intimate Intersections, Forbidden Frontiers*. New York: Oxford University Press, 2003.

Nazario, Sonia. *Enrique's Journey*. New York: Random House Trade Paperbacks, 2006.

Neuendorf, K. A., and P. D. Skalski. *Qualitative Validation of the Four-Part Senses of Humor Construct*. Manuscript in progress. Cleveland, OH: Cleveland State University, 2012.

New York Times. "Immigration Reform and Workers' Rights." February 20, 2013. http://www.nytimes.com/2013/02/21/opinion/immigration-reform-and-workers-rights.html.

Ngai, Mae M. "The Strange Career of the Illegal Alien: Immigration Restriction and Deportation Policy in the United States, 1921–1965." *Law and History Review* 21, no. 1 (2003): 69–107.

Nobles, Melissa. *Shades of Citizenship: Race and Census in Modern Politics*. Stanford, CA: Stanford University Press, 2000.

North Carolina Employment Security Commission. [Additional details redacted]

Núñez, Carolina D. "Fractured Membership: Deconstructing Territoriality to Secure Rights and Remedies for the Undocumented Worker." *Wisconsin Law Review* (2010): 817–73.

Odem, Mary E., and Elaine Lacy, eds. *Latino Immigrants and the Transformation of the U.S. South*. Athens: University of Georgia Press, 2009.

Okamoto, Dina, and Kim Ebert. "Beyond the Ballot: Immigrant Collective Action in Gateways and New Destinations in the United States." *Social Problems* 57, no. 4 (2010): 529–58.

Oliver, J. Eric, and Janelle Wong. "Intergroup Prejudice in Multiethnic Settings." *American Journal of Political Science* 47, no. 4 (2003): 567–82.

Olzak, Susan. *The Dynamics of Ethnic Competition and Conflict*. Stanford, CA: Stanford University Press, 1992.

Omi, Michael, and Howard Winant. *Racial Formation in the United States: From the 1960s to the 1990s*. New York: Routledge, 1994.

Ontiveros, Maria L. "Immigrant Rights and the Thirteenth Amendment." *New Labor Forum* 16, no. 2 (2007): 26–33.

Pachirat, Timothy. *Every Twelve Seconds: Industrialized Slaughter and the Politics of Sight*. New Haven, CT, and London: Yale University Press, 2011.

Padín, José Antonio. "The Normative Mulattoes: The Press, Latinos, and the Racial Climate on the Moving Immigration Frontier." *Sociological Perspectives* 48, no. 1 (2005): 49–75.

Parker, Christopher, and Matthew Barreto. *Change They Can't Believe In: The Tea Party and Reactionary Politics in America*. Princeton, NJ: Princeton University Press, 2013.

Parrado, Emilio, and William Kandel. "New Hispanic Migrant Destinations: A Tale of Two Industries." In *New Faces in New Places: The Changing Geography of American Immigration*, 99–123. Edited by Douglas Massey. New York: Russell Sage Foundation, 2008.

Passel, Jeffrey, D'Vera Cohn, and Ana González-Barrera. "Net Migration from Mexico Falls to Zero—and Perhaps Less." Pew Research Center, April 23, 2012. http://www.pewhispanic.org/2012/04/23/net-migration-from-mexico-falls-to-zero-and-perhaps-less/.

Pastoral Social/Caritas. *Sueños truncados: La migración de hondureños hacia Estados Unidos*. Tegucigalpa, Honduras: Pastoral Social/Caritas, 2003.

Peacock, J.L., H.L. Watson, and C.R. Matthews. *The American South in a Global World*. Chapel Hill: University of North Carolina Press, 2005.

Pine, Adrienne. *Working Hard, Drinking Hard: On Violence and Survival in Honduras*. Berkeley: University of California Press, 2008.

Pope, James Gray, Peter Kellman, and Ed Bruno. "Free Labor Today." *New Labor Forum* 16, no. 2 (2007): 8–18.

Portes, Alejandro, and Ruben G. Rumbaut. *Legacies: The Story of the Immigrant Second Generation*. Berkeley: University of California Press, 2001.

Pressly, Linda. "Honduras Murders: Where Life Is Cheap and Funerals Are Free." *BBC News Magazine*, May 2, 2012.

Quillian, Lincoln. "Prejudice as a Response to Perceived Group Threat: Population Composition and Anti-Immigrant and Racial Prejudice in Europe." *American Sociological Review* 60 (1995): 586–611.

Reskin, Barbara F., Debra B. McBrier, and Julie A. Kmec. "The Determinants and Consequences of Workplace Sex and Race Composition." *Annual Review of Sociology* 25 (1999): 335–61.

Rodríguez, Clara E. *Changing Race: Latinos, the Census, and the History of Ethnicity in the United States*. New York: New York University Press, 2000.

Rodríguez, Richard. *Hunger of Memory: The Education of Richard Rodríguez*. New York: Dial Press, a Division of Random House Inc., 1982.

Roediger, David. *The Wages of Whiteness: Race and the Making of the American Working Class*. New York: Verso, 2007 [1991].

———. *Working Toward Whiteness: How America's Immigrants Became White*. New York: Basic Books, 2005.

Rosenfield, Michael J., and Marta Tienda. "Mexican Immigration, Occupational Niches, and Labor-Market Competition: Evidence from Los Angeles, Chicago, and Atlanta, 1970 to 1990." In *Immigration and Opportunity: Race, Ethnicity, and Employment in the United States*. Edited by Frank D. Bean and Stephanie Bell-Rose. New York: Russell Sage Foundation, 1999.

Roth, Wendy. *Race Migrations: Latinos and the Cultural Transformation of Race*. Stanford, CA: Stanford University Press, 2012.

Sánchez, Gabriel R. "Latino Group Consciousness: Perceptions of Commonality with African Americans." *Social Science Quarterly* 89, no. 2 (2008): 428–44.

Sánchez, Gabriel R., and Natalie Masuoka. "Brown-Utility Heuristic? The Presence and Contributing Factors of Latino Linked Fate." *Hispanic Journal of Behavioral Sciences* 32, no. 4 (2010): 519–31.

Schmalzbauer, Leah. *Striving and Surviving: A Daily Life Analysis of Honduran Transnational Families*. New York: Routledge, 2005.

Schultz, Benjamin J. "Inside the Gilded Cage: The Lives of Latino Immigrant Males in Rural Central Kentucky." *Southeastern Geographer* 48, no. 2 (2008): 201–18.

Schwartzman, Kathleen C. *The Chicken Trail: Following Workers, Migrants, and Corporations Across the Americas.* Ithaca, NY, and London: Cornell University Press, 2013.

Secretaría de Salud de Honduras, Organización Panamericana de Salud. "El huracán Mitch en Honduras." Date unknown.

Shirley, Carla D. "You Might Be a Redneck If . . . : Boundary Work Among Rural, Southern Whites." *Social Forces* 89, no. 1 (2010): 35–61.

Sills, S. J., ed. *Being Brown in Dixie: Race, Ethnicity, and Latino Immigration in the New South.* Boulder, CO: Lynne Rienner Publishers, 2010.

Silver, Alexis. "'Growing Up Gringo': Transitions to Adulthood for Children of Immigrants in a Small Town, New Immigrant Destination." Unpublished PhD diss. University of North Carolina at Chapel Hill, 2011.

Sinclair, Upton. *The Jungle.* New York: Bantam Classics, 1981 [1906].

Skaggs, Sheryl, Donald Tomaskovic-Devey, and Jeffrey Leiter. "Latino/a Employment Growth in North Carolina: Ethnic Displacement or Replacement?" Unpublished paper, 2000. Accessed in 2009. http://sasw.chass.ncsu.edu/jeff/latinos/latino.htm.

Sladkova, Jana. *Journeys of Undocumented Honduran Migrants to the United States.* El Paso: LFB Scholarly Publishers, 2010.

Smith, H. A., and O. J. Furuseth. *Latinos in the New South: Transformations of Place.* Aldershot, England, and Burlington, VT: Ashgate, 2006.

Smith, James P., and Barry Edmonston, eds. *The New Americans: Economic, Demographic, and Fiscal Effects of Immigration.* Sponsored by the National Research Council. Washington, DC: National Academy Press, 1997.

Smith, Ryan, and James R. Elliott. "Does Ethnic Concentration Influence Access to Authority? An Examination of Contemporary Urban Labor Markets." *Social Forces* 81, no. 1 (2002): 255–79.

Smith-Nonini, Sandy. "Back to 'The Jungle': Processing Migrants in North Carolina Meatpacking Plants." *Anthropology of Work Review* 24 (2003): 3–4.

Somers, Margaret R. "The Narrative Constitution of Identity: A Relational and Network Approach." *Theory & Society* 23 (1994): 605–49.

Steinberg, Stephen. *The Ethnic Myth: Race, Ethnicity, and Class in America.* Boston: Beacon Press, 2001 [1981].

Stephens, Thomas. *A Game of Mirrors: The Changing Face of Ethno-Racial Constructs and Language in the Americas.* Lanham, MD: University Press of America, 2003.

Striffler, Steve. *Chicken: The Dangerous Transformation of America's Favorite Food.* New Haven, CT: Yale University Press, 2005.

Stuesse, Angela. "Race, Migration, and Labor Control: Neoliberal Challenges to Organizing Mississippi's Poultry Workers." In *Latino Immigrants and the Transformation of the U.S. South.* Edited by Mary E. Odem and Elaine Lacy. Athens: University of Georgia Press, 2009.

Stuesse, Angela, and Laura E. Helton. "Low-Wage Legacies, Race, and the Golden Chicken in Mississippi: Where Contemporary Immigration Meets African American Labor History." *Southern Spaces* (December 2013).

Stull, Donald D., Michael J. Broadway, and David Griffith, eds. *Any Way You Cut It: Meat Processing and Small-Town America.* Lawrence: University Press of Kansas, 1995.

Tavernise, Sabrina, and Robert Gebeloff. "Many U.S. Blacks Moving to South, Reversing Trend." *New York Times,* March 25, 2011.

Taylor, Marylee C. "How White Attitudes Vary with the Racial Composition of Local Populations: Numbers Count." *American Sociological Review* 63 (1998): 512–35.

Telles, Edward. *Race in Another America: The Significance of Skin Color in Brazil.* Princeton, NJ: Princeton University Press, 2004.

Telles, Edward, Mark Sawyer, and Gaspar Rivera-Salgado. *Just Neighbors? Research on African American and Latino Relations in the United States.* New York: Russell Sage Foundation, 2011.

Terriquez, Veronica. "Schools for Democracy: Labor Union Participation and Latino Immigrant Parents' School-Based Civic Engagement." *American Sociological Review* 76, no. 4 (2011): 581–601.

Thomas, Piri. *Down These Mean Streets.* New York: Alfred A. Knopf, 1967.

Thompson, Gabriel. "New Rules Mean New Hardship for Poultry Workers." *The Nation,* April 25, 2012.

Thornton, Michael, and Yuko Mizuno. "Economic Well-Being and Black Adult Feelings Toward Immigrants and Whites, 1984." *Journal of Black Studies* 30, no. 1 (1999): 15–44.

Thurow, Lester C. *Generating Inequality.* New York: Basic Books Inc., 1975.

Tietz, Jeff. "Boss Hog." *Rolling Stone* (December 2006). http://www.rollingstone.com/culture/news/boss-hog-the-dark-side-of-americas-top-pork-producer-20061214.

Tilley, Virginia. *Seeing Indians: Race, Nation, and Power in El Salvador.* Albuquerque: University of New Mexico Press, 2005.

Torres, Arlene, and Norman E. Whitten Jr. *Blackness in Latin America and the Caribbean.* Bloomington and Indianapolis: Indiana University Press, 1998.

United Nations Office on Drugs and Crime. "Cocaine from South America to the United States." 2001. https://www.unodc.org/documents/toc/Reports/TOCTASouthAmerica/English/TOCTA_CACaribb_cocaine_SAmerica_US.pdf.

United States Census Bureau. "The Hispanic Population." Census 2000 Brief, May 2001. https://www.census.gov/prod/2001pubs/c2kbr01-3.pdf.

United States Commission on Civil Rights. *The Impact of Illegal Immigration on the Wages and Employment Opportunities of Black Workers.* Briefing Report. Washington, DC, 2010.

Vucetic, Srdjan. "Identity Is a Joking Matter: Intergroup Humor in Bosnia." *Spaces of Identity* 4, no. 1 (2004): 7–34.

Wade, Peter. *Race and Ethnicity in Latin America.* New York: Pluto Press, 1997.

Wagner, Ulrich, Oliver Christ, Thomas F. Pettigrew, Jost Stellmacher, and Carina Wolf. "Prejudice and Minority Proportion: Contact Instead of Threat Effects." *Social Psychology Quarterly* 69, no. 4 (2006): 380–90.

Waldinger, Roger. "Black/Immigrant Competition Re-Assessed: New Evidence from Los Angeles." *Sociological Perspectives* 40, no. 3 (1997): 365–86.

———. *Still the Promised City? African-Americans and New Immigrants in Postindustrial New York.* Cambridge, MA: Harvard University Press, 1996.

———. "The Economic Theory of Ethnic Conflict: A Critique and Reformation." In *Immigrant Businesses: The Economic, Political, and Social Environment*, 124–41. Edited by Jan Rath. London: Palgrave Macmillan, 2000.

Waldinger, Roger D., and M.I. Lichter. *How the Other Half Works: Immigration and the Social Organization of Labor.* Berkeley: University of California Press, 2003.

Walzer, Michael. *Spheres of Justice: A Defense of Pluralism and Equality.* New York: Basic Books, 1983.

Waters, Mary C., and Tomas R. Jiménez. "Assessing Immigrant Assimilation: New Empirical and Theoretical Challenges." *Annual Review of Sociology* 31 (2005): 105–25.

Waters, M.C. *Black Identities: West Indian Immigrant Dreams and American Realities.* New York: Russell Sage Foundation, 1999.

Weissman, Deborah, Hannah Gill, Mai Thi Nguyen, and Katherine Lewis Parker. "Legal and Social Perspectives on Local Enforcement of Immigration Under the 287(g) Program." *Popular Government* 3, no. 2 (2009): 2–18.

Williams, Raymond. *Marxism and Literature.* Oxford: Oxford University Press, 1977.

Wimmer, Andreas. Elementary Strategies of Ethnic Boundary Making. *Ethnic and Racial Studies* 31, no. 6 (2008): 1025–55.

Winders, Jamie. *Nashville in the New Millennium: Immigrant Settlement, Urban Transformation, and Social Belonging.* New York: Russell Sage Foundation, 2013.

Wishnie, Michael J. "Prohibiting the Employment of Unauthorized Immigrants: The Experiment Fails." *Faculty Scholarship Series* paper 925, 2007.

Wolcott, Reed M. *Rose Hill.* New York: Putnam, 1976.

Wright, Bill. [Title redacted]. *Fayetteville Observer.* August 8, 1988.

Wrigley, Julia. "Is Racial Oppression Intrinsic to Domestic Work? The Experiences of Children's Caregivers in Contemporary America." In *The Cultural Territories of Race: Black and White Boundaries.* Edited by Michele Lamont. Chicago: University of Chicago Press, 1999.

Yancey, George. *Who Is White? Latinos, Asians, and the New Black/Nonblack Divide.* Boulder, CO: Lynne Rienner Publishers Inc., 2003.

Yelvington, Kevin A. "The Anthropology of Afro-Latin America and the Caribbean: Diasporic Dimensions." *Annual Review of Anthropology* 30 (2001): 227–60.

Zamora, Sylvia. "Racial Remittances: The Effect of Migration on Racial Ideologies in Mexico." (Under review).

Zamudio, Margaret M., and Michael I. Lichter. "Bad Attitudes and Good Soldiers: Soft Skills as a Code for Tractability in the Hiring of Immigrant Latina/

os Over Native Blacks in the Hotel Industry." *Social Problems* 55, no. 4 (2008): 573–89.

Zatzick, Christopher D., Marta M. Elvira, and Lisa E. Cohen. "When Is More Better? The Effects of Racial Composition on Voluntary Turnover." *Organization Science* 14, no. 5 (2003): 483–96.

Zeitlow, Rebecca E. "James Ashley's Thirteenth Amendment." *Columbia Law Review* 112, no. 7 (2012): 1697–731, delivered at the symposium "The Thirteenth Amendment: Meaning, Enforcement, and Contemporary Implications."

Zúñiga, Victor, and Rubén Hernández-León, eds. *New Destinations: Mexican Immigration in the United States.* New York: Russell Sage Foundation, 2005.

Index

Page references followed by *fig.* indicate illustrations or material contained in their captions.

Abelmann, Nancy, 196, 223n16
abjectivity, 225n3
Abrego, Leisy, 42
Accomack County (VA), 99–100
Adriana (Honduran Swine's employee), 56,
    118–19, 126, 131, 211n6
Adrienne (African American Swine's
    employee), 106, 108, 122, 170–71
African American-Korean relations, 223n16
African American-Latino/a interaction: Black
    population size and, 222n12; collective
    action, 132–36, 225–27nn5–6;
    criticisms, 4, 5; ethnic succession and,
    59–64; humor, xvii–xviii, 3–4, 48,
    159–60, 232n10; immigrant worker
    vulnerabilities and, 201; language
    barrier, 179–80; Latina/o migrant
    destination trends and, 98–106; legal
    status and, 84–86; marginalization/
    noncooperation, 167–69; on-the-line
    spontaneous encounters, 1, 10, 16–18,
    111 *figs. 6–7*, 112–13, 114 *fig. 8*; as
    prismatic engagement, 194–201; research
    on, xx–xxi, 12–13, 17, 98–106; sexual
    relationships, 230n4, 232n11; social
    organization of labor and, 224–25n23;
    spatial concentrations of, 33; "structures
    of feeling" governing, 67; whiteness and,
    104–5. *See also* African Americans—

Latina/o view of, as privileged;
    ethnoracial language; Latina/o
    migrants—racialized resentment of
African Americans: anti-immigrant
    legislation opposed by, 193–94; as
    author's coworkers, xviii–xix, 1, 2–3,
    4–5; black utility heuristic and, 233n13;
    collective history/memory of, 182–83; as
    crew leaders, 81–82; employment
    opportunities for, 216n18; ethnic
    succession and, 12, 56–57, 59–64,
    187–89, 209–10n2 (Ch. 1), 216n17;
    ethnoracial language identifying, 78–87;
    as fast food workers, 210n2 (Ch. 2);
    heterogenous Southern population, 7; in
    hog processing industry, 216n15;
    Latina/o migrants as viewed by, 79, 112,
    113; perjorative meanings attached to,
    80–83, 213n10; as poultry farm labor,
    216n15; prismatic engagement and,
    196–201, 200 *fig. 11*; as racially
    alienated, 181; resistance to authority
    by, 149–52; social movements on behalf
    of, 198; Swine compositional dynamics
    and, 47, 210n3; as Swine's supervisors,
    17, 26, 139–44, 191–92, 197, 214–
    15n13, 227–28n1, 229n7–8. *See also*
    African American-Latino/a interaction;
    African Americans—boundary work

257